ALL IN THE DOWNS

Also by Shirley Collins:
America Over The Water (SAF, 2004)

All in the Downs

Reflections on life, landscape and song

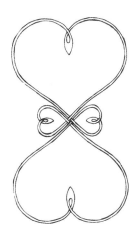

◀ SHIRLEY COLLINS ▶

All In The Downs: Reflections On Life, Landscape And Song
By Shirley Collins

First published by Strange Attractor Press in 2018, in an unlimited paperback edition and an edition of 500 hardbacks, with a signed insert.

All In The Downs © Shirley Collins 2018
Introduction © Stewart Lee 2018

Cover photograph by SF Said
Cover illustrations by Lorna Ritchie

ISBN: 978-1907222-412

Strange Attractor Press
BM SAP, London, WC1N 3XX, UK
www.strangeattractor.co.uk

Distributed by The MIT Press, Cambridge, Massachusetts.
And London, England.
Printed and bound in Estonia by Tallinna Raamatutrükikoda.

Contents

INTRODUCTION

The torch songs of Billie Holiday seem indivisible from the tragedy of her own life; it's impossible to imagine the barbed ballads of post-punk legends The Fall unfiltered by the strident individuality of their singer Mark E Smith; and The Wombles' celebratory anthems about litter collection would not have rung so true had we not known that their daily lives were indeed devoted to selfless off-the-grid guerrilla recycling. But rarely has an artist been as apparently absent from their own work as the writer, song collector and folk singer Shirley Collins.

If I may, in contrast to Shirley, blast my own monstrous trumpet for a moment, I believe it was I who, when penning sleeve notes to Shirley's 2016 return to recording *Lodestar*, wrote; 'To me, her egoless recordings resist stylistic flourishes, remove the obstacle of the performer's personality, and directly channel the listener to the words and music, reconnecting traditional tunes with the strange worlds they emerged from.'

In the run up to the record's release, I put it to Shirley, that in her '50s, '60s and '70s performances she didn't so much inhabit a song as surrender to it. To which she replied, 'All I did was perform the songs in a straightforward way. It's the only way I can sing them, because when people start dramatising or enacting a song, I just become embarrassed. I think the best way is to draw people in, not to stand there and declaim it.'

Partly because of this approach, Shirley's recordings have stood the test of time in a way some post-war folk revival favourites haven't, tied to the identifying sonic and social fashions of the scenes that spawned them. But when she came to write what was to be but her first volume of autobiography, 2004's *America Over The Water*,

Shirley's long-term confidante and cheerleader, the underground musician and archivist David Tibet, of Current 93, confessed, in his introduction to the book, to concerns about the apparent invisibility of the author.

Shirley had based her book around the 1959 song collecting trip she made to the deep south of America as the 'assistant' of her then lover the folklorist Alan Lomax, and upon reading a first draft Tibet noted, 'I felt it was only half-accurate, missing out so much of what I wanted to read about her own life and experience in North America. She had left out practically all information on herself and the book read as an account of Alan Lomax's quest, with a retiring young girl from Sussex assisting, who occasionally mentioned herself. Over many re-writings, Shirley thankfully overcame her modesty to write this luminous account.'

When Shirley published *America Over The Water* in 2004 she had not recorded or performed for nearly a quarter of a century, having suddenly and definitively forsworn singing for mysterious reasons, which she kept private, as she had every right to do. But questions remained unanswered, and one imagined there was a hidden personal drama behind Shirley's apparent accommodation of her former career, the ending of which remained unresolved and more than a little sad.

Then, with no real fanfare, in February 2014, at one of David Tibet's concerts at the Union Chapel in Highbury, Shirley sang again at last, making some kind of public and personal peace with her past. A documentary crew were already trailing her to make what had appeared to be a capstone to her career. But Rob Curry and Tim Plester suddenly found that their proposed film, *The Ballad of Shirley Collins*, had blossomed, in a symbiotic flowering, beyond their wildest dreams into a drama of rebirth and recovery. Given confidence by the realisation that, in her absence, her legend had only grown, Shirley Collins, now eighty years old, set to work slowly on the album that would become *Lodestar*, and on the book that would become *All In The Downs*.

Much as her fans and supporters might want to honour Shirley by allowing whatever work she was prepared to gift to us to stand alone, without the modern mania for full disclosure, the narrative that leads up to *Lodestar*, as documented by Curry's and Plester's magical film, suggested that some major issue had been resolved, that whatever prevented her from singing had been unblocked.

Shirley is a survivor from an age now undreamed of, where social media did not require artists to over-share every last aspect of their lives in a Faustian promotional pact with the audience that feeds them. But nonetheless it would be difficult for the admirably private singer's second volume of autobiography to avoid discussing whatever had prevented her from singing in the first place, and whatever had given her the confidence to begin again.

The 2005 autobiography of the comedian and writer Eric Sykes was playfully called *If You Don't Write It, Nobody Else Will*, but the book's title nonetheless suggests that Sykes was confident he had a story that needed to be told, mainly about playing golf with celebrities admittedly, whether anyone else wanted to tell it for him or not.

In contrast, if Shirley Collins hadn't written this second, and far more open and illuminating and downright literary, volume of autobiography, someone else would have had to at least try. But they would not have made as good a job of it. Like Shirley's, and her sister Dolly's, music, *All In The Downs* dissolves time, darting between distant memory and history and the events of her recent renaissance, dissolving the years between incidents, bringing ghosts, both metaphorical and literal, striding over the downs into life before us.

The history of the post-war working class, and of the pre-war country folk of Sussex, dovetail into and reflect each other. The birth of the '50s folk revival is intertangled with Shirley's own discovery of who she was as a woman, an artist and an archivist, as she scrimps by on scraps in a bohemian London as alien as a distant star. And in the fertile microcosm of Sussex, where the story begins and ends, Shirley, like William Blake, sees a world in a grain of sand, and Heaven in a Wild Flower.

'I feel grateful,' Shirley writes, 'that I lived my youth through an earlier and simpler time, even though in many ways it was hard.

Our childhood and teenage years were free from television and computers and the video games that no child seems to be able to be without nowadays. I feel that Dolly and I were always looking out and around us. We could step outside our front door on a clear night and look up at the skies over old Hastings and gaze at The Milky Way. And if that's not important, I don't know what is…'

And one also feels, that as well as writing *All In The Downs* for us, Shirley had, finally, to write it for herself, to understand the sadness that had stifled her voice, and the circumstances that saw it rediscovered. *All In The Downs* is not a *News of The World* kiss and tell, but, for example, the appearances of her estranged second husband's jumpers in unexpected places serve modestly to speak of Shirley's sense of betrayal, and do so as profoundly as the more emotionally explicit images other writers might have chosen.

When I first met Shirley fifteen years ago, it was beyond any fan or friend's wildest hopes that she would begin to create again, but the last two years have seen her release, unexpectedly, her finest album, *Lodestar*, feature in her own biopic, *The Ballad of Shirley Collins*, and finally deliver the book that makes sense of her story, *All In The Downs*. She is now, though her modesty would forbid her from ever making the comparison herself, the very revered folk matriarch she once went out into the world to document and learn from. And this is Shirley's own story, of Shirley, at last, victorious. But in it, she also gives life to the forgotten and often anonymous forebears of the folk song tradition that sustained her. Their voices, like hers, were once silenced, but now live on through Shirley Collins.

STEWART LEE
Writer/clown, Stratford-Upon-Avon, Shrewsbury,
Hereford, Stoke Newington, Dartford, February 2018.

For my daughter Polly Marshall Taplin, my son Robert (Bobby) Marshall and my grandsons Joe Miller-Marshall (musician) and Louis Miller-Marshall (cricketer); Chris Taplin; Daphne Dahrendorf; Pip Barnes; Ian Kearey; David Tibet.

And with thanks to my publisher Mark Pilkington for his unfailing patience.

Above: Shirley at the fundraising event for *The Ballad of Shirley Collins*, June 2015 (Stephen Hopper).

PROLOGUE: *Long Looked For Come At Last**

On 8 February 2014 I stood at the side of the stage at The Union Chapel in London's Islington, waiting, with almost a feeling of dread, to sing in public for the first time in over thirty-five years. I had finally agreed to do this for my friend and supporter David Tibet at a concert by his band Current 93, and that after two decades of his asking. Ian Kearey was there to accompany me on guitar, and my daughter Polly was with me to give me courage. I sang just two songs, 'All The Pretty Little Horses' and 'Death and the Lady'. It was a shaky performance, but at least I did it, and a door had opened again that I had thought was closed for ever…

Within two years I had recorded *Lodestar* for Domino, my first new album since 1978.

Three years later, almost to the day, on Saturday 18 February 2017, I stood in the wings at The Barbican ready to go on stage to sing the *Lodestar* concert with the seven-piece Lodestar Band. I felt a huge responsibility towards the audience, the musicians, and the songs. I invoked the presence of the old singers I had learned these songs from; I was singing back to them, for them. When I thanked the audience for their warm welcome, everything was in place, and I knew I could open my mouth and sing – a changed voice, but still my own. After almost forty years I was Shirley Collins, the singer, again.

You might wonder why I had stopped. Why it took so long for me to sing again. Did it matter in any case? One thing is for certain, none of us ever knows what life is going to throw at us, good or bad, or how we might react; but here's my story, the whole story.

*Song collected by George Gardiner, from William Winter, Andover, Hampshire, July 1906.

ONE: *It's Hard To Hold Them That Will Not Stay*

Now after a morning there comes an evening
And after the evening another day
And after a false love there comes true one
It's hard to hold them that will not stay*

'Why did you stop singing?' is the question I'm most frequently asked. Some people assume that I chose to give it up, but that's not the case; and I can't bear for it to be thought that I was no longer interested in the English folk music that I love. My life as a singer was overturned against my will; it's a long story, spread over many years.

I had first met Ashley Hutchings one night when I had a booking at the folk club in Cecil Sharp House. I was still living with my two young children, Polly and Robert, at 15 The Keep, in Blackheath, London at the time. Their father, and my then husband, Austin John Marshall, and I had separated more or less amicably; he had moved into central London with his girlfriend, and I was awaiting my divorce. That must have been around 1970, after I'd finished recording the album *Love, Death & the Lady* with my sister Dolly; it was a rather sombre album that reflected the difficulties and sadness of the time, although tinged with relief.

Ashley, or 'Tyger' as he was called then, had phoned me out of the blue one day. It was the first time I had ever spoken to him, although I knew of him as a member of Fairport Convention and Steeleye Span. He wanted to ask me what it was I said when I introduced

*'The Streets of Derry', from Mrs Sarah Makem, Co. Armagh. Recorded by Peter Kennedy in 1953.

Opposite: Shirley at Red Rose, circa 1974 (Toni Arthur).

the song 'The Whitsun Dance', as he'd heard it when Dolly and I appeared on the same concert as Steeleye Span a little while back; he said he was moved by it. I told him it was about the women who had lost their sweethearts or husbands in the First World War, and were left to dance alone or with other bereft women; and that the memorial stones for the dead had replaced the maypoles on so many village greens. He asked if I'd mind if he came along to hear me at a gig I was doing in a couple of days at Cecil Sharp House. 'Of course I wouldn't mind,' I said, and thought no more about it.

At the end of the folk club evening, a rather slight young man came up and introduced himself as Tyger Hutchings. He said he'd been fascinated throughout my performance by the way I tapped my feet as I sang, because it didn't seem to bear any relation to the rhythm of the song! I was a bit nonplussed, but when he laughed at what he'd said, I realised I liked him. When he invited me for a drink at The Volunteer, I said, 'yes'; when he asked me what I'd like to drink, I couldn't think straight (I didn't drink except for brandy egg-nog at Christmas, a tradition I'd brought back from America), so I said, 'Brandy, please,' and then, when it was time for me to leave to catch my train home, he cradled the back of my head in his hands and kissed my lips. Everything had changed; I'd fallen in love and it seemed it was mutual.

We started to see each other, one of the highlights of which was a trip to the Whitby Folk Festival together in August 1970, where we were both appearing. We travelled on the train, and to my surprise he insisted on buying lunch for us both – the first meal I'd been treated to for a long time; in those days you sat in the dining room and had waiter service. When it was time to pay, he pulled a thick wad of notes from his jeans pocket. I expressed my surprise at the amount of money he was carrying and learned that he didn't have a bank account, and always carried his earnings in this way.

Some time later, when we had decided to marry, we had to find an engagement ring, and while wandering up the Charing Cross Road one day, we spotted in a jeweller's shop window a gold Victorian ring with a spray of flowers formed from seed pearls. I loved it straightaway and we went into the shop to try it on. It fitted perfectly and Ashley said he'd buy it. The jeweller asked if we'd like the original box it came in; we both gasped when he showed it to us, a little maroon leather box with initials embossed in gold A S H – Ashley's initials, Ashley Stephen Hutchings. This was all meant to be!

Following my divorce from John on 16 June, 1971, the little house on a new estate in Blackheath was sold. I had long wanted to get out of London and back home to Sussex, and I found a cottage to rent advertised in *The Lady* magazine. Ashley arranged for Steeleye's lovely roadie, Dennis, to hire a van and drive us down to Etchingham, and with all our worldly possessions off we went, with our cat Copper sitting on the children's knees.

There was such anticipation as we turned off from the village and drove down Borders Lane. Red Rose was the name of the enchanting cottage; it was part tile-hung, part white weatherboard, late seventeenth century, with a yellow front door that had an iron fox-head knocker, an old cast-iron Phoenix Fire Insurance sign, and a beautiful hawthorn tree on the corner. Inside, we loved the sloping wooden floors in the upstairs bedrooms and the doors with their latches on knots of string. We threw open the casement windows, breathing in the clean country air and listening to the silence.

A sweet country life is to me the most endearing
All for to walk abroad on a fine summer's morning*

On the third night there, starting to get used to the quiet and the stillness and the clotted darkness at night, we settled down in front of the TV to watch a drama about witches, and found ourselves growing nervous. We had noticed in the grate of the big open fire a couple of bronze urns that were filled with a strange, rather sinister-looking green substance that neither of us had seen before. We convinced ourselves that it was something to do with witchcraft, and Ashley took the urns right down to the bottom of the garden. I showed them to Dolly when she came to visit a few days later, and

*From the singing of Sussex singer Bob Lewis.

was quite unprepared for her to burst out laughing – too scornfully I thought – at how scared we'd been at simple florists' floral foam!

We soon settled in well. Red Rose was halfway down Borders Lane, which looped around from the top of Etchingham, joining the Burwash road at the end of the Straight Mile. It was peaceful, except when the milk lorry went by in the early morning, or the occasional herd of cows. In the summer the cow parsley grew to head height on the verges on both sides of the lane, and for two years running a pair of fire-crests nested in a small oak tree fifty yards away. We'd creep down on summer's evenings to see if we could spot these tiny birds, such a great pleasure to derive from something so very small. Robert, my son, became a keen ornithologist – I have proof of this in the many photographs he took, mostly of empty telegraph wires, the birds having just flown. Polly and Rob went to the Primary village school in Burwash which held just forty pupils. It stood behind the church on the edge of a meadow, with a garden where the children grew carrots and lettuces to feed the pet rabbits, and it had its own small swimming pool. It was perfection, and to top it all, the school dinners were cooked by women from the village. We quite envied the kids when we heard what they'd eaten each day. I'd pick them up after school, and we'd wander back home across the fields; there was a stand of beautiful horse-chestnut trees where we could knock down plenty of conkers in the autumn.

It was a quiet and contented life in the Sussex countryside. Ashley proved to be a kind and patient stepfather, and the children thrived. We had a large garden with a stile at the far end which we climbed over to get to the meadows beyond.* The meadow led down to the Dudwell, a tributary of the Rother into which it flowed lower down in the village. Ashley and Rob fished for minnows, a peaceable occupation, although it distressed Rob to have to unhook a fish on the rare occasions he caught one. Beyond the Dudwell were a couple more meadows leading up to the wood where bluebells grew so profusely in spring that their scent was overwhelming – indeed almost narcotic.

*Where the pictures were taken of Ashley and me for the *No Roses* album, and later of me alone for *Amaranth*.

Rob and Polly Marshall playing in the garden at Etchingham.

    The garden held a wooden hen-house, a tyre swing hung from a tree, a see-saw and a couple of apple trees (I had no idea how hard apple wood was until I tried to prune them). The garden had been neglected, but we slowly brought it back into use and dug a vegetable patch, although it was heavy clay soil and rather unproductive; but Ashley persisted. We brought an old wooden wagon wheel in Heathfield and planted herbs in between the spokes (how original, we thought!), set up a badminton net on the lawn, and discovered the simple pleasure of archery, shooting arrows ahead in the meadow, wandering to retrieve them and shooting them again; hours happily spent. Polly and Rob discovered a Victorian rubbish tip in one of the fields next to the farm slurry heap and brought home a selection of old ginger-beer bottles complete with their marble stoppers, clay pipes and, rather alarmingly, some old medicine and poison bottles

– still with residue inside them! We lined them all up outside the back kitchen door that was visited twice daily by two black-and-white Muscovy ducks who waddled up from the farm along the lane and fussed about on our red-brick path.

We had mice aplenty, both inside and out. One Christmas they gnawed their way into a box of chocolate liqueurs that were placed by the Christmas tree and, maddeningly, just chewed the corners of all the chocolates, which had to be thrown away. We hoped we might find the tipsy mice and shoo them down to the end of the garden, but no, they'd gone to some hiding place to sleep it off. One afternoon as I was climbing the stairs I heard a scuttering in the wall. I banged hard with my fist and said 'Be quiet you mice!' A loud, angry buzzing was the response – I had disturbed a wasps' nest and had to run around closing all the windows before calling the pest control man from Burwash to come and remove it. When he'd smoked the wasps away, he showed me the nest, an intricate woody thing of real beauty. But it had to go. Another time, a swarm of bees collected on the big chimney breast outside, just as Ashley and I were preparing to leave for an Albion tour of Sweden. Fortunately the local beekeeper came and lured them away, to the great relief of my mother, who was looking after the children while we were away.

Occasionally we were woken – why was it always so very early in the morning? – by heifers or sheep who'd jumped the ditch from the field at the side of the garden and biffed their way through the hawthorn hedge, invariably trampling the vegetable patch rather than the lawn. One morning five sheep wandered down the lane and along the path by the back door. We ran out to head them off, but three had already run down into the garden, while a fourth one jumped into the wheelbarrow that was always left there, and the fifth got up on its hind legs and pushed it down the garden…

A favourite children's TV programme that we all enjoyed watching was *Catweazle*, the adventures of an eccentric medieval wizard who found himself in present-day England. He was amazed by modern day objects, such as the telephone, which he called 'telling-bone' while electricity became 'eleck-trickery'. One memorable

Title ALL IN THE DOWNS: REFLECTIONS ON
Condition Good
Location Aisle K Bay 5 Shelf 6 Item 1653
Description This paperback book shows normal wear and tear. Shipped to you from Goodwill of the Valleys, Roanoke VA. Thank you for your support!
Source TAP - Unprocessed
SKU 3BJTTV002SYD
ASIN 1907222413
Code 9781907222412
Employee cstarkey
Listed Date 2/19/2024 9:41:14 AM

3BJTTV002SYD

1653

1653

1653

high summer's day, at the village fete held in the Etchingham churchyard, where crowds of children had gathered, a figure with unkempt hair and beard, dressed in tattered robes, yelling wildly at the top of his voice, leapt over the tombstones. 'Oooh,' screamed the children in fright as the figure ran towards them, and then, in wonder and delight, 'Aaah – it's Catweazle!' It had been arranged by Moray Watson, the actor, who lived in a big Edwardian house on Etchingham's Straight Mile and was friends with Geoffrey Bayldon, who played Catweazle. What a splendid and unforgettable thing it was for them to have done.

While the children were at school, and we had some leisure time, Ashley and I walked or cycled around the local villages – Burwash, where Rudyard Kipling's former home, Bateman's, was a favourite visit, as was Socknersh Manor, a Tudor house set well away from the road and said to be owned by a famous but unnamed rock star. There was a lake there, at the side of which was a huge dug-out boat hollowed from a single giant tree trunk, covered in many years' growth of moss and lichen. Legend had it that it was an African tree-boat that had been towed back from there behind an ocean-going liner. When Ashley climbed into it, all that was visible were his head and shoulders. A photograph of him in it was used on the inside back cover of a song book he put together, *A Little Music*, with these words, as best I can remember:

> *Ashley Hutchings is my name*
> *England is my nation*
> *Etchingham's my dwelling place*
> *And music's my salvation*

But our favourite day out was to first play pool at The Fuller's Arms at Brightling, then head on to the village to explore 'Mad Jack' Fuller's follies – The Needle, an obelisk 40 foot high, The Sugar Loaf, The Temple and, far from being a folly, the beautiful Observatory from where Turner painted many sunsets. Jack Fuller was an iron-master, an MP for over forty years, and the local Squire from 1777–1834. As a landowner he was reputedly kind to his tenants; in one very lean winter, he gave employment to his men by having them build a wall round his estate. It still stands there. We'd save the Parish Church of St Thomas à Becket for last.*

In the grassy churchyard, often grazed by sheep and with a treacherously slippery brick-paved path, is a 25-foot-high pyramid, made of blocks of sandstone, now blackened with age. Inside this mausoleum, which Jack Fuller had ordered to be built some twenty-four years before his death, lies the man himself. Or rather, if legend is to be believed, he sits on a chair with a bottle of claret at his side. However, some say the truth is that he was buried beneath the floor. I'll go with the claret, wondering how well it has aged.

Inside the church, there are beautiful wall paintings, brasses and effigies, rubbed and no longer clear, but they still hold the power to move me these centuries later; perhaps they are even more precious because that is all that remains. My favourite, dated around 1470, reads:

> Rest blameless sovle. Friends
> Neighbovrs, all bidd sleepe
> Thou hast noe foes waking thy
> Ghost to keepe.
> Sleepe neare thy mate: Aprill yov
> Both intombs
> Why should one fleshe, one hart take
> Vp two roomes

We had neighbours, Will and Fanny Eastwood, a couple in their eighties, in Rose Cottage, a Victorian home where they had spent all their married lives. One day I asked Fanny if she'd had any boyfriends before she met Will. She told me she'd walked out with one young man. 'So why didn't you marry him?' I asked. She sounded rather put out. 'Oh, I couldn't marry him, he was too outlandish.' When I asked her what that meant, she replied that he came from a village three miles away!

*Why is it considered the right thing now to delete the à? Thomas Becket simply doesn't have the same ring.

Will was a retired railway worker and a keen gardener, and more than happy to give advice to us outlandish Londoners. The second summer we were there I was keen to grow strawberries. Will scoffed, 'You'll never grow strawberries here – the soil's too heavy.' Nevertheless, I went ahead and brought half-a-dozen plants; they grew rampantly, and for the rest of our time in Etchingham we were overwhelmed. We made strawberry jam, milk shakes and ice-cream; we gave plenty to Will and Fanny (much to Will's chagrin, I'm sure) and kept the blackbird population fed. But, tellingly, I remember a conversation I had with Ashley, after our divorce and when we were able to talk things over more rationally, when perhaps he had made some excuse about life in the country being too quiet or too dull. 'Yes, Ashley,' I remarked, 'It was just you, me and the strawberries.' He smiled wryly, or was it ruefully, and nodded. But we both knew there had been far more to it than that.

Ashley had proposed marriage to me as we walked out of Hastings Railway Station one afternoon, adding, as I turned to him to accept, and as though it had some significance, 'What colour are your eyes, blue or green?' And then he said, 'I can't promise it will be forever.' Why didn't I pay heed to that?

Days later, we went to Battle Registry Office to apply for a marriage licence, and to book the date for the wedding. As various questions were asked of us, we started to be amused as we realised how little we knew of each other's histories, although we had lived together in Etchingham for a while.

We both gave the same address, and I was embarrassed by that, as the clerk would know we were 'living in sin'. It was like that in the early 1970s. Ashley was asked for his father's name. 'Leonard Arthur Hutchings.' 'Good Lord,' I said. 'My dad's middle name is Leonard!' We had to state our fathers' occupations. Ashley gave his dad's as a lettering artist for the Post Office. 'Good Lord,' I said again. 'My dad works for the Post Office, too!' His occupation was duly noted as 'Post Office Engineer' by the clerk whose eyebrows were by now raised. It was as though we scarcely knew each other at all. When we were outside again, we sat on a wall, collapsing with laughter – but we had set the date: 6 August 1971. We'd missed the date of the classic English folk song 'Brigg Fair' by one day.

It was on the fifth of August, the weather fair and mild
Unto Brigg Fair I did repair for love I was inclined

I rose up with the lark in the morning, my heart was full of glee
Expecting there to see my love, long time I'd wished to see

I looked over my left shoulder to see whom I could see
And there I saw my own true-love come tripping down to me

I took hold of her lily-white hand, and merrily sang my heart
And now we are together I trust we ne'er shall part

For the green leaves they will wither and the roots they will decay
Ere ever I prove false to her, the girl who loves me well

The evening before the wedding I went for a walk alone up the lane, anxious and almost depressed, wondering if I was doing the right thing. Perhaps it was a premonition.

However, the next morning, the taxi, a black Ford Zephyr – 'To hire for Weddings and Funerals' – arrived from Burwash, driven by a kindly Mr Farley wearing his best grey suit and peaked cap, and with Polly and Rob we drove off to Battle in high spirits. My sister Dolly and her then husband Dave Busby (a very fine Morris dancer with Chingford Morris, later to become Albion Morris) came in from Bodiam along with my mother. Ashley's parents chose not to attend; they disapproved of our union because I was older than Ashley and had two children. His father and brother Greg came down to visit us in Etchingham just once in all the time we lived there; his stepmother never left her house.

I wore a simple Laura Ashley dress that I'd had for a while; it started out life cream, but I had dyed it a soft, faded, moth-like brown. Polly had a Laura Ashley dress, too (she was just coming up to ten years old), and we were both holding posies that we'd picked that morning. Robert, who was nearly eight, had been persuaded to have his hair combed.

After the ceremony, carried out by registrar Mr Leonard Tree and his assistant Miss Daisy Field – happily propitious names I thought – Ashley and I walked hand-in-hand down through Battle High Street to The George Hotel, where we'd arranged to have lunch. We had a private room and we sat at a long wooden table. We had champagne, except for mum who never drank alcohol as she reacted badly to it, so she ordered a glass of ginger wine, which of course contained alcohol. Within minutes of sipping it she complained that her hat was too tight and it was making her head ache. Dolly suggested she take it off, but no, she wouldn't, as then her hair would be a mess. And as she kept sipping ginger wine, this conversation went on throughout the whole of the lunch, to such an extent that this is the most abiding memory I have of that day – my wedding day. As for me, I never wear hats.

The next day, Ashley and I were off on a long weekend's honeymoon down to Cornwall, where Steeleye Span were playing at the splendid open-air Minack Theatre. Ashley was still a member of Steeleye, and had been busy recording two albums in 1970 and '71, *Please to See the King*, and *Ten Man Mop* – the last he was to make before he left the band later that year. They'd had a great success in Keith Dewhurst's play *Corunna* at The Royal Court Theatre in London, and were touring it too, so Ashley was away quite a lot of the time.

And yet somehow in that first year at Red Rose, we got married, recorded *No Roses*, and in subsequent years the albums *Morris On* (1972), *The Battle of the Field* (The Albion Country Band, 1973, although it wasn't released until 1976) and in 1974, *A Favourite Garland* (a compilation album of my songs), *Adieu To Old England* and *The Compleat Dancing Master*. In 1976, we recorded *Rattlebone and Ploughjack*, *Son of Morris On*, *Amaranth* and *The Prospect Before Us* (released in 1977); and in 1977, *Kicking Up the Sawdust*. And during the time of the short working week in 1974, when often there was no electricity, at the suggestion of Martin Carthy we formed the acoustic Etchingham Steam Band with local Sussex musicians Terry Potter and Ian Holder, Ashley replacing his electric bass guitar with a beautiful acoustic Earthwood. We played by candlelight in a few folk clubs; memorably at the Lewes Arms where Ashley turned up with his left arm in a plaster cast and sling. There were groans of disappointment throughout the audience, and dismay from Terry and Ian, until he slipped off the false cast. Only joking…

All in all our marriage felt like a good and certainly productive one.

The making of *Morris On* was great fun, especially the memorable day when the musicians came down to Red Rose to be photographed in our garden for the album sleeve. What a gathering, and what larks. A cricket match was soon under way, and Richard Thompson broke our bathroom window with a splendid hit, a story that my son Rob, who was nine at the time, still loves to recount, somewhat embellished! All of the musicians were dressed as updated characters from the Morris tradition. Richard Thompson was a dashing Robin Hood with a modern cross-bow; John Kirkpatrick a chimney sweep complete with a vacuum cleaner; Ashley as a Morris man, albeit with short trousers, his hat trimmed with flowers and a straw love-knot, playing an electric guitar; Dave Mattacks dapper in smart grey suit and bowler, sitting on the latest model of a bicycle, with our hobby horse (from Liberty's!) leaning up against it. Old and new… And, best of all, was the devilishly handsome Barry Dransfield in a long frock, bonnet and boots looking blowsy and buxom, languidly dangling a balloon on a stick. It's one of my children's favourite memories, Polly in charge of Barry's make-up, while Robert blew up the balloons that were Barry's bosom.

On the whole we were happy. We both took jobs locally when we were short of money, such as delivering Christmas post, clearing Lady Valentine's garden, or burning the apple-tree prunings in Bill Youdale's orchard in a thrillingly large bonfire. The kids loved that. But little cracks were appearing.

One October day I'd done really well picking apples at Bill's. He only ever hired women as he found they worked faster and caused less damage to the fruit. This day I'd earned more than usual picking splendid Lord Lambournes. I burst through the front door at tea time – 'Guess what, Ashley! I made £7 today!' All I got was a glare and a pained, 'Don't make so much noise.'

One time Ashley asked me if it was alright for him to take a break, that he needed to be alone for a few days. Well of course I said yes; I knew that he had lived through some dark and difficult times ever since the Fairport road crash in May 1969 in which their drummer Martin Lamble and Richard Thompson's girl-friend Jeannie Franklyn had been killed, and Ashley had suffered, among other injuries, a broken jaw. So away he walked up the lane to catch the train, and Dorset was his destination. But after he'd gone I was aware that the camper van which was the home of a young Australian woman who'd set up on the smallholding further down the lane, was gone, too. I didn't challenge Ashley about that on his return; I let it go, although the young woman's attitude towards me had changed. Once friendly, it was now aggressive; she was clearly angry with me. I suppose things were starting to crumble, but I wouldn't, or couldn't allow that thought.

A bigger crack, more of a gulf, appeared when Ashley suggested to me that, as we were away either recording or gigging so often, it would make life simpler if we didn't have to ask my mother out to Red Rose to mind the children; he and she found each other irksome to say the least. He thought a school nearby would be the solution, where Polly and Rob could be weekly boarders. After a lot of soul-searching, I agreed. It would make life easier, and it did. What was hard for me to bear, though, was the guilt, and the desolation of how much I missed them. And it wasn't enough of a concession to Ashley. Perhaps he saw it as a sign of weakness on my part, perhaps he even despised me for it, for instead of holding us together, things started to fall apart.

It started the day after a fifth wedding anniversary. Ashley and I were walking hand-in-hand down Borders Lane on our way home to Red Rose. We'd spent the day in Battle, celebrating with lunch at The George where we had held our wedding reception.

We spent the afternoon wandering in and out of bookshops, where Ashley bought me a still-treasured copy of Ella Mary Leather's *Folk Songs of Herefordshire*.*

There was a jar of handmade beeswax candles on the counter (fancy candles not being as ubiquitous as they are now), and Ashley said he thought he ought to buy a couple as a thank-you present for an actress (who we shall call Actress A) who was 'putting him up' in London when he couldn't get home to Etchingham after meetings there. It was a frequent occurrence during runs of the productions of *Lark Rise* and *The Passion*, then in full swing at the National Theatre, that members of The Albion Band would stay with various company people. I wasn't suspicious that anything was awry; Actress A seemed equally overtly friendly with all the musicians.

No, I was far more worried about another, unknown woman. A few weeks earlier the phone had rung at home in the cottage. 'Etchingham 305,' I said. A man's voice asked, 'Mrs Hutchings? Are you aware that your husband is having an affair with a secretary at the National Theatre?' My legs turned to water. I slammed the phone down and collapsed onto a chair, my heart thudding. When I'd recovered, I decided to keep this to myself, for a while at least. And when Ashley stayed overnight at Actress A's, I knew she was an actress and not a secretary and, I thought, far too naïvely, that if Ashley was lodging occasionally with her, then at least he wasn't with 'The Secretary'.

But into my mind drifted odd incidents that had happened recently at Albion Dance Band gigs. These dances were unique events at the time, bringing a thrilling energy to English country dancing which for far too long had been thought of as something done on wet afternoons at school when you couldn't get out to play hockey or football, or prissy pointed-toe dancing by genteel, middle-aged, middle-class people at Cecil Sharp House. No, this

*It was in this book that I found 'Awake Awake', which became the first track on *Lodestar*, my 2016 album for Domino Records. More on this song, and the work of Mary Ella Leather, in chapters 5 and 9.

was different, perhaps outrageous to some: it was the first time the dance tunes, dating from the fifteenth century and through to the eighteenth and nineteenth centuries, were played LOUD on electric and early-music instruments by consummate musicians: Simon Nicol on electric guitar, Mike Gregory on drums, John Rodd on concertina, Ashley on electric bass, Phil Pickett, the master of all things wooden that you could blow into, John Sothcott on viele, and Eddie Upton and me singing. Eddie also was the dance caller, resplendent in his green velvet Tudor-style jerkin and breeches. It was a great, pioneering band; the music powerful and beautiful, especially 'The Horse's Branle' (or Brawl) that was taken up in later years by many a band. 'The Brawl' was a splendid dance that everyone relished. It had a unique sideways-and-backwards step that flummoxed me at first. I remember attempting it as I was standing with Ashley on Platform 2 at Tunbridge Wells railway station – possibly not the best place to practise.

At gigs Ashley and I would go out onto the floor to demonstrate a dance, after which the audience surged on and danced to the band in full flight, filled with energy. The atmosphere was electric, joyful and fun, although the dances were taken seriously and done properly. At last we could rightly be called 'the dancing English' again, something we'd been renowned for in earlier centuries. They were such good times… until things began to falter. One evening, as Ashley and I walked onto the floor together, instead of partnering me, he went to the crowd and picked out a girl to dance with, leaving me standing alone. When we walked back on stage I hissed at him, 'Don't ever humiliate me like that in public again.' He didn't look at me, or even respond.

Apart from this, Albion Dance Band gigs were such happy events. There was always laughter on stage, especially when Simon Nicol was playing a stunning solo. It was a delight to be in his company; always easy-going, funny and a sublime guitarist. He could toss a tambourine high in the air and catch it on the beat as it fell; that always drew loud applause. I was a good frontwoman, able to make people laugh. One evening I said, 'I'll tell you what happened last night when Ashley and I were in bed.' There was a catch of breath from the audience and the band both. I told them how Ashley had been kicking in his sleep, so I woke him up, asking solicitously if he was being chased by someone or something. 'No!' was the enraged answer. 'I was just about to score the winning goal for Spurs!' Simon laughed particularly hard as he knew Ashley had been an ardent supporter of Tottenham Hotspur from an early age.

One afternoon before an Albion Dance Band concert in the National Theatre's Cottesloe auditorium, as I walked into the dressing-room I was sharing with Ashley, a young woman who was talking to him leapt up and ran away in terrible haste through the empty theatre. That, I guessed, was The Secretary. Then several times throughout the evening Actress A popped into our room. 'God, isn't she tiresome', I complained.

But the sight of The Secretary had shaken me, and I forgot the words of one of my songs that night – 'Edi Beo Thu Hevene Quene'. Not that the audience would have been aware: it was all sung in Middle English, and had been the one song I'd found it difficult to learn. I sang through the three verses, making some words up on the spot. I thought I'd got away with it, until I saw Ashley glaring at me.

One of my duties was to keep the Albion Band's accounts, and while going through the chequebook one day, I noticed a stub that Ashley had written for a double room in a hotel, along with another for single rooms for the rest of the band. Fear clawed at my heart, and I asked Ashley about it. He explained that the hotel had insufficient single rooms that night and that he'd had to share a double room with Simon Nicol. I half believed him, although I wondered why that needed a separate cheque. A couple of days later I tackled him about 'The Secretary', telling him about the phone call I'd had. He admitted that he'd had a brief fling with her, but that it was over.

A couple of days after our fifth wedding anniversary, Ashley headed off to London for meetings, taking the beeswax candles, the thank-you gift for Actress A, with him. When he stepped through the door that evening I could tell by the look on his face that something was up. 'What is it, Ashley?' I asked. 'Are you still in love with The Secretary after all?'

'No,' he replied, 'but I am consumed with love.'

'Then who with?' I managed to ask.

'Actress A. And if you say anything against her, I shall walk out of the door and never come back.' All I managed to say in reply was, 'She's got very strong hands.'

As I stood there I remembered what Ashley had said when he asked me to marry him: 'I can't promise it will be for ever.' I reminded him of this and that I had accepted him on those terms, not thinking that it would happen, and said, 'So I have to let you go.' How noble was that?!

But as I spoke the words, I half hoped that by showing a bit of integrity, Ashley would be shamed into staying with me. It didn't work. But he looked at me with such sweetness (or so I thought) and said, 'You are a remarkable woman. Haven't you had enough of me then?' 'No,' I replied and started to weep, and couldn't stop. He held me, for hours it seemed, but said he had to be with her.

You may well wonder how, after some forty years or so, I remember the scene and the exact words, but I just do; they were seared into my mind.

The next morning I went out of the cottage very early and walked through the fields for hours, trusting that he would be gone before I returned. But he was still there in the early afternoon, packing a few belongings.

And then he left.

The next few days were a blur of shock, bewilderment and grief. I couldn't eat, except, for some reason, melon and milk-chocolate half-covered biscuits, and I shed weight drastically (great diet!). After a month or so had passed, several members of the Albion Band came down to visit me at Red Rose. As we were eating lunch they told me they were playing a benefit gig that evening for the Actors' Benevolent Fund. 'We won't ask you for a donation,' joked John Tams. 'You've already given.' I managed a weak smile. I appreciated the fact that they had come down to see me until another musician delivered a message from Ashley – that I was a strong woman and had to make a new life for myself. I turned on him in a rage. 'I know that! But tell Ashley to deliver his messages himself and not be such a coward!' I sent them away soon after, but I did feel for them – it was a wretched position that Ashley had put them in; after all, we had worked closely together, we were friends, and the Albion Band was their livelihood. It was also mine, and I, too, had a living to make, for Polly, Robert, and me; but we obviously weren't considered Ashley's priority.

But that dear stalwart John Tams visited me again a while later. I met him at Etchingham station on a rainy day, wearing a new bright yellow waterproof. He smiled when he saw me and said it was clear that things were getting better. And so they were.

Ashley was a changed person – I think he'd been fed some New Age nonsense – and when he said to me, without a trace of irony, 'I'm marching to a different drummer now,' I laughed out loud. 'Oh Ashley,' I reproached, teasingly. He wasn't pleased. But it all helped, as my respect for him was starting to erode.

Ashley left it to me to tell Polly and Rob that he'd walked away from us. I know they were his stepchildren, but Ashley himself was a stepchild: his mother had committed suicide when he was a little boy, and he was raised by his father and stepmother. He never saw Polly and Rob again, indeed, he didn't even say goodbye. I delayed telling them, just in case Ashley had a change of heart, but that didn't happen. I broke the news to Polly first as she was the older of the two; she was tearful and bewildered. Then after a month or so, I sat Robert down on the stairs. When he heard what I had to say, his face blanched, it was deadly white. I had never seen that before in my entire life, and at that point I hated Ashley for what he had done to us all.

I knew that he was capable of ruthless behaviour, I had seen it a few times when he sacked members of the band. Perhaps I should have been more prepared for him to act like that towards me.

During this time the Albion Band was working at the Cottesloe in a production of *Lark Rise*, Keith Dewhurst's adaptation of Flora Thompson's book *Lark Rise to Candleford*, about life in an Oxfordshire village before the First World War; Martin Carthy and I were the singers. It was agreed I could still keep my place there provided, as Ashley said, I could leave our 'difficulties' out of it. But things started to go awry. It was a promenade performance, the action taking place on the floor of the theatre with the audience milling around us. Actress A often turned up to the performances, standing right in front of the band, directly in front of me, and more often than not wearing one of Ashley's sweaters, which of course I recognised. I especially remember a red and blue striped one. Over those evenings I was attempting to sing through tears; my throat swelled up, my voice cracked, and sometimes, nothing came out at all. But Martin Carthy came to the rescue, standing by me, singing with me or, on some occasions, singing for me. Ashley was furious with me for 'letting the band down' and said he thought we'd agreed to leave our problems behind. 'Well', I said, 'You aren't keeping to your side of the deal. Why do you allow Actress A to stand right in front of me, wearing your clothes. That's unnecessarily cruel. She's got you, she doesn't have to rub my face in it.' He said he hadn't noticed. Well, they say love is blind…

But I believed I'd earned my place in the theatre on the strength of my past career (and also I needed to earn some money), so however painful it was I continued throughout that run. Sometimes I managed to sing well – and thank heavens I did so on the night the BBC came to film the show.* The Albion Band and some of the back-stage crew were supportive, and often gathered at the end of the evening to hear my final song, 'The Bonny Labouring Boy'. It was a beautiful and moving moment when it went right; I had learned it from my Grandad, and it was the first song that Alan Lomax recorded from me in 1957.

As I roved out one May morning all in the blooming spring
I overheard a maid complain and grievous she did sing
How cruel were her parents, they did her so annoy
And would not let her marry with her bonny labouring boy

---

*That bit of film appears in *The Ballad of Shirley Collins* and is still out there on the Internet.

Now Johnny is my true love's name as you may plainly see
My father he employed him his labouring boy to be
To plough the soil and reap and mow all on my father's land
And soon I fell in love with him, as you may understand

They courted for some twelvemonth long but little did she know
That both her cruel parents did plan their overthrow
They watched them close one evening down by some shady grove
And heard them pledge each other in the constant bands of love

Her father he strode up to her and took her by the hand
He vowed he'd send young Johnny unto some foreign land
But boldly made she answer, which did them so annoy
It's single I shall always be for my bonny labouring boy

His hair is like the raven's wing, his eyes are black as jet
His face it is the finest that ever I've seen yet
He's manly, neat and handsome, his cheeks are like the snow
And in spite of both my parents, with Johnny I will go

And with a last verse added by John Tams:

So fill your glasses to the brim let the toast go merrily round
Here's a health to every labouring man that ploughs and sows the ground
And when his work is over, it's home he speeds with joy
And happy is the girl that weds her bonny labouring boy

To end the show, there was a country dance after the song
for both the cast and audience to join in. But one night, after
a particularly poignant performance of The Bonny Labouring
Boy, with the emotion still hanging in the air, John Tams
switched off the Band's electricity supply on stage, saying
'You can't follow that, you can't deny the truth of what's just
happened'. Ashley was furious, as were most of the cast, and
especially the director and playwright, as they liked an uplifting
finale so that the audience would leave the theatre happy.

There was a palpable silence; but John Tams refused to budge.*

I was touched by Tam's action and support, but it didn't really help; I was already up against it with several members of the cast, one actor telling me that I ruined the show each evening. 'Well,' I retorted, 'At least I'm not drunk!' 'Then there's no excuse, is there,' he said. That particular company was known for the amount of alcohol the men consumed. I remember well, when we were playing in a production of *The Passion* (another promenade show at the National Theatre) as the actor who was playing Jesus passed by, you could smell the whiskey on the air. I was rather anxious, too, when it came to the moment the actors raised Jesus onto his heavy wooden crucifix, and hoped they were sober enough to loft him safely!

At the end of each performance, I'd race across to Waterloo Station to catch a late train back home to Etchingham, arriving there at around one o'clock in the morning to a dimly lit station, fumbling to unlock my bicycle chain, then riding up through an unlit village and down the dark lane to Red Rose. I felt that I'd been totally abandoned, uncared for, unprotected. It was the bleakest of times.

Over that autumn, Ashley came down sporadically to collect more of his belongings; these were painful visits, and finally I'd had enough. I packed up the rest of his things, put them in the garage and told him to collect them, and to never come again. When he arrived, he was angry with me; so I retaliated and asked how he could have done this to me, to cause such pain, such grief and such chaos. 'Why,' I asked 'did you ever allow yourself to be seduced by her?'

'No, I seduced her,' he said.

I laughed bitterly. 'Didn't you notice her dropping in at rehearsals, batting her eyelashes at all of you in the band? And you're the only one that fell for it. God, how I despise you.'

I could tell by the look on his face that I had hit home. Even so, there was still a part of me that hoped, in those early months, that Ashley would come back. But as time wore on, I knew that our life together at Red Rose was over.

---

*Interestingly, when we recorded an album of the *Lark Rise* music, 'The Bonny Labouring Boy' was left out, perhaps as a petty act of revenge on Ashley's part.

After holding on at Red Rose for a few months, I knew I had to get away. I had taken Polly and Rob out of their boarding school, and they were now attending secondary school in Bexhill. They had to catch a school bus early in the morning, then straight back after school, which meant they had very little social life with the new friends they had made there. So I decided that Bexhill would be our new home. I found a flat, the two top floors of a large Edwardian house on Sea Road, two minutes from the sea. It was ideal, as the top of the house would be Polly and Rob's bedrooms, there were two further bedrooms, a lovely hall and staircase with a huge casement window that let in bright seaside light, a large lounge – plenty of room for the three of us. I took the children to see it, and Rob asked tentatively whether I was renting it or buying it. I reassured him that I was going to buy it. We all needed security. To his credit, Ashley, who had just received a royalty cheque for £1800, gave me £900 towards the deposit; it was to be the final settlement when my divorce came through. This good deed was slightly undermined when he told me that he'd given Actress A the same amount to pay her outstanding Income Tax bill. How come, I thought, that a loving relationship of several years gets the same pay-off as one of a few months?

I wanted a mortgage, and I needed a larger deposit. I wrote to Austin John Marshall's mother and stepfather, who I knew were fairly well-heeled, and they were, after all, Polly and Rob's grandparents. They sent me £1000 and their good wishes from Australia where they were living in comfortable retirement. So now all I had to do was apply for the mortgage. In those days women couldn't get a mortgage on their own, so I applied in both my name and Ashley's and signed any documents that I had to. What was the worse crime – me being denied the right to buy a property just because I was a woman? Or me forging Ashley's signature? It wasn't doing him any harm, but I felt very nervous all the time this was going on, and each time a meeting was called by the bank or the building society, I had to pretend that my husband was away touring with the band, and that he'd sign on his return! So eventually I got the mortgage, and we moved into the Bexhill flat in, I think, the winter of 1978.

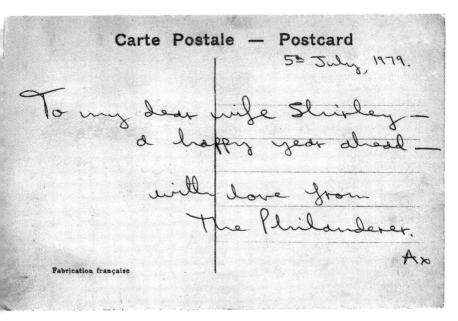

5ᵗʰ July, 1979.

To my dear wife Shirley —
a happy year ahead —
with love from
The Philanderer.

A x

Fabrication française

Birthday card sent to Shirley by Ashley Hutchings, July 1979.

One day, not a month later, I had a phone call from Ashley with a request: did I still had the green Egyptian cotton sheets that we had treated ourselves to a couple of years back? He said he wanted them. Little did he think that this would be another stage in my healing. Could I really love a man this insensitive? So I agreed, cheerfully (on the surface at least). Then a week or so after he called again and said he'd like our television set! This time I laughed out loud and said, 'Oh dear, Ashley haven't you anything better to do?' Another step in my recovery. It seems there are often three things that signify an end: the third was Ashley's reaction on hearing Dolly's and my 1978 album *For As Many As Will*. He was angry that I had recorded three or four songs from *The Beggar's Opera*; he said he was planning to do a complete version of it, and that I'd jumped the gun and ruined his plans. No mention of the wonderful songs on it, 'Gilderoy', 'Never Again' or 'Lord Allenwater'…

But events had caught up with me, and that first Christmas at Bexhill I came down with acute bronchitis. Even so, needing some income, I had taken a job delivering Christmas post, and struggled each day to complete the round feeling really ill. And to cap it all, when I went to collect my wages on Christmas Eve, I was told that payment would be made after Christmas. That was hard! In early January I took a job that was cash-in-hand as a weekly cleaner at Penhurst, the second country home of the literary agent who had years back been a boyfriend of my sister Dolly's. The gardener came and collected me once a week and I had money at the end of the day.

In the spring I started running most mornings along the Bexhill seafront, passing the arcades below the beautiful white domes on the promenade on the beach side of the De La Warr Pavilion, those domes that glowed so luminously in the evening light. In one arcade hung a sign: GYPSY ANITA LEE – YOUR FORTUNE TOLD, YOUR PROBLEMS SOLVED. Well, I certainly had enough problems, and could do with a bit of good fortune to come my way. One morning, I plucked up my nerve, parted the plastic strip curtains, and went in. There sat Gypsy Anita Lee, wearing a turban, with lipstick on her teeth and chipped red fingernails.

'What do you want, dear?' she asked.

'What have you got?' I replied.

'Well, dear, there's palm readings, crystal ball or tarot cards.'

I thought the tarot might be a bit heavy, so I plumped for the palm and crystal ball – £5 the two. She held my hands open, and peered down at my palms.

'Oh yes,' she said, 'born under the sign of Cancer.'

'Yes.'

'Born early July?'

'Yes.'

'The fifth?'

'Yes,' I breathed.

Then she bent my little finger and said 'Oh, married twice?'

'Yes.'

'Two children?'

'Yes.'

'Girl and a boy?'

'Yes.' I was beginning to perspire…

'Now, dear, your husband is a philanderer. Always will be.'

This was extraordinary. A few days before I'd received a postcard from Ashley, a beautiful French WW1 silk-embroidered one. He had written on the back, 'To my dear wife with love from The Philanderer' and added a single kiss.

Then Gypsy Anita Lee paused, looked a bit concerned and stated, 'You ride a bicycle.'

'Yes.'

'But you're not riding it at the moment.'

'No.'

'What's the matter, dear? Has it got a puncture?'

'Yes.' I was finding it difficult to mumble my responses by now.

'Well, dear,' she said, looking me quite hard in the face, 'I wouldn't get it mended if I were you. Just leave it.'

So my bike rusted away in the salt air of Bexhill. I never dared ride it again.

Mind you, I was still heartbroken, but the humiliation of having a complete stranger point out to me that my husband was a philanderer, hardened my heart a little more.

Time passed, and I was invited back again to join the company at the Cottesloe for a new run of *Lark Rise*. I thought I felt strong enough to give it another try, to claim what I believed was my rightful place there. The first day of rehearsals, as the Albion Band musicians were warming up by playing dance tunes, in stepped 'Actress M' who was in the play. She wore a long rehearsal skirt, and she tripped prettily around the floor, skirt whirling. I looked at Ashley; he was watching her, and it was clear he was entranced. 'Oh here we go again,' I thought, and indeed that was the case. Actress A was ousted.

I grew reasonably friendly with Actress M until the afternoon we were rehearsing in a church where that night we were due to give a performance of *The Life of Thomas Chatterton*. As I was preparing to sing 'O Sing Unto My Roundelay' – one of Chatterton's poems that

I had set to music, she appeared wearing one of Ashley's sweaters, a white Aran knit that I had washed umpteen times over the years. Much of the progress I had made vanished, and that evening my throat closed up, it was as much as I could do to croak my way through the ballad I had to sing.

It was then I knew I must divorce Ashley – get it over and done with finally. When I told him of my intention he asked if that was really what I wanted. 'Well, I don't have a husband, do I?' He didn't have an answer to that. So I started proceedings. I didn't cite either woman; at that time I couldn't bear their names to be there. So the grounds for divorce were given as 'marriage broken down irretrievably.' How sad it felt that two people who had been so close, so good together and so productive, should have become so completely estranged. I now dreaded the thought of seeing Ashley at all.

> *So slowly passes the winter's night,*
> *So slowly dawns the day*
> *It's many's the time I wished you were here*
> *Now I wish you were away* *

The Decree Nisi arrived in the post on 4 July 1980, the day before my 45th birthday, and the Decree Absolute on 24 November with the words: 'Made final and absolute and that the said marriage was thereby dissolved.'

On 12 July 1982 I renounced my married name by Deed Poll – the only way to make it legal to claim back my own name: 'BY THIS DEED I the undersigned SHIRLEY ELIZABETH COLLINS... A British subject... do hereby absolutely renounce and abandon the use of my surname of HUTCHINGS and in lieu thereof do assume the surname of COLLINS'.

But it would be many more years before I could sing again.

---

*'The Old Garden Gate', sung by a Mr Broomfield in East Hornden, Essex, to Ralph Vaughan Williams in 1904.

TWO: *Little Dorothy, Little Shirley*

So here we were, Polly, Robert and me, living in Bexhill, just a couple of miles westward along the coast from my home town, Hastings, where I had lived for the first eighteen years of my life.

I know I have a good memory, after all I can remember the words of a few hundred songs. But I wonder, how truly personal are those earliest memories, are they really mine or are they what have been recounted to me by my parents and grandparents?

But I'm sure I remember the Christmas (I was probably three or so) when we still lived in our 'old' house on Emmanuel Road, on the West Hill, Hastings. I'd been so excited to get a china doll as a Christmas present that I tossed it up and up in the air. I was told to stop, warned that it would break if I dropped it; but I couldn't stop, and of course it fell and smashed on the lino floor. I can see myself at the age of four, rummaging in the neighbours' dustbins for discarded flowers, then trying to sell them from door to door. Another time, I persuaded the assistant in the shoe-shop on the corner of the next street that my mother said I could have the pair of blue shoes that I'd spotted in the window display, and coveted. She let me take them away, but soon followed after me to ask Mum (Dorothy Florence Collins) if this was the case. It wasn't, and the shoes were taken away again. But how, I wonder, did I get out of the house? I don't think my mother was careless or unwatchful. In a notebook of hers that I found after she died, she had written some of her memories down, and it said that I'd open the front room window, climb out onto the sill and fall down into the garden. Soon after this, Dad (George Leonard Collins) nailed the window shut!

I have a photograph of me at perhaps a year old, sitting on the grass in our unkempt back garden, scowling at the sun. We had a tortoise called Fu; I was fascinated by how slowly he blinked his eyes, how deliberately he munched and gulped lettuce leaves, and how he appeared to move his legs sideways and backwards in order to move forward. We had a large ginger cat, Mickey, that Dad had brought back as a kitten from a farm, a gift from a customer on his milk round. Mostly he was given dead rabbits, so this made a nice change and Mickey stayed with us for fourteen years.

I can still recall the smell of the savoury braised heart that Mum cooked when Granny and Grandad came down on Friday evenings for supper, followed by a game of cards. My sister Dolly and I sat on either side of Grandad begging for tastes.

At our infants' school on the West Hill, we always had a nap after lunch, lying on the floor on individual oval rush mats – no complaints from any of us how hard they were, just obedience to the ritual. It was a pleasant and sensible thing for pupils and teachers. It worked in schools then, so why not nowadays? Why has time become so compressed?

I just about remember my great-granny, Mary Ann Easton, who lived on the top floor of our tall house (or so it seemed to me), at the top of dark stairs which we had to climb up to visit her. She's important to me as it was she who sang 'The Cuckoo is a Pretty Bird', which was one of the songs I sang on my album *Sweet England* (1958) recorded by Alan Lomax and Peter Kennedy. I have a clear picture of her, however, only from her presence in the photograph of my parents' wedding. She was tiny, shaped like a bell, in her long, full skirts with a high toque hat and dressed entirely in black ever since she had lost her son George Cyril Easton (my mother's uncle) in the First World War. He served in The Royal Flying Corps, and was shot down over Italy on 5 August 1918 aged eighteen and a half. At first he was reported missing, but the story came down through the family that on that night his mother awoke to see her son standing at the foot of her bed. He said to her, 'Don't worry, mother, I'm alright'. Then he turned to the door, waved a hand in farewell and raised his head; his mother saw that it was a skull. Next day the telegram came telling of his death.

I have the bronze plaque his parents were presented with after the war, a beautiful thing in its way, with Britannia holding her trident in one hand, and an olive wreath – or is it a laurel wreath? – in the other, a lion padding at her side, and with two leaping dolphins circling around her. HE DIED FOR FREEDOM AND HONOUR is inscribed around it, and it's set in a solid wooden circular frame. The letters that form his name are a little rubbed, and I picture his mother touching them over and over. When I hold it, I feel such pity and anger for her, and for the many thousands of other grieving mothers, wives, sisters and sweethearts, and wonder how they found the courage to endure their losses. I also have the memorial book that Great Granny made for him, full of cuttings and verses from newspapers and magazines – such sentimental platitudes, and such hypocrisy it seems to me now – though not on her part. It must have been a consolation for her, a comfort, albeit, surely, a bitter one. On the first page is this from a local newspaper:

> **WAR CASUALTIES** – 2nd Lieut. George Cyril Easton R.A.F. was reported missing on 5th August, and no further news has been received. Lieut. Easton was a boy in our choir; he has done well, and thoroughly deserves the position he has won for himself in the army.

Deserves what?! Lying dead somewhere in Italy, shot out of the air! His mother placed these words in the local paper: 'In loving memory of our only son Lieut. Easton R.A.F. killed in the air on August Holiday 1918.' All deaths in this conflict were unbearable, but somehow it seems extra cruel to lose your child so close to the end of the war.

There was such pride in him at first. He had, unsuccessfully, tried to join the army when he was sixteen; his father followed him to the recruiting office and hauled the under-age boy home. But at eighteen he successfully enlisted. Although but an under-gardener, his natural intelligence was noticed, and he was sent for a short while to Oxford University. As his nephew Fred FC Ball sardonically wrote, some 45 years later, in his book *A Breath of Fresh Air*:

> What had happened was that the war had got in a tangle and the government had decided, to the dismay

of some regular officers, that certain men from the ranks should be commissioned. So Lance-Corporal Uncle Cyril was interviewed to see whether he could be taught to speak an officer's version of the King's English. And, needing a little practice, had been sent to Oxford University for three months as a cadet in the Royal Flying Corps.

Great Granny survived until 29 January 1938, missing, mercifully, yet another world war; so I would have been two and a half when she died. My memories of her are faint now; all I can recall is the tiny celluloid bath with metal taps she gave me one Christmas, with a celluloid doll and a scrap of cloth for a flannel. I never knew her husband, George Easton, who had died before I was born. My mother told me he had been a builder and decorator, part-owning the business until his partner made off with all their money. He then had to join the work force and at one point had a job at the Woolwich Arsenal, 'helping to make widows and orphans.' He had been a lay preacher, but his troubles ruined him financially, and led him to drinking heavily. He became increasingly irascible, disgusted with the social set-up, and deeply affected by the loss of their son in the Great War; they received a small pension for this – he called it 'blood money'. They had to move from their rented house into two rooms, and from there into one room and were evicted even from that because of his temper. Uncle Fred remembered him as a fiery man, and a cynic: 'A cynic is a man who takes comical things seriously, and serious thing comically.' George died in 1931 following a fall in the street in which he broke his hip, and at this point my parents, newly married, gave his widow a home and took care of her.

My own maternal grandparents I remember clearly. I see Grandad drinking his tea from a saucer. Of course, it was given to him in his large special cup, and he'd pour it into his saucer, blow on it and slurp it into his mouth. But when Dolly and I attempted to follow suit, it was forbidden. He had his own knife, with which he did everything from whittling wood to cutting cheese – always with the knife blade towards him, as did Granny when slicing a loaf of bread held against her pinafored bosom. Our favourite trick of Grandad's was peeling an apple in one go, ending up with a beautiful long curling peel – if it was intact you could make a wish. He held his thumb against the back of the blade, which was worn to a sliver; it was a knife he had used for a very long time.

We were given tasks by our grandparents. With Granny, we helped cut apple rings and thread them on string to be hung up in her scullery to dry; we trimmed runner beans from Grandad's garden to salt away in big stone jars, but we also had to scrape the big blocks of salt – and that was painful. You couldn't help grazing your knuckles and you couldn't keep the salt from them. Grandad grew tobacco in his greenhouse, and we'd help him slice the leaves as finely as we could before packing them into bowls to have black treacle poured over them – he called it a sweet-cure! We'd sit and watch while granny darned our socks over her wooden mushroom, and patiently help unravel old jumpers, winding the wool into balls ready to knit scarves and mittens. We loved them both absolutely. Every Christmas we'd buy Grandad a small pot of Gentlemen's Relish, the rather expensive (we thought) anchovy paste. How could anyone like anything so salty and fishy! And Granny's Christmas treat was pickled walnuts – even the tiniest nibble gave me heartburn. What odd creatures grown-ups were. Still, Granny did always have a glass jar of striped mint humbugs on hand.

I was fascinated by the way Granny did her ironing; she'd cover the kitchen table with a blanket that was mottled with scorch marks, wrap a wad of cloth around the handle of her flat iron and heat it on the kitchen range, testing its readiness by spitting on the iron until it sizzled. We children were forbidden to spit… another example of what adults could do, but children mustn't. In our house, Mum plugged her electric iron into the light socket overhead. No wonder she was nervous of electricity – much like Thurber's cartoon of his Grandmother worrying about it leaking all over the place!

I've often told of my grandparents singing to Dolly and me as we lay in their Morrison shelter during World War II. Grandad sang a couple of songs – 'The Bonny Labouring Boy' was one of

them. Granny sang 'Barbara Allen' and mostly sentimental Victorian or Edwardian songs… What were we supposed to make of these songs I wonder now? There was one about two little girls – one rich, one poor. The two of them are sitting under a tree, and the rich girl, whose daddy is a gentleman, mocks the poor one because her daddy is clearly not.

> *My Daddy's a gentleman, I'm so glad*
> *My Daddy's a gentleman but not your Dad…*

And that's all I remember until the verse when, as the little rich girl is about to get run over by a carriage, the poor girl's father dashes into the road, saves her, is crushed by the horses and dies… and the last chorus, sung first by the rich girl goes:

> *My Daddy's a gentleman, I'm so glad*
> *My Daddy's a gentleman, but not your Dad*

And the poor girl…

> *Then the other girl replied 'God bless you!*
> *'But my Daddy,' she cried, 'Saved your life and died,*
> *So my Daddy's a gentleman, too'*

So that's alright then…

The other memorable cheery song of Granny's had a chorus that ran, 'For we all must die like the fire in the grate.'

My Dad served in the Army in the Second World War, and while he was gone, Dolly and I were evacuated from Hastings to Welwyn Garden City – the whole primary school was sent, with our teachers, but without Mum. I have a rather touching photograph (opposite) of Dolly and me in our wellington boots taken in the school playground at Welwyn; Dolly has a protective arm around my shoulders, and an anxious smile on her face. Obviously, we have both been told to stand up straight – our arms are held firmly at our

Little Shirley

Now who knows little Shirley
A darling little girl
She has got such a pretty face
Her hair is all a-curl

She's staying up at Welwyn now
And happily at play
Her daddy sends her pennies
To buy sweeties every day

Each week she gets a parcel
One which her daddy sends
And when she finds some sweets inside
She shares them with her friends

Dear little Shirley Collins
I long to hear your laughter
God bless you little darling
I know you're well looked after

— — — — — — — — —

sides! Mum said that she and Dad came to visit us once, when he was on leave, but I have no memory of it. What I do have, from a book of poems written by him while on active service, are these two simple verses; doggerel, if you will, but I treasure these pages written in Dad's hand, the paper now dog-eared and foxed.

The entire system of evacuation seemed chaotic to say the least, for the extraordinary thing was that soon after we were taken away, Mum was sent two evacuees, young boys from London's East End. They were so impressed when Mum

Little Dorothy.

Does anyone know a little girl
A girl whose name is Dolly.
She's such a pretty little miss
Her face is nice and jolly

She loves to play at hop-scotch
And skipping with a rope
And she is very well behaved
At least thats what we hope

She has a parcel too, from Dad
She shares the one with Shirley
And when she sees the postman come
She gets up nice and early.

God bless you little Dorothy
You're well looked after too
And here are two big kisses
One for Shirley, one for you.

– – – – –

cooked fish and chips, as they'd only ever had shop-bought. They arrived with fleas, and in the following years Dolly and I would sit patiently on Sunday evenings our heads bent over newspaper, while Mum worked through our hair with a fine-toothed flea comb, just to make sure. We were away for just a few months before being returned to Hastings, united with Mum again. Not long after this we were evacuated, this time with Mum, to Llanelli in Wales for a few weeks. But soon after we had been sent back to Hastings again, an incendiary bomb hit the house next door on Emmanuel Road and took half of ours with it; luckily we were out at the time.

So Mum, Dolly and I moved up to 27 Canute Road in Ore village to share Aunt Grace and her husband Cyril Winborn's home, with their children Bridget and Lesley. Their railings and iron front gate had long since been officially requisitioned 'to help with the war effort.' We weren't free from bombing or strafing raids from German planes. Many nights we slept in the broom cupboard under the stairs on eiderdowns; three children, a baby and two adults (Uncle Cyril was in the Fire Brigade and out on duty most nights). The front door was blown in by the blast from a bomb that landed two streets away and brought down our ceilings, covering us with plaster. Dolly and I were strafed one day as we walked down Alfred Road pushing baby Lesley in her pram. We saw a huge grey plane coming straight up from the sea, realised as we saw the black cross on the underside of its wings that it was German, and flung ourselves, and the pram, under a hedge, and watched machine-gun bullets tear up the road.

Uncle Cyril had been a snob – a cobbler – in civilian life and still had his iron last. He mended all our shoes, paring away the leather on the soles, his thumb firmly pressed against the blade of the knife, and hammering in the blakeys, the metal studs that made your shoes last that bit longer, which also were great for striking sparks on hard pavements. He made sure our shoes were polished, too. He kept rabbits in hutches in his side garden; we loved playing with their soft ears. Aunt Grace was a very good cook; she'd gone into service at fifteen, and had risen from maid-of-all-work to become cook over the years. She could conjure meals out of very little; she made the lightest pastry and her rabbit pie was memorable. Wartime, with its food rationing, was not the time for sentiment.

So deprived were we of sweets during the War that one day, when I spotted a bar of chocolate on the mantelpiece, I took it and ate it all. The theft was discovered, and retribution was speedy; it turned out to be a bar of Ex-Lax – yes, the laxative. When things had calmed down, Mum stood me in a corner with a piece of cardboard tied round my neck with the word THIEF written on it – a double humiliation. I didn't quite learn my lesson though.

That punishment was repeated when I polished off a half-full tin of sweetened condensed milk that I found in the larder, and which the grown-ups were saving to sweeten their tea. We weren't punished often; just the threat of 'a clump' or a 'thick ear' would sort us out. The worst was being sent to bed without any supper, although generally Mum relented and would bring up a bowl of 'bread-and-milk', cubes of white bread soaked in warm sweetened milk. Very comforting. There were so many things to be alarmed about, too – bombs and doodle-bugs; spiders and

thunderstorms; attacks by lurking strangers. Mum insisted that we walk down the middle of the road if we were walking down to Granny and Grandad's after dark – an impenetrable dark due to the blackout – no lights were allowed anywhere. She warned us that someone might jump out at us if we walked close by the hedges! And after the War, if there was a thunderstorm during the night, she'd wake us and take us downstairs to sleep under the table.

At the end of the War Mum rented a house at 117 Athelstan Road, two doors down from Granny and Grandad at 121. One day, she told us that Dad was coming home, he had been 'demobbed' – what did that mean? I scarcely remembered what my father looked like as he'd been in the Army during the war, rarely coming home on leave, although we did have a photo of him (above) in his uniform. Dolly and I were playing outside one day after school, our bikes leaning up against the wall, when a man appeared, walking down the road – a man I didn't recognise, although Dolly, being two years older than me, did, and ran to meet him. I hardly knew what the word 'Dad' meant. And yet I still can picture a smiling, curly-haired man in a navy suit that was just a little too tight for him – the 'demob' suit that all returning soldiers were issued with. I still have his 'demob' suitcase, a wooden one with a simple but very secure metal fastening. A couple of faded green labels are still stuck on it, one 'British Railways Local' and the other '4d paid.' It sits in my study and is full of Dolly's compositions and arrangements, holding about a tenth of her work.

It took a while for all of us to get used to being together again, and the joy of having Dad safely home didn't last. Mum had a job as a bus conductress. She'd worked on the trams in Hastings towards the end of the war, and had battled to be paid a man's wages. She now seemed to fight everybody. Dad wanted her to stop work, he wanted to be head of the household again, but Mum refused; she was used to earning her own living and she wasn't going to give that up. So the love that these two people had once felt for each other was now replaced by loathing. Here's one love-song to her from Dad's wartime book of poems.

To My Lady – September 1943

She is to me a gem of beauty, never was one so fair
The sunlight fades to nothingness in the gleam of her golden hair
The stars of heaven their utmost try to dim her radiant eyes
Her smile so gay, like dancing beams mirrored from April skies

And who could help but fall in love with her whom my heart seeks
The softest winds of eventide just stay to kiss her cheeks
And murmuring on, swell to a hymn to praise her wondrous grace
And all the love and tenderness within my lady's face

Their reunion wasn't the happy one told of in so many folk songs, lovers re-united despite the great odds of a soldier returning safe home after serving abroad for seven long years 'fighting for strangers'.

And here is the ring that between us was broken
In the depths of all danger, love to remind me of you
And when she saw the token she fell into his arms
*Saying 'You're welcome lovely William from the Plains of Waterloo'**

By now Mum was scornful of Dad for what he had become – a mildly conservative man, joining the Ratepayers' Association (perhaps to annoy, or spite Mum), and also because he was a Football Pools agent, something she didn't approve of. I can still feel the paralysing misery of meals together in the kitchen, the tension: Dolly and me sitting on the wooden bench on one side of the scrubbed pine table, not daring to move, Mum and Dad on the other. Mum would bang the dishes and plates down hard on the table – a habit she retained all her life – then throughout the meal complain that she couldn't put up with the way Dad ate, gobbling up his food she'd say, being a noisy eater; then him retaliating by pushing his plate away and leaving the table – and the house – before he'd finished his meal.

Dolly and I were caught between the two of them, and often sought refuge at Gran and Grandad's, needing to be with grown-ups who loved each other as well as us. We knew that something horrible was happening, but we didn't understand why. Granny told me how fond they had become of Dad over the years, although initially they had taken against him because his grandparents were Irish and lived outside Ore village in Red Lake. The match wasn't approved of, as Red Lake was considered to be a bit of a rough district. But Dad was a pleasant, intelligent, straightforward man, handsome, too, with thick, curly dark hair. Mum had fair, wavy hair. (Dolly got Dad's colour but Mum's wave, while I got Mum's colour with Dad's curls.) And when I see photos of a young Dolly I think of the lines in the song 'Rolling in the Dew': 'with her red rosy cheeks and her coal-black hair.'

*From 'The Plains of Waterloo', sung by OJ Abbott, Ottawa Valley, Canada, to Edith Fowke 1957.

Shirley and Dolly during World War Two.

Naturally Dolly and I had grown to love our father again and we were just happy to have him at home. He took a job with a laundry firm, delivering to customers out in the country – the rural route. He'd take us out sometimes in his delivery van. He was a genial man, and his customers liked him, giving him presents of eggs, rabbits and teenagers' magazines for Dolly and me. When he took us 'down town' or to the seafront, he'd buy us ice-cream wafers instead of cornets (they weren't called 'cones' then), and that felt much more grown-up. He'd take us into amusement arcades on the pier to play on the penny slot machines, an activity of which Mum really disapproved. But surely it was harmless fun in those days and to me, thoroughly enjoyable, as you could – though rarely – win prizes of sweets, or sometimes a little packet of cigarettes, though both would have been too stale to either eat or smoke. Even more exciting were the times he took us to speedway racing at the Pilot Field to watch Split Waterman, so dashingly clad in his black leathers; how handsome he was with his dark hair and elegant moustache, thrilling us as he screeched at speed round the bends, his bike almost horizontal to the track, one booted foot dragging on the ground. The noise was so exciting and the air was charged with the smell of a unique combination of hot fuel and the burning cinders of the track.

Before too long, though, the situation between Mum and Dad became intolerable. He left home and moved in with a red-haired widow and her two children who lived close by. Dolly and I would see them out as a family together, leaving us not only bewildered and bereft, but having to live with an embittered mother, now faced once again with bringing up two children on her own. Not only were Dolly and I sad, we felt ashamed, too. I thought this was only happening to us, but I'm sure it must have been repeated in many families although it was never spoken about, not with Mum or Gran, nor our friends at school.

Then Dad moved away from Hastings, and settled in Shirley, a district of Southampton. How could a place be named Shirley? Was it done to spite me? And I remember a story my mother had told me – quite recently – that when I was born, my parents hadn't thought of a name for me. And while they were at Granny and Grandad's one day, showing them the new baby, Dad looked out of the window, and noticed the bungalow opposite was named Shirley. Problem solved! At least, I thought, Mum could have pretended I was named after the Charlotte Brontë novel.

I only saw my father once more in my life; he turned up at a concert Dolly and I were giving in Southampton when we were in our thirties. He had brought us a quarter pound box of Milk Tray chocolates each, and spoke to us almost as if we were still the school children he had abandoned – or been driven away from.

So what do I remember of my Dad? His hazel eyes, his tanned arms on the steering wheel as he drove his van and his own father's name, Leonard Collins, on the World War I memorial outside the church in Ore Village.

Hastings, forever associated with the date of the Battle, 1066, is, in its oldest part an ancient fishing port and one of the Cinque Ports. Nestled between and below two great hills, the East Hill and the West Hill, the Old Town is picturesque and charming, but still a working place and full of character. It has a large fleet of fishing smacks that are launched from the shingle beach as there is no natural harbour there. Any attempts to build one were thwarted by the sea, the English Channel. I watched, as a teenager, the boats being winched up the shingle slopes, the fishermen sliding wooden planks under them to make the task easier. My mother told me that in her day, a donkey was tethered to a capstan and plodded round and round, drawing the boats up.

In this end of town, called The Stade and Rock-a-Nore, what many of us think of as the 'real' Hastings, are many beautiful old houses lining the narrow All Saints Street and the High Street. From the top of the East Hill you can look over a captivating roofscape, and continue a walk on to the picturesque, damp, mossy, ferny Ecclesbourne Glen to Fairlight and glorious countryside beyond. On the green sward of the West Hill, are views of the sea, and the ruins of the castle that William the Conqueror ordered to be built. Both hills have funiculars – cut right through the steep sandstone cliffs.

In the many good fish and chip shops, fresh local fish is served to cater for the holiday-makers and day-trippers, or 'Londoners' as we disparagingly called them as children. Visitors love the old rope houses, tall black weatherboard huts built to house the nets and fishing tackle. More recently the rather splendid Jerwood Gallery has been built right on the beach, with sea and sky views. Small wonder that so many artists, musicians and writers have chosen to make Hastings their home. My favourite church is St Clement's, just off the High Street where, in the seventeenth century, a cannon ball fired from a Dutch ship hit the church tower and lodged there; the authorities ordered an identical one to be carved in stone adjacent to it, to balance things up!

The newer part of Hastings is fairly unremarkable. It's true there are some handsome Regency buildings on the sea front that have survived many years of neglect, and Marine Court, built in the late 1930s to resemble an ocean-going liner, is now being restored to its former glory. Our gym teacher had a flat there, and I still remember these lines of a poem she wrote for the school magazine:

> *The sea lives at my door.*
> *Night and day I hear him roar*
> *And grumble up the shingle*

There's the spacious and attractive Alexandra Park, three parks actually, with a boating lake and tennis courts where Dolly and I spent carefree times. And when I worked as a tram conductress for a summer season, and was on early shifts and had to walk through the parks to the bus depot, the clamour of bird-song at dawn in the third park by the dank and dark reservoirs, was almost deafening, and helped take your mind off how isolated a spot it was.

Things come, things go. In my childhood, the centre of the town was the Albert Memorial, a tall, extravagantly ornamented Gothic clock tower built of Portland stone in 1862, a year after the death of Prince Albert. All the traffic from the main streets had to manoeuvre around it, and eventually it was demolished in 1973, following an arson attack. Also removed – and this was a disgrace – was the Cricket Ground in Queens Road. Built in 1864, it saw many County matches, but in 1995, Hastings Town Council voted to demolish it and replace it with a shopping mall. There was fierce and bitter opposition to this, the understanding being that the land had been left in perpetuity to the people of Hastings. Commerce won out. I have fond memories of the Cricket Ground; pushing Grandad down in his wheelchair to watch matches, and seeing my son Robert hit a six that soared out of the ground and smashed through a Town Hall window! Advance revenge!

An old Hastings tradition has been revived, the splendid Jack-in-the-Green celebrations on May Day. It was a custom that had died out in the last decade of the nineteenth century, but thanks to the imagination and ambition of, notably, Keith Leech, and Mad Jack's Morris, it sprang to life again in 1983, and has continued ever since, growing in size and splendour. It now is a full-blooded, vibrant and sexy, wonderfully-costumed, thrilling and often moving day of music, dance and procession. One tune is played throughout the day, the lovely seventeenth century Playford Dance tune 'To Drive the Cold Winter Away'.

'Jack' brings back to life the boisterous, bawdy, somewhat dangerous anti-establishment May Days that were held in England in past centuries, where 'Mis-rule' was key. 'Jack' is firmly planted in the past, present and future. I hope he represents a happier time for Hastings; it has been a poverty-stricken town for a long time – you can read about it in Robert Tressell's *The Ragged Trousered Philanthropists* which gives a true picture of working-class life there at the beginning of the twentieth century. He named the town 'Mugsborough'.

Hastings has long been a place people wanted to go to; the most famous visitor was William Duke of Normandy, but I prefer my mother's memory of her childhood jaunts to the town to spend the day on the beach and, as a special treat, have a cornet of hokey-pokey. If there was no money to spare, my Gran and her five children would walk the six miles from their home in Telham; but when Gran was in funds, they'd travel to see the sights on a four-horse wagon that bore the sign:

**FAIRLIGHT – LOVERS' LEAP
BATTLE ABBEY – TWICE A WEEK**

My early life in Hastings was parochial, compared with the way things are nowadays, with the choices that people have of moving away from home and travelling all over the world. And yet what my sister Dolly and I had, as youngsters, was a simple freedom that was a normal part of life, and one that I don't see kids having nowadays, although they have more licence. It wasn't that we were free from worries or danger – after all, we grew up during World War II, our Dad was away for four years serving in the Royal Artillery, and we had very little money. And although we hadn't been outside Hastings as children apart from the two times we were evacuated, we weren't distracted by today's gadgets; probably the most exciting things we owned were a magnifying glass through which, with the aid of the sun, we could scorch bits of paper, a small pen-knife that we weren't supposed to have, and a torch that would enable us to read under the covers in bed. And there was time; hours in which to explore our town and its close surrounding countryside. We just had to walk to the end of Fairlight Avenue and hop over the stile into a field of buttercups and clover that led to more unspoiled countryside. We'd sit and open up Grandad's old khaki army haversack, with its worn-out leather straps, and take out our picnic – a couple of slices of Hovis, hard-boiled eggs and a tin of baked beans, hoping we'd remembered the tin opener. We'd save a couple of crusts for our companion, the loveable Jim, an ugly little mongrel with liver-coloured splashes on an off-white coat, but with an irrepressible tail and boundless energy. He belonged to an old couple down the road who were happy to get him out from under their feet for the day.

Turning left outside Aunt Grace's house, the road led down to Ore Village. Never the prettiest place, it is even uglier now that the old shop fronts have been replaced by the garish neon strips of fast-food outlets. Ore was the place that travellers passed *through* – it was the old road out of Hastings that eventually led to London if you took the left turn, or if you continued straight ahead, up through Red Lake, you'd reach Kent.

There was a row of shops on just one side of the road except for the fish-and-chip shop opposite them: the butcher's, with its blood-stained, sawdust-covered floor and the sweetish smell of meat heavy on the air (Dolly fainted there a couple of times), where we'd hand the butcher a shilling wrapped in a slip of paper from Grandad, not aware that it was an illegal bet on the horses; there was the draper's where, at the age of fifteen, I purchased my first bra, which was lifted out from a glass-fronted wooden drawer behind the counter by an assistant who helpfully decided what size I needed as I had no idea, and was too embarrassed even to hazard a guess – I'd earned the money for it doing a newspaper round before school. The newsagent's was part of the Post Office, run by a mean and grumpy man who deprived Dolly and me of our newspaper rounds' Christmas tips (boxes as they were called then) by doing them himself in the week before the holiday.

The end shop was the dairy, always so cool inside with its tiled walls where, on the very rare occasions we bought cream (Mum's birthday), it would be carried to the counter in a jug with a beaded muslin cover and poured into the tiniest cardboard carton. The grocer's, Swatlands I think it was, had a bacon-slicing machine, a wire cheese cutter and board, and covetable (at least I coveted them) wooden butter pats. I was fascinated watching the lady behind the counter cut the butter from a large square then shape it, a pat in either hand, into a perfect oblong with squiggly lines pressed into the top, before she wrapped it in waxed paper. This all took time, of course, and you had to be fairly patient, although I don't remember there ever being much pressure on time. The shop smelled of the stale broken biscuits that lay in a large metal canister, temptingly placed in front of the counter. If we had enough pennies to buy some, the assistant scooped the pieces out, tipped them into a rough blue paper bag and slapped them onto the scales to be weighed, making sure they really *were* broken. The baker's smelled of the artificial vanilla of the so-called rice-cakes – our favourites, solid pink rock buns scattered with tiny lumps of sugar on top to represent the 'rice' element of the cake, I suppose, and which we nibbled off first.

The hardware shop on the other side of the church smelled of tarry twine and animal feed; and across the road was the little corner shop – and it was an actual corner, a narrow triangular sweet and tobacco shop, where we'd spend the pennies we'd earned running errands on licorice dabs, gob-stoppers that changed colours in such a satisfying way as you sucked hard, licorice comfits (what great lipstick the red ones made), a packet of sweet cigarettes, or a couple of Woodbines for Aunt Grace – there was never enough money for a whole packet. There were two pubs, a telephone box – and that was Ore village.

So, not a very exciting place, except for the forge, tucked up at the end of the bank at the bottom of Harold Road. It had once been owned and worked by my Great Granny's brother-in-law Charlie Easton, and Dolly and I were still allowed in to stand and watch a horse being shod. We were thrilled by the whole process, the leather-aproned blacksmith, his face covered in grime and running with sweat, his bare arms pumping the heavy bellows, making the fire glow even more intensely and the flames leap into life – how did he bear that heat day after day? Next he'd hammer an iron horseshoe into shape on the anvil, sparks flying, the shoe hissing and steaming as he plunged it into cold water; then, holding the horse's fetlock firmly between his legs, he pared the hoof, his thumb right up against the blade of his knife, finally placing the shoe strongly and cleanly on the hoof, raising another hiss and the acrid smell of ammonia.

Small wonder then that later one of my favourite songs would be 'A Blacksmith Courted Me':

> *I love to watch my love with his hammer swinging*
> *I love to hear it fall on the anvil ringing*
> *The notes are loud and clear, the sparks are flying*
> *My love is handsome then, there's no denying…*

And there's a verse sung by Queen Caroline Hughes, the great Dorset gypsy:

> *With the hammer in his hand, cold iron in t'other*
> *Well, he made the sparkles fly all around my middle…*

Was Caroline aware of the gentle eroticism of those words?

We had to go through Ore to get to school once we were

both at the Hastings High School for Girls. Most days we went by bus, walking through the passage from Athelstan Road down to Pinders. That mysterious name still casts a spell on me; there didn't seem to be any sign that said Pinders, and the word itself didn't seem to have any association with the surrounding area but, there you were, it was Pinders. Whatever the weather, Mum would make us go to school – she was such a great believer in education – or perhaps she just wanted us out of the way. So, even in the winter of 1946–7 when there was a heavy snowfall and such a bitterly cold spell that the trees froze and there were great snowdrifts, Dolly and I walked the couple of miles to school, each with a pair of Grandad's heavy woollen socks over the *outside* of our wellington boots, to give us better purchase on the frozen snow. I can still hear the sound, unlike any other, of the tinkling and creaking of the unhappy trees trapped in ice. Very few pupils made it to school, and not many teachers, so it was a couple of days of playing quizzes and spelling bees. It was fun, but Mum might just as well as let us stay at home!

We knew Hastings so well. A favourite haunt was the ruin of the Norman castle on the West Hill, where, although Mum had forbidden it, we clambered up and down the treacherous, crumbling sandstone cliffs, pieces of rock skittering away from our feet down the slopes. From our home in Athelstan Road we could see the Fire Hills, and it was a short walk down Harold Road to where we'd turn left past the two reservoirs (that provided us with the tadpoles we'd put in jam jars in the spring) and up through Barley Lane to get to the Golf Links, a proper links course, windswept and bare, except for the gorse bushes which gave the Fire Hills their name.

Sometimes, when there were storms and high seas, Dolly and I would venture onto the seafront, holding on to each other as we were buffeted by gale-force winds, running to safety away from the waves and the shingle as it was thrown up onto the promenade. The town centre flooded frequently, and it was fun to see rowing boats used as transport around the Memorial. The public toilets, which not only had been built within yards of the beach, but were also well below sea level, flooded more often than not. Great planning!

The two main department stores, Mastins and Plummers, still used the system of canisters sent on overhead tracks that conveyed your money to the cash room, then minutes later whizzed back with the change. It was here that we bought the green- or blue-checked gingham that would make our school uniform dresses for the summer term, and I loved watching the assistant throw the bolts of material across the counter, shaking out enough lengths for our needs, then expertly cutting it through with a large pair of scissors. What skills people seemed to have.

I cannot remember ever being bored as a child. If it rained hard enough to keep us indoors, we'd read, or play Chinese Chequers, or play the wind-up gramophone, but as we had only three records it didn't detain us long. They were 'The Laughing Policeman' by Charles Jolly, 'In a Persian Market' and 'In a Monastery Garden' played by Troise and his Mandoliers, and 'Will The Angels Play Their Harps for Me?' by Carson Robson. And often we'd run out of needles anyway. Otherwise we'd be entertained by our pet wild rabbit, Tosh, who Dad had found by the side of a lane on his delivery round. He brought it home, Mum wrapped it in a blanket and put it in the upturned lid on top of the copper, where the sheets were washed. Tosh survived, and was with us for a couple of years. He would scamper around inside the coal cellar, which was right in the kitchen underneath the stairs, then race all over the house leaving a trail of sooty pawprints. When he was a bit bigger he was allowed out into the back garden and once ate so many strawberries that within a couple of days, a huge boil appeared in the middle of his forehead. As time went on, he'd vanish for a while, and when he came back, he'd leap straight onto his blanket on the copper lid and collapse exhausted. And one day, he didn't come back. We hoped he was with his own family somewhere.

At Bank Holidays the funfair came to Silverhill, on the outskirts of Hastings. The best ride was the swing boats – we'd sit at opposite ends, and the harder you pulled the thick twisted rope (although it burned your hands), the higher the boat would fly. And of course, we loved the merry-go-rounds with their magnificent painted horses and cockerels. I expect they'd seem tame to today's children, but they were thrilling enough for us. As a special treat in the summer holidays we were allowed to camp at Uncle Wally's Tudor farmhouse up at The Harrow on the road to Battle. It had a built-in dairy – three slabs of stone steps down from the scullery, always so cool with its sweet and milky scent. Not so pleasant was the outhouse in the farm yard – just a wooden seat with a deep hole – how we held on to the sides! Our camp was on the front lawn where we'd string our tent up between the two concrete tank traps that were still there despite the war being over, and we'd always be woken early in the morning by Aunt Nell's geese landing on top of the canvas. The farmhouse was a magical place, dark wooden panelling along the hall, feather mattresses upstairs that you'd float on and sink into at the same time. Magical or not, it was demolished in the 1950s, and a ranch-style house built there.

When the war ended, and the tank traps and barbed wire that had kept us off the beaches were removed, we'd go out to Pett Beach in a big family group and spend the day there, those lovely long days of childhood. We paddled and pretended to swim, we played rounders or beach cricket on the long stretches of sand, but had to be careful of the black patches of soft sinking-sand. And oh, the memory of those dreadful homemade knitted woollen bathing costumes we children wore; they filled with sand and water and bagged down to your knees. Our skins rasped with sand and sun at the end of the day.

The end of the year was marked by our visit to Kings Road, St Leonards, to do our Christmas shopping and to listen to the traditional carols played by The Salvation Army Band, a sound that can still move me to tears. We walked there and back with Mum and Aunt Grace, a distance of a few miles from home, and it was always an outing we looked forward to. We'd got our earnings from carol singing door-to-door and our newspaper round money to spend. When I venture there now, I see an uninspiring street with a hodge-podge of shops that simply leads to Warrior Square Station, but in those earlier days we loved it so, perhaps because it was the first street to put up Christmas lights after the war, and its shops the first to decorate their windows.

The Old Town was the most attractive and characterful part of Hastings, but Mum didn't really like us to go there on our own, as she considered it 'rough'. Mum was a bit of an alarmist and she enjoyed, frequently, recalling how once her brother, our Uncle Robin, had been set upon as a teenager by a gang of Old Town youths (this was years before I was born!), but because he'd had boxing lessons was able to turn the tables on them. Even so, we *did* go there, and survived. In any case, we had to go there to catch the funicular that cut up through the cliffs to start the walk over to Ecclesbourne Glen, and once past there, we'd do another forbidden thing – climb through the windows of the old coastguards' cottages that were crumbling over the cliff edge – and which are no longer there, taken years ago by the sea.

I feel grateful that I lived my youth through an earlier and simpler time, even though in so many ways it was hard. Our childhood and teenage years were free from television and computers and the video games that no child seems able to be without nowadays. I feel that Dolly and I were always looking out and around us. We could step outside our front door on a clear night and look up at the skies over old Hastings and gaze at The Milky Way. And if that's not important, I don't know what is…

In many ways, of course, life continued as normal after Dad left. Dolly was going to Hastings High School for Girls, while I was struggling to pass the 11-Plus entrance exam for the High School. It took me two goes and I passed at the second attempt, but I think I was badly affected by the bitterness between our parents. After I'd done that first year at school, I was kept down, and made to do the whole year again, three whole terms with a new batch of pupils, while my friends had moved up. I felt so ashamed of myself. I had so longed to join Dolly at school, and to wear a navy gymslip and cream Viyella blouses – even to have homework to do! But clearly I didn't live up to its expectations.

But at least I had my big sister there, and in the morning and afternoon breaks when all the girls were expected to go outside to the playgrounds, Dolly and I would practice shooting netballs into the net or, at the longer lunch-time break, race down to the playing field and play catch with rounders balls. Sport became our consolation; we were in our school netball, hockey and tennis teams, and we were both made Games Captains of our Houses. A lesson in class differences was given on the day our school played a tennis match at Roedean, the posh public school for girls on the coast east of Brighton. They beat us – and as was the courtesy we, the losers, called first for three cheers for the victors – 'Hip Hip Hooray!' They called for three cheers for us – 'Hip Hip HOORAH!' Yes, they'd defeated us twice!

Mum was now free to attend her Communist Party and Labour Party meetings and sometimes sent us out to sell the *Daily Worker* in Hastings town centre at the Memorial, on Saturdays. How nervous I felt, how embarrassed, praying that no-one from school would see me. But most Saturday mornings Dolly and I went 'down town' to the Library – we were avid readers. I loved Richmal Crompton's *William* books and anything by Enid Blyton, especially those set in boarding schools, where apparently you had loads of midnight feasts and tuck-boxes; but after Dad left I came to prefer Malcolm Saville. He was born in Hastings and some of his books were set locally – *The Gay Dolphin Adventure*, for instance took place in nearby Rye – although mostly Shropshire was the location; I was intrigued by the names of The Stiperstones and Long Mynd. I was drawn to these books because one or two of the children in them had parents who were divorced, and that made me feel a little less ashamed, and not alone in that sad situation.

Mum would give Dolly a ten-shilling note, enough to buy our lunch at Lyons Corner House and then go to the pictures in the afternoon. Going to the flicks might have proved more risky than playing on the slot-machines on the pier with Dad, as occasionally, if there was an A-certificate film (over-16s only) which you could only see if you were accompanied by an adult, we'd hang about outside the cinema and ask a grown-up to take us in. Sometimes, if it was a man, he'd come and sit by us, too, and you'd feel a hand on your knee from time to time. I froze when that happened, but we only felt free to move to different seats when we could forget how grateful we were to him for taking us in!

When Mum was out at work and Dolly and I weren't rambling, perhaps on a rainy day, we'd sneak into Mum's bedroom to explore her dressing table. In one drawer we found an upper set of yellowing and bitter-tasting false teeth which we'd cram into our mouths, laughing at our reflections. I think they might have been Great Granny's – but why would you want to hang on to them?

There were some hairnets, faded and smelling of old powder. We'd slip our fingers through their cobwebby lightness, lift them over our hair and pretend we looked like film stars Margaret Lockwood or Patricia Roc, or glamorous land-girls. We tried out Mum's make-up, too: Pond's cold cream which felt pleasant on your skin, and a posher-looking one in a tube, Crème Simone. It sounded classy and French, but you could buy it in Woolworth's and it was so highly scented it brought me out in a rash. Mum used an orange Tangee lipstick so dry you had to scrub your lips to get it off. Her face powder had the same artificial vanilla scent that Bird's custard powder did, and almost the same consistency.

One day we found Mum's sapphire engagement ring wrapped up in a scrap of paper in a corner of a drawer. I put it on my finger; it fell off and disappeared between the floorboards. We tried, but failed to find it; I dare say it's still there. We never confessed this to Mum. And yet I wonder if she *did* know. When Granny died, Mum was left two sapphire rings that Grandad had brought back from Burma at the end of his six years' service in the Army there during the First World War. Decades later, she gave one to Dolly, but bypassing me, gave the other to my daughter Polly. Retribution?

At sixteen I got a boyfriend of my own. I can't remember how we met, but his name was Ted, and to my teenage eyes he was very handsome. His family owned a pig farm; he invited me there one day to see the pigs. It was a very hot day, and at one point he took off his shirt; I nearly swooned at the sight of his tanned and very fine torso and the male smell of his sweat. Then he put his shirt back on! It wasn't a relationship that could last, however, both mothers doing their best to undermine it. My mother called him 'Pigs' in a scornful way; and one Christmas Ted turned up with a present – the box had the words Kayser Bondor on the side, thus raising my hopes that there would be gorgeous lingerie inside (even though surely that would have been a bit forward of him). Instead, it contained the drabbest mustard-coloured woollen cardigan with holes in it that his mother had knitted. My young heart couldn't overcome the disappointment. Fairly soon after we parted, he wrote me a poem which he put through the letter-box, but it turned out to be the words of a pop song, and that didn't seem to quite count:

> *Answer me, O my Lord*
> *Just what sin have I been guilty of?*
> *Tell me how I came to lose her love?*
> *Please answer me O Lord*
>
> *She was mine, yesterday*
> *I believed that love was here to stay*
> *Won't you tell me where I've gone astray*
> *Please answer me O Lord*
>
> *If she's happier without me*
> *Don't tell her I care*
> *But if she still thinks about me*
> *Please let her hear my prayer*
>
> *Let her know I've been true*
> *Send her back so we can start anew*
> *In my sorrow may I turn to you*
> *Please answer me O Lord*

It was a song I knew, sung by a favourite singer of mine at the time, Frankie Laine; it got to No. 1 in the Hit Parade of 1953, when it was then banned by the BBC for its religious content! Poor Ted. I'd have been far more impressed if he'd composed something himself. In any case, I didn't like his crabbed handwriting. I had the memory of my Dad's fine hand, and was endeavouring to copy the italic writing of Miss de Gruchy, our headmistress at The Hastings High School for Girls.

While Mum had politics, Dolly and I had music.

We were now avid listeners to *Country Magazine* and *As I Roved Out*, two BBC programmes that had begun to play genuine folk songs on the radio. We were learning them as well as some more pop-oriented songs, and those we sang at school mostly from Cecil Sharp and Sabine Baring-Gould's book *English Folk Songs for Schools*. And we had our songs from the family. Miss West, our school music teacher, gave me nine out of ten marks in a music test for my singing of the 'Eriskay Love Lilt'. It was encouragement that I still feel a little rush of gratitude for all these years later. And, as the 1950s dawned, although we didn't realise it at the time, Dolly and I were embarking on our lives' work.

One morning in the month of May
When all the birds were singing
I saw a lovely lady stray
Across the fields at break of day
And softly sang a roundelay
The tide flows in, the tide flows out
Twice every day returning

A sailor's wife at home must bide
She halted, heavily she sighed
He parted from me, me a bride
Just as the tide was a-flowing
The tide flows in, the tide flows out
Twice every day returning

Aunt Grace Winborn sang this – it was all she remembered. More complete versions of it have been collected, but to me, this is a perfect fragment.

My dear Uncle Fred, the author FC Ball, my mother's brother, became the most important man in Dolly's and my life after our father left. He introduced us to the music of Purcell, Monteverdi and the boogie of Jimmy Yancey. We'd sit on the floor in the large front room of his house in Edmund Road in Hastings, while he played records on the wind-up gramophone. He wasn't afraid to show his passion – his eyes would light up, and he'd say, 'Christ! Just listen to that!' And listen we did, and soaked up the sounds. Sometimes there would be a group of friends there, talking about politics and literature, and there is one person I can't forget – Gregory Gildersleeves. What a remarkable name! I used to think he should have been a knight, and not a chap who wore horn-rim glasses.

Dolly and I loved going round to Uncle Fred's, occasionally staying overnight with our cousin Jean. Theirs was a much grander house than ours, a semi-detached Victorian villa with a back garden on two levels. The top tier was a walled path that led through dark and dense laurels and rhododendrons – wonderful places in which to play hide-and-seek. From the lower level you could run down the steps and into the huge cool cellar that had dark corners, a more scary place to hide, feeling that there might be something unknown lurking behind you.

I wished that we had a lavatory like they had at Uncle Fred's (ours was out in the back yard, dark and narrow). Theirs was not only indoors, it was upstairs as well. It was a mahogany settle, with a floral lavatory pan completely decorated with violet-coloured flowers inside and out; and at the side was a wood and enamel handle that you lifted up to flush, unlike the temperamental pull chain we had at home.

It wasn't till years later that I came to appreciate what a remarkable writer Uncle Fred was, drawing on the family's history with his books *A Breath of Fresh Air* (1961) and *A Grotto For Miss Maynier* (1965). Or what a scholar he became, researching the life of Robert Tressell, author of what is known as the first working class novel, *The Ragged Trousered Philanthropists*, and writing Tressell's biography *One of the Damned* (1973). And this from a man who was employed by the Gas Board in Hastings to read the gas meters and collect the pennies that had been fed in by householders – this was his working day – then writing in the evenings and at weekends. And he knew more about English literature than anyone I ever met, and loved discussing it.

Fred's temper flared occasionally, but the anger subsided just as fast. He always got very cross if he was asked to join in a game of rounders or cricket on the beach or in a field, saying he preferred to watch, but on the whole he was a cheerful and humorous man, in spite of the tragedy he had experienced.

My mother told me that as a young man, Fred was engaged to Elsie, but was in love with another young woman, a friend of his brothers Robin and George; she was a fellow art student. He wrote this poem for her…

Come My Love

Come my love, my only love and you're the best of all
Let's dance the stars down from the sky and the moon from off the wall
And if we cannot share a bed, because of what they'll say
Let's share a bit of field instead until the break of day

For dreams are things that stay awhile, and we must dream apart
But while our stars are still aligned, give me your hand and heart*

Elsie came to know about this state of affairs and threatened to sue Fred for Breach of Promise, a serious offence in those days. His mother (my Granny) advised him to marry Elsie, as they couldn't afford to pay any court costs or compensation, and in any case, she didn't want the scandal. So Fred and Elsie married. As far as I knew they had two children, Jean and Colin; tragically, Elsie was a

---

*Years later I set it to the tune of 'Dives and Lazarus' and it was one of Dolly's loveliest arrangements: I sang it in the Sydney Opera House in 1980, with Winsome Evans playing harpsichord; it was recorded, and included on my 2002 box set *Within Sound*, released by Fledg'ling Records.

carrier of haemophilia, and Colin was infected. I remember him as a white-faced, sharp-featured, pale blond-headed boy, painfully thin, slow-moving, sweet-natured. He died around the age of 12. Uncle Fred was grief-stricken.

What I didn't know was that Colin was their second son; their first was Robin Charles Ball, who lived for just two years. Early in 2014 the American poet Justin Hopper sent me a cutting from *The Hastings and St Leonard's Observer*, dated from the 1920s, with the tragic story of a two-year-old boy who, while toddling, bumped into a stool, and fell, forcing a tooth through his gum. The bleeding couldn't be stopped, and within 24 hours he had died. The father was named as FC Ball of 27 Edmund Road, Hastings. It was, of course, Uncle Fred. But I had never heard, nor been told, of this first-born son of Elsie and Fred's, nor of the tragedy of his death.

I hope he found consolation in his writing, and the music that he loved; I know he found it in his second wife Jacquie and their daughter Clare – their time together was filled with laughter. And in Jacquie he had found a helpmeet, and a typist! Talented though he was, he never sought fame. He hated being away from home and he often declared that he was proud to be a provincial man. In his novel *A Grotto For Miss Maynier* he wrote this frontispiece about himself:

> F C Ball was born in 1905 and comes from a long line of wheelwrights, ironsmiths, building tradesmen, dress-makers and domestic servants. He was educated at village school in Battle, Sussex, and from workers' educational lectures and from books. The son of a gardener, he himself began life as a garden-boy. He was a shop-assistant for eighteen years, a meter collector and clerk for twenty-one years. At twenty-three he decided that he ought to be a poet and wrote verse, mostly unpublished for twenty years. After that he decided to try prose. He found and edited the original manuscript of Tressell's *The Ragged Trousered Philanthropists*, published a biography, *Tressell of*

Mugsborough, then wrote an autobiographical novel, *A Breath of Fresh Air* followed by a novel *A Grotto For Miss Maynier*, three radio adaptations of these, and an unpublished novel. At the moment he is working on a commissioned biography of Robert Tressell and a new novel.

The 'commissioned biography', entitled *One of the Damned*, was published in 1973 by Lawrence & Wishart. Fred took the title from *The Ragged Trousered Philanthropists*' original subtitle: 'the story of twelve months in hell, told by one of the damned'. The unpublished novel is *To Live Like A Man*; I have the manuscript in my study.

Fred became fascinated with genealogy through his Tressell research, and he found his own family tree on the paternal side, the Balls, going back to 1555 in Hastings and came across this will:

> In the name of God amen the fifth day of April anno domini 1645
>
> I Richard Ball of the town and port of Hastings... Fisherman, being sick in body but of sound and perfect mind and memory... do make this my last will and testament in manner and form following...
>
> **Item.** I give unto Bridgett my wife my house and garden with the appurtenances wherein I now dwell for the term of her natural life...
> Always provided that my said wife shall maintain and keep the said house... in good and sufficient repair the whole term of her natural life.
> **Item.** I give unto John my son the said house and garden and appurtenances after the death and decease of Bridgett my wife... He shall pay out of the said house five pounds... to his sister Elizabeth my daughter within twelve months space after he shall enter upon the said house.

Item. If it happen my said son John do die, then I will and give the said house to my daughter Elizabeth.

Item. I give to my two children John and Elizabeth each of them two Yarmouth nets apiece and two shott nets apiece, ready fitted and made to go to sea to be delivered to them upon the day that my said executrix Bridgett shall be next married, and to each one of them a pair of sheets to be delivered upon the same day of marriage. All the rest of my goods I give unto Bridgett my wife.

Item. I intreat and desire Peter Stanbynorth my father-in-law and my loving cousin Richard Stanbinorth to be overseers, and as a token of love I give them two shillings apiece…

Signed Richard Ball

Witnesses: Peter Stanbynorth his mark, Richard Stanbinorth, Thomas Haynes.

I remember my uncle Fred with great fondness and admiration. His clear view of the world was frank and honest, forgiving and kind, but critical when he needed to be. It was much later in life that I came to value the knowledge that he had been a good friend to my father, right from when they were young men and dad was courting Fred's sister, my mother, and up to the time of Dad's leaving us. Fred never spoke ill of him. It was quite a while though before I started to see things in a different light, understanding Dad's position more, feeling kinder towards him and his actions and, much later, able to forgive him.

FOUR: *The False Young Man*

Dolly and I first sang in public at Oakhurst Hotel, on The Ridge at Hastings; it was a large Edwardian building set back from the road, and not too far along from another guest house, Netherwood, where Aleister Crowley had lived for a couple of years, until his death in 1947. Known as 'The Great Beast', among other titles, he had a reputation as a person to keep clear of – and I know that when Dolly and I were walking along The Ridge to The Harrow where our Uncle Wally and Aunt Nell lived in their Tudor farmhouse, we'd always cross to the other side of the road and creep by. Then run!

Oakhurst itself might have been equally alarming to some people, as it was where the Hastings Communist Party held their meetings and social weekends, and it was on these occasions, because of our mother's Party membership, that Dolly and I were invited to sing. So out would come the Czechoslovakian guitar that Dolly had bought on instalments from an advertisement in *The Daily Worker*, and which, since she hadn't learned to play it properly, she put in open tuning, laid across her knees and strummed. We sang, in two-part harmony, our rather limited repertoire: some were family songs, some from school, others we'd picked up from the radio. Josh White was our favourite; an African-American, he had a series of radio programmes on the BBC in the early 1950s called *My Guitar is Old as Father Time*. He had a lovely gentle presence that came across the airwaves, and he sang blues and spirituals in his soft, sweet voice. His theme song was:

> *I can tell the world about this*
> *I can tell the nations, I'm blest*
> *Tell them what Jesus has done*
> *Tell them that the Comforter has come*

Opposite: Shirley, Dolly and their mother Dorothy on the Railway Bridge at Coghurst.

It wasn't until recently that I learned that he'd had a long recording and singing career also as Pinewood Tom, that he'd been blacklisted by the McCarthyite witch hunts of the 1950s in the States, and later was an activist in the Civil Rights movement. So he was a hero. Recently, when I was checking his name, I came across the fact that at some point in the 1940s there had been a plan afoot in Hollywood to make a film: *Alan Lomax & The Adventures of a Ballad Hunter*. It was proposed that Josh White would play Leadbelly, and Bing Crosby, Alan! Josh was honoured in June 1998 when his likeness appeared on a US postage stamp.

Other radio favourites included Frankie Laine, Guy Mitchell and Jo Stafford, who sang folky pop songs such as 'Shrimp Boats'. The only one we learned was 'Two Brothers', a song about the sweethearts of two brothers on opposing sides in the American Civil War.

> *One wore blue and one wore grey as they marched along their way*
> *A fife and drum began to play there on a beautiful morning*

It ended with the loss of one of the brothers:

> *Two girls waiting by the railroad track for their lovers to come back*
> *One wore blue and one wore black…*

It really touched us: it was anti-war without the point being hammered home; it had a lovely tune and we could harmonise it in a way that pleased us. We practised our singing at the top of the stairs where there was an enhancing echo, and we thought we sounded really good. We sang a few other anti-war songs that Dolly had written. I still can't get out of my head the line 'a bullet hit him in the battle', which always made me smile to myself back then, wondering which part of the body was 'the battle'. How callous and superficial youth can be.

There were other advantages to be found at Oakhurst, too, such as the Christmas that Mum won a chicken in the raffle! (It

The Oakhurst Hotel, Hastings.

was still the years of chicken being a Christmas-only treat). Another was that one of the more earnest members of the CP fell in love with Dolly, but she scorned him. So he'd take me to the pictures instead as second-best, and he'd always bring a box of chocolates for me to take home to Dolly. He chain-smoked, and kept offering me cigarettes, which I accepted and tucked behind my ears to give to Mum.

Romance did blossom for Dolly, however; it was at Oakhurst that she first met a young conscientious objector, Jonathan Clowes, an intellectual and an activist who was then earning his living as a painter and decorator. He was a dark-haired, black-bearded young man, very thin, who wore brown corduroy trousers that were too large for him and which he continuously hitched up, chuckling as he did so. It's a gesture that I still associate with him, as he didn't lose the habit later in life, even when he became a very successful literary agent.

I, too, was to meet a man at Oakhurst who became of importance to me, although not romantically. John Hasted was a Marxist and a lecturer in physics at London University. He was a tall, rather gangly man with a cheerful but vague manner. He was a poet, too, but more essentially for me, he loved folk music. He told me about Cecil Sharp House in London, the headquarters of The English Folk Dance & Song Society, about the library there, where there were hundreds of books of folk songs for me to pore through. He played guitar and five-string banjo and had enthusiasm and a generous spirit. Later I would see how much like Pete Seeger he was: the same tall, rangy figure, exhorting his audience to join in the choruses as he sang; the same light of fervour in his eyes. In John I found my first Communist folkie, a man whose passion for Socialism (in which I had very little interest, feeling bludgeoned by it at home, and blaming it for the loss of my father) meshed with a passion for the folk songs in which I was very, very interested.

He encouraged young people like me to sing; I would later join the evenings in London when he ran 'singarounds'. He was also a supporter of The Workers' Music Association (the WMA), an organisation founded in the 1930s to promote songs of the working-class struggle. In 1939 the WMA founded Topic Records, still to this day the most important folk music record label in Britain. By the early 1950s, left-wing politics and folk music were drawing even closer together. It was John who suggested that Dolly take lessons in classical composition from the WMA's founder, the composer Alan Bush, and for two years Dolly travelled every fortnight from Hastings to the WMA in Paddington. She flourished under his tuition. But that was all a little in the future.

Like so many ordinary people then, I hadn't been away from Hastings, or travelled at all (apart from being evacuated). The furthest we went from home as children was when Mum and Dad treated us all to an evening or Sunday afternoon outing on the Maidstone & District Buses. The coaches were lined up along the promenade, each with a wooden noticeboard denoting a destination. By far our favourite was the 'Mystery Tour'. You didn't know where you were going but you were certain to end up at a pub out in the countryside. Children weren't allowed inside pubs, but Dolly and I were always content to sit at an outside table with a glass of fizzy lemonade and a packet of Smith's Crisps – no flavoured ones then, just a twist of blue waxed paper with a helping of salt to shake over the crisps. The salt sank to the bottom of the packet, making the crisps almost inedibly salty; but we still ate them, *and* licked our fingers clean.

Sixty miles up the road from Hastings, the post-war world was awakening in London, but by the age of sixteen I had been there just twice. Once was a school trip to the Festival of Britain on the South Bank in 1951. It was all thrilling, but I was especially taken with Richard Huw's 'Water Mobile' sculpture, a series of elegant steel containers. As water poured down through the arrow-shaped funnels, each in turn tipped as they filled, the water cascading to the one below; a beautiful sight and sound. It was a great outing, only spoilt by having to write an essay about it the next day at school.

The only other time was when Dolly and I travelled, in our early teens, to World's End, the more lowly part of Chelsea, to stay for a few days with Uncle George and Aunt Edith – or Dixie as she liked to be called, a far racier name that she'd acquired when she served in the Auxiliary Territorial Service during the War. George was an artist, and his flat was filled with his satirical paintings of workers and bosses. It was from here that Dolly and I ventured out into the posher, more exclusive streets in search of Laurence Olivier: Uncle George lived among painters and actors, and he knew where 'Larry's' London home was. We lurked across the road, and by some miracle, he appeared, and gave us a jaunty salute. We both burst into tears, overwhelmed. But we deserved this little bit of attention – after all, we'd spent all of our newspaper-round earnings to see all his films. *Henry V* thrilled us, and we'd seen *Hamlet* at least ten times when it was showing at The Gaiety in Hastings for a special fifteen-day run. In those days, you could stay in the cinema and see the whole thing a second time round – no wonder we virtually knew *Hamlet* by heart. We sobbed over *Wuthering Heights*, and I can still sing the music composed by Alfred Newman that played over Heathcliff's words as he holds the dead Cathy in his arms:

> *O Cathy, my heart's darling; hear me this time Catherine at last. I cannot live without my life; I cannot die without my soul…*

Once we'd cycled the thirty-six miles to Cranbrook and back to see him as Lord Nelson in *Lady Hamilton*, although it turned out to be our least favourite. We didn't really like to see our hero with only one arm and one eye.

Around 1952, when I was seventeen, I went to Furzedown Teachers' Training College in South London. It had been proposed by the head teacher of my school, and as Mum was very keen on girls being educated, I went along with it, living in one of the student halls, but I felt at such a disadvantage there with very little and sometimes no money. Dad was supposed to send me a postal order for a few shillings each month, but it mostly failed to arrive. In any case, teaching wasn't what I wanted to do with my life, and I left after the first year. At home, things had changed a bit in the time I'd been at college. Together with other Oakhurst regulars, Jonathan Clowes, our Uncle Fred (Mum's brother), and Barbara and Henry Chapman, a would-be playwright* met at one another's homes to discuss writing, music and politics. Jonathan, although politically committed, wasn't over-earnest. There was a lingering sense of wry humour and fun about him. Dolly found him handsome, intelligent and excitingly different, and it wasn't too long before they had a committed relationship. He soon moved in with Dolly – and the rest of us! – to Athelstan Road. What Mum made of this I don't know; she was enough of a prude to object, but sufficiently romantic to allow it.

My own sights were set on London. I took a job as a tram conductress in Hastings for the summer season, to save enough money to move there and start 'being a folk singer'. I felt grown up at last; I was managing my own money – not that there was much to manage, and my savings didn't last long. On arrival in the capital I rented a bedsit in Highgate for fifteen shillings a week and immediately had to find work.

My first job was in Marks & Spencer in Oxford Street where I was a counter assistant on jumpers, the garments all neatly folded

*Who actually had a play set on a building site, *You Won't Always Be on Top*, put on by Joan Littlewood's Theatre Workshop in 1957.

and laid out on display. The customers couldn't touch the goods – they had to ask to be shown them. I'd lift out a jumper and hold it up for the woman to look at, and perhaps feel. All well and good if they decided to buy it, but if not, you had to fold it up and return it in pristine shape to the others.

My time-keeping was hopeless – I simply couldn't sort out how the Underground worked, because from Highgate Tube the line separated at Camden Town, one going to the City, the other to the West End; I'd end up rushing to another platform but getting hopelessly muddled. One morning this made me so late I decided not to go in to work. The next day, my supervisor sent for me to explain my absence. I had to think fast! 'I had to go home to Hastings to see my mother. She's ill.'

'What's the matter with her?'

'Oh, she had a heart attack.'

I was trying to cry to make it more convincing.

'And how old is your mother?' asked the supervisor.

'Ummm' – a quick reckoning here – 'thirty-nine? Forty?' It didn't work. She gave me a very hard look and what sounded like a suppressed snort before she handed me my notice.

My next job was in Collets Bookshop on Haverstock Hill – a much easier Underground ride from Highgate. The manager was Edgell Rickword, a First World War poet. Just the two of us worked there; it was reasonably quiet, and I was more than happy looking through the bookshelves 'acquainting' myself with the stock. It was here I found the two volumes of Cecil Sharp's and Maud Karpeles's *English Folk Songs From the Southern Appalachians,* a collection that was, at that time, unknown to me. They were priced at sixty-three shillings for the two volumes, one of ballads, the other of songs. I bought them with my first two weeks' wages – thirty-two shillings a week. I had to live very frugally for a while, buying buns for lunch from the baker across the road, and a packet of dried chicken noodle soup for my evening meal. With no protein and no vitamins I got very run-down that winter, and had painful chilblains on my heels. It's called 'suffering for your art', but I maintain to this day that it was the best money I ever spent.

First published by GP Putnam's Sons in 1917, the year following Cecil and Maud's field trip to the Southern Appalachians, the two volumes were then put out by Oxford University Press in 1932, with a reprint in 1952 – these were the volumes I bought. They were hardbacks and quite weighty, the boards of a deep blue/green linen cloth (though faded now), with a green Foyle's label stuck down on the inside left-hand corner, and the price – '63/– 2 vols'– lightly written in pencil. *Volume 1 (Ballads)* included a fold-out map showing the counties in Kentucky, Virginia, West Virginia, Tennessee and North Carolina, where the songs had been collected. I pored over the songs, delighting in their number and variety, enthralled by the thought of their survival and discovery in the mountains – songs that had travelled over with early settlers, indentured servants and 'transports'. (Yes, people were transported as criminals to America before Australia was even discovered.) I was thrilled, too, that I knew some of the English versions of the songs, and I was utterly beguiled by the names of some of the singers: Philander and Napoleon Fitzgerald notable among the men, and by the given names of the women: Luranie, Zilpha, Tempa, Sina, Memory… Where did those names come from? And crucially, in many of the songs and ballads, although they remained remarkably intact, the names of the characters were often changed, the place names, too; and sometimes the stories were muddled, parts of one ending up in another. Well, of course that also happens in our tradition at home, too, but here in these books it was right in front of me on almost every page.

It was the intensity of many of the love songs in particular that held me.

The False Young Man

Come in, come in my old true love
And stay for a while with me
For it's been three-quarters of a long year or more
Since I spoke one word to thee

I can't come in, I won't sit down
For I ain't got a moment's time

Since you are engaged to another true love
Then your heart is no longer mine

But when you were mine, my old true love
And your head lay on my breast
You could make me believe by the falling of your arm
That the sun rose up in the west

There's many's the star shall jingle in the west
There's many the leaves below
There is many's the damn shall light upon a man
For treating a poor girl so…

Sharp collected and published several versions of each ballad, and it's fascinating to compare them to other Appalachian versions, let alone our English ones.

I love, for instance, the absolute forthrightness in 'Little Musgrove', when the adulterous pair, Lady Barnard and Matty Groves, first clap eyes on each other in church: 'He looked at her, she looked at him, The like was never seen…'

So that's that! Not much you can do about such a *coup de foudre* – but it does result in a lot of bloodshed!

I learned some of the songs straightaway and started to sing them. 'The False Young Man'* was one of the first. 'The Foggy Dew'* another, with its closing two verses, so unlike the twee and rather misogynistic ending of some English versions taken up by trained singers, sung so coyly with a knowing half-smile: 'Now I am a bachelor, I live with my son…'

And despite the crudeness of the American words, there is real tenderness, and it is set to a wonderful mountain tune:

I taken this girl and I married her
I loved her as my life
And I taken this girl and I married her
She made me a virtuous wife

*Both on *False True Lovers*, Folkways 1959.

I never throwed it up to her
Damn my eyes if I had
For every time the baby cried
I'd think on the foggy dew

In many of the ballads it's the directness, the instant power of the words, that hits me hard, such as in 'Lady Margaret and Sweet William':

Sweet William arose one May morning and dressed himself in blue
We want you to tell us something about the long love between
Lady Margaret and you
I know nothing of Lady Margaret's love, I'm sure she don't love me
But tomorrow morning at eight o'clock, Lady Margaret my bride
shall see…

It's cold, it's cruel and you know there's tragedy to follow.

The Appalachian books were newish when I bought them all those years ago; now they have a slightly fusty smell and the covers are faded, but I still treasure them. As I pored over them when I first owned them, I could never have dreamed that in 1959 I'd be in Appalachia collecting songs myself, or that in 2014 I'd be asked to write the preface to the book *The Dear Companions*, a selection of the Sharp/Karpeles Appalachian collection, published by the English Folk Dance & Song Society.

As my repertoire began to grow, so too did my experience of life in the big city. It was while working at Collet's Bookshop that I paid my first ever visit to a bank, to pay in the week's shop takings. I felt so nervous; the bank felt so grand and imposing, even though it wasn't a large branch. I had pretty much the same feeling on entering it that I used to have when seeing a policeman on his beat – guilty, although entirely innocent, as if the bank staff might suspect I was a robber or, more likely, that I had no right to be there. I didn't have my own bank account until I was twenty-six; I'd only ever had savings stamps books. It was a common feeling in the society of the 1950s, a time in which seemingly every situation drew a distinct line between the classes.

A couple of times a week I'd go to Birkbeck College where John Hasted was running the evening singarounds he'd told me about back at Oakhurst in Hastings. I was so nervous, and so excited the first time I walked through the tall iron gates at the entrance to the college, and stayed that way all evening, waiting for it to be my turn to sing, longing for it, but dreading it. John was always generous with his comments to us young singers; he encouraged everyone, was never critical, and sometimes accompanied us, playing guitar or five-string banjo. How good it was to hear the songs enhanced by simple harmonies. There was quite a mix of singers there, some members of John's London Youth Choir. Judith Goldbloom (later Silver) was one, Fred (later Karl) Dallas another. Fred wrote political songs with choruses which we all dutifully sang.

> *In the month of July in the year of '54*
> *There were slates off the roof and there were holes in the floor*
> *There were rats in the cellar, and we hadn't got a cent*
> *And the landlord came and told us he was putting up the rent*
> *Oh that greedy landlord, oh that landlord o*

So no change there then…

'Wimoweh' was another favourite tune, and again we'd all join in the choruses. I sang some of the songs I'd heard at home, and others that I was learning from my first incursions into Cecil Sharp House, the HQ of The English Folk Dance & Song Society. Sometimes it felt to me a bit like singing very earnestly around a campfire – although the only experience I'd had of that was in the Brownies, before I'd been thrown out at the age of eleven. I was really upset by that; I had loved my uniform!

I sang occasionally with John and Judith at the recently opened Troubadour Coffee Bar in Earl's Court where there was a folk club in the basement, known as the Cellar. The 'Troub' was owned by a

charismatic Canadian couple, Mike and Sheila van Bloemen. They had leased the premises – a grocer's shop – on the Old Brompton Road and decorated it in a way that for its time was completely innovative. The Troubadour stood out splendidly on the street (and still does). Sheila made a large birdcage out of wire containing two artificial birds, and placed it in the window. It drew a great deal of attention from passers-by and inspired friends to make their own birds, which Sheila hung inside. The walls were covered in murals and political posters and hung with various artefacts that the couple found in markets and junk-shops. The coffee tables were low, their surfaces of colourfully decorated tiles, while the handsome heavy wooden front door was carved with medieval figures.

Mike and Sheila had transformed the basement with various musical instruments hung from the walls. Like all folk clubs at the time, it was very smoky, lit by candles with very little fresh air coming in. The fug was added to by several male singers who, before they started a song, would light up a cigarette and stick it onto the end of a guitar string, letting it burn away under their noses. Of course, it wasn't only folk clubs that were full of smoke in those days, it was virtually everywhere – pubs, cinemas, offices, buses, even the doctor's surgery.

Mike and Sheila needed an assistant in the coffee bar, and offered me the job. I gave up my bedsit in Highgate and moved to one in Earl's Court, where I could walk to work. I served in the café, learning as I went. I can only remember serving coffees and pastries, spaghetti bolognese and scrambled eggs with herbs. In those days though, you couldn't buy fresh herbs, only dried, acrid so-called mixed herbs. The first time I served the eggs, the customer came straight back and asked what quantity of herbs I'd added. 'A heaped teaspoonful,' I replied. She laughed, quite kindly though, and advised me to put only a pinch in, and waited while I made a fresh serving. I'd never had spaghetti before, unless it came out of a Heinz tin, so I was rather bemused when I was instructed to boil the pasta

Opposite: Shirley in the basement of the Troubadour Cafe, Earl's Court, London circa 1954 (Herb Greer).

itself in a massive pan, then transfer it to tall sweet jars, ready for almost instant use – just a plunge in hot water before I served it. I learned how to make the bolognese sauce (more dried herbs!) and to make the dish look tempting by grinding parmesan all around the outside. And all this while serving coffees and such – it got pretty hectic sometimes. I preferred the customers, like a rather grumpy Richard Harris, who sat nursing a mug of coffee all morning – much less trouble.

I sang occasionally at the folk club downstairs, where there was quite a variety of guest singers from all over the country; Alex Campbell, a tall roguishly attractive Scot; a young Martin Carthy (well, we were all young then, weren't we?) who inflamed the passions of the ladies, and impressed with his guitar playing and his repertoire of songs; Dominic Behan who sang Irish rebel songs and who grew more vicious the more he drank; Louis Killen from Newcastle, a fine singer of a great many long ballads about sea-battles, which he sang in his strong Geordie accent and which, I must confess, I gave up trying to follow. There was the Scots duo Robin Hall and Jimmie MacGregor who went on to become household names with their regular appearances on BBC TV's *Tonight* programme and *Hootenanny*.

I loved it when the genuine traditional singers came down occasionally, such as Seamus Ennis, the sublime uilleann pipe player, singer and story-teller – 'a lean greyhound of a fellow' as Alan Lomax described him.* There was The McPeake Family from Belfast, whose song 'The Wild Mountain Thyme' became surely the most sung anthem in the folk world; and the great Irish singer and tinker Margaret Barry, knocking people out with the power and intensity of her voice and her remarkable presence. But the most popular of all was the American Ramblin' Jack Elliott, wearing cowboy boots and a Stetson hat, who sang a lot of talking blues in a very laconic style. He was joined by another American, the very laid-back Derroll Adams, who wrote 'Portland Town', a song

---

*Seamus played whistle on the song 'Long Years Ago When I Was Young' which I recorded for the album *A Pinch of Salt* in 1960.

that the audiences loved and sang themselves into a trance-like state with its repetitive chorus. So when another visitor arrived from the States, he was thought of as a young upstart. His name was Bob Dylan. Jenny Barton (now Hicks), who was running the club at the time, told me that he asked to sing, so she gave him two songs: he sang them, then disappeared for the rest of the evening into the toilet, smoking some substance or other. I didn't reckon him much at the time, but other people said – years later – they recognised his genius straightaway…

In these early years of the 1950s, I also made two journeys behind the Iron Curtain, so-named by Churchill in 1946. I went to Warsaw first, with John Hasted's London Youth Choir, and a couple of years later to Moscow, with a Theatre Workshop production directed by Joan Littlewood and written by Ewan MacColl. I was only asked to do it because the actress and singer Isla Cameron was ill. It required me to act as well as sing, and I didn't go down at all well with Joan and Ewan.

Ewan was a looming figure that you couldn't ignore, although I had taken an instant dislike and mistrust of him the first time I heard him sing. I found him pretentious and pompous, although those probably aren't the words I'd have used then. I simply knew that here was a vain, conceited man and, to my ears, not a convincing singer. And his habit of turning a chair round, straddling it backwards, before tipping his head back and cupping one ear with his hand made me giggle – it looked so silly. This image of him hovers into view in my mind occasionally; I try to dismiss it as quickly as I can, along with the memory of the evening he invited me to his home to look at his collection of books. He was already undressing the minute I walked through the door. I fled, furious that I'd wasted money on the bus fare.

But I have to acknowledge that he sang some very fine songs, and I even learned three and later recorded them, 'Proud Maisrie', 'Richie Story' and 'The Cruel Mother'. I entered a folk-singing competition at Cecil Sharp House singing 'The Cruel Mother'. I was so nervous that at the end of every verse I lost control of my voice and sang every last line in a sort of tremolo. There was nothing I could do about it, and it certainly didn't go down well with the adjudicators, who criticised it as if it had been intentional! I longed to tell them it was entirely involuntary. I didn't get placed in the competition, but at least I was put forward to sing in the evening concert.

Even so, wary as I was of Ewan, in the mid-1950s I accepted the part in the production. All I remember of it now is the one song, its tune, and the lines 'I may be gone a year or more in Kenya or Malay'. What I remember far more clearly is how inept I was as an actress, and Joan Littlewood's attempts to turn me into one, admonishing me because I couldn't make my moves across the stage while emphasising the rhythm of my song. I was far too self-conscious. It was the same paralysing embarrassment that I felt when walking past a building-site where the labourers wolf-whistled anything female that went by; your legs wouldn't work properly and you knew your bottom wobbled. I'd invited Mum up to see the final dress rehearsal with an audience, in a hall near King's Cross, and at the end, after we'd taken our curtain calls, I jumped down off the stage to greet her. Joan fetched me back and tore me off a strip for being so unprofessional. She was quite right though about my behaviour – it was absolutely against theatre etiquette. I cringe now when I remember it.* But for good measure she also told me not to wear eyeliner! And it was Ewan who had told me off for wearing nail varnish – according to him it wasn't what folk-singers did. Ewan and Joan had been married at some point; what was it with these people and cosmetics?

I've written about the trips to both Warsaw and Moscow and the time I sang in the Kremlin in my book *America Over the Water* (2007). But I hadn't included that it was in Moscow that I met a tall, slender young New Zealander, Tom Shanahan. He was from a farming family, and was travelling the world before settling

---

*Although when I mentioned it to my actor friend Pip Barnes recently, he said he was rather surprised that Joan Littlewood reacted that way, knowing of her passion for all things Brechtian!

down back home. He had light straw-coloured hair, pale blue eyes that had a distant look about them, and I was thrilled when he said he was travelling to London after the festival, and would get in touch.

We saw a bit of each other in London while I was working at the Troubadour. It was Tom who first introduced me to curry. I can picture it clearly. I sat opposite him reading the short, typed menu in its stained plastic cover. I didn't want to appear ignorant or unworldly, and I thought it wise to be safe, so I ordered egg curry. It was tasteless; hard-boiled eggs in what passed as a curry sauce on a mound of boiled white rice. On the next occasion I thought I'd be bolder, and ordered a vindaloo. I ended up with streaming eyes, a dripping nose and a red face. How could romance survive that? Still, it did for a little longer.

Our relationship was an unnerving experience as I had to smuggle him up three flights of stairs to my bedsit, tiptoeing as quietly as we could – visitors were forbidden. My landlady, who lived on the premises, kept an ear and an eye open – and a very sharp eye it was, too. We were caught (although not in flagrante), but still embarrassing enough. I was given notice to quit, kicked out of my London room in disgrace.

However, it wasn't that that ended the romance; it was scuppered by my mother. Tom played a trombone, and he brought it with him when I took him down to Hastings to introduce him to Mum and Dolly. We all sat round the fire in the front room to listen to him play, and although he played very well, he emptied the accumulated saliva from his trombone into the fire, where it sizzled. My mother's distaste was palpable. In any case, he was here in Europe to travel, and that was that.

Back in London, while I was still attending John Hasted's evening singarounds, another person had entered the scene – Peter Kennedy, son of the then Director of the English Folk Dance & Song Society, Douglas Kennedy. Peter was working for the BBC, recording folk song and traditional music throughout the British Isles. Douglas was rather patrician, Peter far more egalitarian, and he too started running evening events at Cecil Sharp House. It was virtually the

Shirley performing at Cecil Sharp House, 1950s.

same set-up as John's, except that every once in a while Peter would bring up a genuine traditional singer from the country and set him or her down amongst us. What a revelation this proved to be. It was here that I first heard George 'Pop' Maynard sing and Harry Cox, Bob Roberts and Phoebe Smith. Quite simply, George and Harry both stole my heart, reminding me of my own Grandad, who had died while I was in college.

Both in their seventies, modest, courteous men, they sat in the basement café in their country clothing, knitted waistcoats, flat caps on the table beside them, drinking tea, before coming into Storrow, the room where we all awaited them. And then they sang. Their voices were perhaps not as strong or melodious as they once had been, but there was a gentle dignity about them both that felt heroic; it was authentic, honest and with a direct beauty that simply wasn't there in younger singers; and they sang in their own local dialects. Their songs were a revelation, too; songs that they had known and loved for many years and which went directly into my heart. I had my first real inkling then of how a song should best be sung, simply and directly. That became the touchstone for the rest of my life – no dramatising a song, no selling it to an audience, nor over-decorating in a way that was alien to English songs, and most of all, singing *to* people, not *at* them.

I now had a foothold in Cecil Sharp House, but I wanted to gain access to the famed Vaughan Williams Library. It was almost like storming a fortress there was such a resistance to letting me in. You'd have thought they'd be pleased that I cared so much, but it wasn't like that. Perhaps it was a class thing: the Society was very upper middle class at the time. Just imagine, the presumption of a girl from the same class of people the songs had been taken down from over many years! Eventually, with Peter Kennedy's help, I was allowed in. I worked my way through the books; their allure was more powerful than any obstacles put in my way.

Because I couldn't read music, I first went for words that appealed to me: certain songs just leapt off the page, as if demanding to be sung, to have life breathed into them again. I copied the notes of the tunes down on manuscript paper, and later when I went back down to Hastings, Dolly played them on the piano for me. If I liked the tune, I learnt the song, and this was how I first started to build my repertoire. Later I had the opportunity to listen to the field recordings of collectors such as Peter Kennedy, Bob Copper and Alan Lomax, and that was a cornucopia. It's also the best way to pick up songs, learning them in the same way as they had been handed down over generations – by heart.

Recently, before Malcolm retired, he and I were in the library and I mentioned that the first song I ever copied down there was 'I Drew My Ship Into the Harbour' from John Stokoe's *Songs & Ballads of Northern England*, published in 1899.*⁻ I told Malcolm I could still visualise the moment I took the book off the shelf some fifty or more years back. He went to a shelf and held out an edition of the book. 'No, that's not it,' I said. 'It wasn't on that shelf, and in any case it had a dark blue cover.' He then went to another shelf (where I knew I'd first found it) and lifted another book out. 'That's the right one,' I told him. He was impressed by my memory, and I was pleased that I'd been vindicated, and had also proved to myself that those memories that are so clear to me are true ones.

And I was growing to understand and appreciate that my working-class, semi-rural background wasn't an obstacle but an advantage. I began to recognise that I had a responsibility for the songs and for the people who had sung them before me. This feeling endured. Whenever I sang I felt the old singers standing behind me, and I wanted to be the conduit for them, for their spirit, these people who'd kept the songs alive.

Most of all I felt I was part of them and of the music of England.

---

*←It was to be one of the first songs I ever recorded; it appeared on *False True Lovers*, the album that, along with *Sweet England*, was recorded by Alan Lomax and Peter Kennedy in 1958. In the liner notes Alan wrote: 'The listener who cares to compare the recorded version with that published by Stokoe, will see how Miss Collins has breathed life back into the print and made something lovely and alive out of an unimpressive folk fragment'.

FIVE: *Bogie's Bonnie Belle*

Not only was Peter Kennedy encouraging us youngsters to sing, he was also a major part of the BBC's project to collect traditional songs all around the country. This might never have happened had it not been for one crucial letter sent to the BBC in 1950.

There was a popular radio programme, *Country Magazine*, to which Dolly and I listened without fail. Every week it included a traditional song, but sung by a trained singer with a piano accompaniment. The BBC postbag was full of letters from listeners saying how much they enjoyed hearing the songs, and often adding that they, too, knew some old ones. Most notable of these letters was one from Jim Copper, Bob Copper's father. Bob recollected that Jim said to him one day in 1950, 'They sung one of our songs on the wireless last week in a programme called *Country Magazine*.'

'Oh yes,' said Bob, 'And what kind of job did they make of it?'

'Bloody awful!' was Jim's reply. 'They had some chap tinkling away on a joanna all the time t'other one was singing. Anyway, they didn't know the song properly.'

Bob suggested that his Dad write to the BBC to say how *pleased* he was to hear on the wireless one of the many old songs that his family still sang at home. On reading Jim's letter, Francis Collinson, the programme's musical director, sent him a telegram saying he'd be down to Rottingdean in Sussex, the family's home, and true to his word, he arrived the next day. Francis looked through the songbook in which, in 1936, Jim Copper had written out all the seventy songs the family sang, and listened to them singing. Francis then arranged for Bob and his Dad to broadcast live for *Country Magazine* from the garden of The Eight Bells at Jevington in Sussex, singing one of their family songs, 'Claudy Banks'. This proved to be a catalyst. More excitement followed – Brian George, a senior director at the BBC, loved it and was impressed by what he heard. Convinced that

there must be more songs and singers like the Coppers out there, and aware of how essential it was that such an important, but largely unknown and neglected part of British culture should be saved, he convinced the BBC to fund the recording of songs from ordinary people throughout the British Isles, while they were still there to be heard.

Bob Copper himself was chosen to do the work in Sussex and Hampshire (his 1973 book *Songs and Southern Breezes* recounts his adventures), while Peter Kennedy collected all over the British Isles for the next decade or so. In between field trips Peter found time to host singing sessions at Cecil Sharp House; and it was at one of these that I first met his wife, Eirlys, who was to become my best friend for many years. Eirlys Thomas, known as 'Tommy', was Welsh, and had the widest and sweetest smile I'd ever seen. She and Peter had two infants, David and Jonathan, who I babysat from time to time. Occasionally Tommy and I would go to the West End for a day's window shopping, always starting off at Dickins & Jones to have what we believed was a very sophisticated lunch – Swedish open sandwiches. Exotic ham and pineapple was our favourite.

In 1955 Peter gave me my first big break when he recorded a track from me for an album he was making for HMV, a ten-inch LP, *Folk Song Today*. My song was 'Dabbling in the Dew', and I accompanied myself on an auto-harp, an instrument which automatically changed chords when you pressed the right button. How ruefully I listen to it nowadays, not only pitched far too high, but it's a bowdlerised version of the song that I'd learned from *English Folk Songs for Schools*. It would be some time before I heard George Maynard's 'Rolling in the Dew' with its far franker words and vastly superior tune. And my singing sounds so naïve… But I was thrilled because on the album my track was placed next to three of my heroes, Bob and Ron Copper, and Harry Cox, although in all honesty I didn't really deserve it at that time.

Since the start of the 1950s, while I was starting to delve into the tradition of English song, a craze had been sweeping the country – it was called skiffle, music that almost anyone could play, mostly souped-up, speeded-up American songs and blues, thrashed out on guitars, home-made basses, and washboards played with thimbles. The longer this craze lasted, the more frantic it became, the young enthusiasts basing themselves on its worst (in my opinion) perpetrator, Lonnie Donegan. Skiffle was thought of as working-class music because anyone could afford to buy or make the instruments, and could play their music wherever and whenever they wanted, free of the constraints of the pop music business.

John Hasted wanted to capitalise on the craze, and formed John Hasted's Skiffle and Folk Group, even going so far as to change the name of the folk club he'd started, The Good Earth, to The 44 Skiffle Club. He justified this by hoping that audiences who came in for the skiffle would be interested in the folk element of it. And I became part of it, singing folksongs in between sets of raucous skiffle which, while they may have lacked finesse, were certainly full of energy, played by a band fronted by Redd Sullivan, a merchant seaman, and Martin Winsor. One evening when I was in the audience at Martin's Soho club Folk & Blues, I grew so incensed that no-one had sung any folk songs at all that, as I left, I took my lipstick and crossed out the word 'Folk' on the poster outside. Martin spotted me and confronted me with a knife, telling me that if I ever went there again, he'd use it. I believed him…

John's skiffle group played further afield, too. I recall one trip to Suffolk, travelling in John's rather ancient Morris van, sitting on a blanket on the floor in the back, while John's girlfriend took the passenger seat for the whole bumpy ride. An important lesson learned there; the group's singer doesn't take precedence over the bandleader's sweetheart.

Then life changed, and it was a sea change.

Ewan MacColl invited me to a party that he was giving for Alan Lomax, who had just returned to London after three or more years collecting music in Spain and Italy. He had come to Europe in 1950 to record for, and edit, *The World Library of Folk & Primitive Music* for Columbia, and also to escape the attentions of the Un-American Activities Committee in the States – apparently collecting American folk music was considered too subversive an occupation. Europe wasn't necessarily any better: in Spain, which was still under the heel of General Franco, Alan attracted the attention of the Guardia Civil, who, he wrote, always appeared in the background 'like so many black buzzards carrying with them the stink of fear.' And even in Britain the police were keeping an eye on him at the request of the FBI.

> *I'm a rambler, I'm a gambler*
> *I'm a long way from home*
> *If the people don't like me*
> *They can leave me alone**

I was thrilled to be invited to Ewan's party as Alan was one of my heroes – I'd listened to all his programmes on the radio, and I loved the music he played, some of which he'd recorded in the British Isles from the Hebrides to Cornwall. He spoke with such warmth about the people he met, so vividly about their lives and their music. I was so nervous of meeting him, though, that when I stood before him I blurted out that one of my ambitions was to go to hear more of his field recordings in The Library of Congress in Washington. He expressed surprise that I'd even heard of it. And that's all I remember of that first meeting, except that he bought me a strip of raffle tickets!

I had fallen in love on the spot with this charming, tall, burly Texan with shaggy dark hair and, as I have said before, because it's true, he reminded me of an American bison. Some days later he got in touch with me, and we met a few times at Peter Kennedy's home. Then he started asking me out, perhaps for a drive, or to visit friends of his. One evening, Frances and Nat Brown, socialist friends of his in Hampstead, invited us to dinner. They still talked about an earlier visit that Alan had made when he was first in London in the early 1950s when foodstuffs, including butter, were still rationed; on

*'The Rambling Gambler' from *Cowboy Songs and Other Frontier Ballads*, John Avery Lomax and Alan Lomax, 1938.

the dinner table had been a small dish that held all of the Brown's precious butter ration for the week, and Alan swiped it all to put on his mashed potatoes!

I'd go over to Alan's flat occasionally to do some typing and transcribing for him, and then it seemed the simplest thing was for me to move in with him. So there I was in a three-bedroom upper floor flat of a semi-detached house at 10 Cholmondeley Park in Highgate, which Alan rented with his ex-wife Elizabeth and her new partner Herb, with whom she was writing a book about post-war Spain, and with Anne,* Alan and Elizabeth's ten-year-old daughter.

It was a strange set-up, fraught with difficulties for us all, but especially Anne. It was a situation she shouldn't have been put in, but it was the only way financially, as none of them had enough money to afford separate accommodation. Elizabeth and Herb spent all day locked in their bedroom, writing, and Alan was always occupied with his various projects, too, compiling his *World Library of Folk & Primitive Music* albums, putting together his radio programmes for the BBC, occasionally performing, and writing a new book *The Folk Songs of North America*. Materially they gave Anne almost anything she wanted, but they didn't part with enough of themselves or their time. They bought her a black poodle puppy, Blue, but Anne would leave the front door open, partly I believe because I told her to keep it shut. But since I was only a few years older than her, I had no authority. One day, Blue ran out and was run over on the main road. It was an unnecessary tragedy.

The atmosphere was often edgy. We had 'house meetings' as the need arose where complaints were raised. Elizabeth was angry with me one morning because I'd taken the top of the milk for my coffee instead of shaking the bottle first, thus depriving Anne of nutrition, she said… Well, I thought, there are far more important things that she is being deprived of. Once Alan slammed away from the table, refusing to eat the dinner that Elizabeth had prepared for one of

*Anne later became Anna Lomax Wood, a noted anthropologist and folklorist.

Herb's Jewish festivals – matzos with cottage cheese, sprinkled with paprika, and that was all. I rather liked it.

Elizabeth was often angry over trifles, but I can understand now that she felt I was an interloper, and so I suppose I was, but it hadn't been my idea or even my expectation that I should be there. It was bad enough to be made to feel unwelcome, and I was also coping with the guilt and embarrassment of living with a man I wasn't married to. How different attitudes were then, or perhaps I was too unworldly.

When visitors came to the flat I tried to pass myself off as Alan's secretary. I don't suppose anyone was fooled, and I now realise that probably no-one even much cared. And what did my mother think of all this? She didn't like Alan, after all, he *was* a man. She told me some years later, though, that she felt I was safer in London living with him than being on my own – all those dangerous coffee bars! And my sister Dolly had after all set a precedent by sharing a home, unmarried, with Jonathan Clowes back in Hastings. All I know is, when I reflect on it, that I was a most useful girlfriend for Alan, having as I did a love of folksong, an instinct for it and intelligent understanding of it – and the ability to type! I'll admit I was quite scared of Elizabeth, she had a remarkable way of showing scorn with a curled lower lip, especially at my attempts at cooking. They all refused to eat my liver and onions, saying it would give them liver flukes, though my scrambled eggs had improved since the Troubadour days.

Alan had many guests who arrived from America; among these were Guy Carawan and his wife Candie, young folksong enthusiasts who stayed a while. They insisted on cooking occasionally, and their most frequent meal was beef heart, sliced and flash-fried. They ate it for the iron in it they said, but no-one else could stomach it; but it gave me a flashback to childhood and the savoury smell of the braised heart that Mum cooked for Grandad.

Guy played guitar accompaniments on my first two albums, *Sweet England* and *False True Lovers*, recorded by Peter Kennedy and Alan in 1958. I remember the couple as handsome, decent, sweet-natured and a bit awestruck by things English. One day, as I was cutting a bunch of grapes into 'snippets', they were entranced by that word, thinking it must be an old Elizabethan usage. They went on to great achievements. Guy became the music director and song leader at The Highlander Research and Education Centre in New Market, Tennessee, and they helped popularise the song 'We Shall Overcome', making it the anthem of the Civil Rights Movement for which they both worked.

All this time my world was expanding, and not just musically. One evening Alan took me to the Venezia, a restaurant in Soho. He ordered *pollo sorpresa* for me. I didn't know what the surprise was going to be, but was delighted when the waiter cut open the crusted chicken breast and golden garlic butter flowed out over the plate. It was the most delicious thing I'd ever eaten. It was followed by Strawberries Alexander, the fruit tossed at the table by the waiter, in brandy, sugar and cream.

One of the first tasks I was given when I'd settled in was to transcribe the words of the work songs, blues and field hollers of Alan's 1947–8 recordings made in Parchman Farm, the Mississippi State Penitentiary. The Nixa Record Company was releasing an LP, *Murderers' Home*, along with a booklet containing all the words. This material was new to me, sung by the convicts in their deep Southern accents, which I found impenetrable. At first I was baffled. One song in particular that I couldn't figure out:

> *There ain't no more cane on the Brazos*
> *They done grind it all in molasses*

What was the 'Brazos'? I hadn't at that time heard of that Texas river, and for some reason I didn't associate the word 'cane' with sugar, and had to ask Alan for an explanation. Gradually, though, I grew accustomed to the language, and listened enthralled to the songs, over and over again. I still think of those recordings as being some of the most noble music I have ever heard, tempered by feeling guilty knowing that the men were incarcerated, often for no other reason than that they were black. And, of course, I had no inkling then that a few years later I'd be with Alan recording in Parchman Farm.

My growing understanding of the Southern accent stood me in good stead when visiting American blues men arrived at the flat –

among them Muddy Waters, Sonny Terry and Brownie McGhee, and Memphis Slim. I was better able to understand their speech, although occasionally I had to concentrate hard. What wonderful men they were, courteous and charming, humorous, wearing sharp clothes and with sharp minds. Alan relished their company, and it was good to see the respect and affection, the ease and the laughter, that flowed between them – and they weren't above joshing Alan, too. It was a privilege for me to meet them, and I loved their music. We went to the occasional gig: seeing Muddy Waters perform for the first time was a revelation; I had never seen such explicit eroticism before, menacing, arousing, teasing and joyful. Nowadays when I see pop performers being gratuitously 'sexy', grabbing at various parts of their bodies, making the now-ubiquitous choreographed provocative moves, it strikes me as coarse and just plain tiresome. Muddy could spontaneously arouse his entire audience with a charge of genuine virility (as Elvis Presley could – but then who had he learned from?). The British audiences were thrilled to see these bluesmen that they'd only ever heard on recordings, actually performing live, and they greeted them with warmth, love and respect, and that was reciprocated by the musicians.

I was also meeting singers from the British Isles, people that Alan and Peter had recorded on their many song-hunting trips. I had some favourites, although sometimes they could be challenging. Davy Stewart, a Scottish tinker, energetic singer and passionate talker was one I got to know well and grew very fond of. He came down to London in December 1957 to do some recordings for the BBC and stayed with us, and it was my duty to escort him across London and deliver him to the studio on time. Invariably though, on the Underground he'd engage fellow passengers in conversation, more often than not totally bewildering them; his Scots accent was so strong and his words indistinct as he had more gaps in his mouth than teeth. And every time we got to the bottom of an escalator he'd whip out his accordion and start busking. It was the very devil to get him to move on! His voice was loud and penetrating, after all, that's what he did for a living, and the sound must have carried through several platforms. His accordion playing matched the keen power of his singing – it had a chaotic grandeur. This tinker/busker was a man of worth, too. He'd fought in the Great War on the Western Front, and had been wounded three times, but before that he had busked around farms and bothies, fairs and markets in Scotland and Ireland, and had acquired a remarkable store of songs. For me, his greatest was 'Bogie's Bonnie Belle', a ballad that is sometimes sung as a love song, which in part it is, although to me it's a heart-breaking tragedy of the highest order, and with one of the most beautiful melodies. Louis Killen, the Northumbrian singer, got it absolutely right, describing it as 'a small tragedy stemming from the class system that determines who is fit to be with whom, with a bitter sting in its tail.' It's a song that can make almost any singer sound good because of its powerful words, its story and exquisite tune, but many can't resist the temptation to sing it too romantically. I know of only one other singer who can match Davy's passionate performance, both as singer and accordionist, and that is John Kirkpatrick. He understands all the implications of the story, and sings it straightforwardly with a touch of pain, anger, bitterness, and yes, male pride.*

Bogie's Bonnie Belle

As I came down to Huntly town one morning for to fee
I met with Bogie of Carney and with him I did agree
To work his two best horses, to cart and harrow and plough
Or anything about the farm that he would have me do

Now Bogie had a daughter, her name was Isabelle
The lily of the valley and the primrose of the dell
Her cheeks they shone like roses, her eyes like the morning dew
She stole my heart completely, so comely for to view

When she went out walking she chose me to be her guide
Down by the banks of Carney to watch the fishes glide
And I put my arm around her waist and gently down did slide
And there we had our taste of love down by the waterside

*You can hear it on John Kirkpatrick's CD *One Man and his Box.*

*But when three long months had come and gone the lassie lost
her bloom
The rose fell from her bonny cheeks and her eyes began to swoon
And when nine long months had come and gone, she brought
forth to me a son
And I was quickly sent for to see what could be done*

*I said that I should marry her, but no that wouldn't do
He said 'You're no match for my Bonnie Belle and she's no
match for you.'
And he sent me packing down the road without a penny of
my fee
So all you lads of Huntly town a long farewell to thee*

*And now she's married to a tinker lad that comes from Huntly town
He mends pots and pans and paraffin lamps and he scours the
country round
Maybe she's got a better match, old Bogie he doesn't tell
But 'twas I that had the maidenhead of Bogie's Bonnie Bell
Maybe she's got a better match, old Bogie he doesn't tell
So a long farewell to Huntly town and Bogie's Bonny Belle*

I recorded a long interview with Davy while he was staying with
Alan and me. I'd forgotten all about it until recently, when Vic Smith*
unearthed a tape of it. Vic said it was one of the best interviews he
had ever heard, because it gave free rein to Davy. Well, I didn't exactly
plan it that way, Vic – I simply couldn't stop him talking!

Another notable visitor was Margaret Barry, the Irish tinker,
singer and banjo player. Alan had first heard her when he was
recording in Ireland in 1951. He told how, while walking down a
street in Dundalk, he heard a woman singing. He went round the
corner to find out who she was, and saw a handsome dark-haired
woman playing a five-string banjo and singing powerfully at a wall,

*Vic is a stalwart of the folk scene in Lewes, East Sussex. He and
his wife Tina ran the Royal Oak Folk Club for twenty-five years.

ALL IN THE DOWNS

throwing her voice against it so that the sound would carry further. He was entranced and thrilled – here was one of the greatest Irish singers he had heard, and quite by chance. The first time I heard her was at a Folk Festival concert in the Royal Albert Hall. Standing on stage, a stately figure with her ropes of black hair, she took command as she struck on her banjo the opening notes of She Moved Through the Fair, and then sang, contorting her mouth, singing out of the side of it. It was a blazing, triumphant performance; everything else that evening paled into insignificance.

She was a unique character and an unstoppable talker – and how she could down the Guinness! Exhausting as she could be, I knew that I was honoured to be in her company. Alan was determined that people should hear her. He had a series of broadcasts on the BBC at the time, his producer was a young David Attenborough, and they booked Margaret for one of the TV shows, *Adventures of a Ballad Hunter*. Both men got into hot water from the Head of Programmes for 'inflicting a toothless wild Irish gypsy on the public.'*

Margaret came to Alan's home several times. She was a voluble talker, like Davy, and it was hard to stop her; she confided in me about the difficulties she faced as a traveller (and since they were confidences, that's how they'll remain). I hope the prodigious amounts of Guinness that she drank helped her.

I grew to love both Davy and Margaret and their music, and I still cherish the memory of the time I spent with them both, people who were so full of life, so vivid, and so uniquely themselves.

In 1956 Peggy Seeger arrived in London from America and was spending time at Alan's working on her guitar arrangements for his book, *The Folk Songs of North America*. She was the half-sister of Pete Seeger and daughter of Ruth and Charles Seeger, composers, musicians and musicologists, and friends in the States of the Lomaxes. She stunned people here with the brilliance of her guitar

*At the BBC Folk Awards in 2008 when I was given the Good Tradition Award, I was sitting at the same table as David, and I reminded him of this. He spoke warmly of Alan, and still remembered what he called 'the Margaret Barry experience' with glee.

and banjo paying, the like of which we hadn't heard before, the level of accompaniment in London being, on the whole, still fairly rudimentary. She was about the same age as me, but I was a little wary of her as she appeared so self-possessed, brisk and a little aloof in her manner, yet with a merry laugh. I also felt aware of a class divide. Generally speaking though, we got on well together, playing tennis, whizzing around London on her scooter, me holding on at the back.

Crucially, though, she and Ewan MacColl had fallen in love. This was around the time that Alan and Ewan formed The Ramblers with Peggy and me, and Brian Daley, a jazz guitarist. I was amused recently to read in a biography of Peggy that, when she was asked who was in The Ramblers, she said there was 'a girl who worked the London bus lines.' So perhaps I'd been right all along about the class divide – although of course I had worked one summer season as a tram conductress in Hastings!

Being in The Ramblers wasn't the happiest experience. We sang mostly songs that Ewan had written, such as 'Dirty Old Town', a song about Salford, and 'Hard Case', a song about Broadmoor Prison, alongside jail and railroad songs that Alan had collected in the States back in the 1940s and which he sang without finesse and a lot of pounding foot-stamping. I remember the embarrassment I felt at this when we were rehearsing in the flat – it seemed so excessive, and I understood the anger and despair of the family who lived beneath us on the ground floor. The songs meant very little to me, the subjects having nothing to do with me. I sang 'The Water Is Wide' as a solo, and joined in on the choruses of the other songs. I wasn't enjoying it, but at least I was earning some money. Being around these two alpha males was often uncomfortable. There was one occasion at Ewan's Ballads and Blues Club when he introduced Alan to the audience as 'the Big Lummox'. Alan smiled to cover his anger.

Despite the rifts within The Ramblers, an EP was released on 2 August 1956, Alan and Ewan's nod to skiffle. All the while that craze was still going strong, Lonnie Donegan singing, purloining and claiming copyright on Lead Belly's songs. The Lomaxes – John, Alan's father, and Alan – had discovered and recorded Huddie

Ledbetter in 1933 while he was a prisoner in Angola, the Louisiana State Penitentiary. The next year, they took their recording of Lead Belly singing 'Goodnight Irene' to the Louisiana Governor Oscar K Allen, who released him from prison on parole to them.

In 1957, on 21 October, Alan made his first recordings of me singing two songs from home, 'The Bonny Labouring Boy' and 'The Bonny Cuckoo'. He took down two versions of each, one unaccompanied, the other with simple guitar accompaniment, to see what, if any, difference it made to the way I sang the song. I don't think there was a verdict. It was a private and personal thing, unreleased until 2002 when David Suff used it to open my box set *Within Sound* on Fledg'ling Records.

One day Alan drove his ex-wife Elizabeth down to Hastings to meet my mother and sister; she was in tears as she listened to the three of us singing 'The Bonny Cuckoo'. I never quite understood why.

> *My bonny cuckoo I tell thee true*
> *That through the groves I'll rove with you*
> *I'll rove with you until the next spring*
> *And then my cuckoo shall sweetly sing*
>
> *The ash and the hazel shall mourning say*
> *O bonny cuckoo don't go away*
> *Don't go away but tarry here*
> *And make the spring last all the year*
> *Cuckoo, cuckoo pray tarry here*
> *And make the spring last all the year*

One of Alan's most ambitious undertakings was his broadcast for the BBC on Christmas Day 1957, the groundbreaking *Sing Christmas and the Turn of the Year*. It was done live. Studios all over the British Isles were hooked up ready with mostly amateur singers and musicians from every part of the country, from Cornwall, Wales and Northern Ireland, Yorkshire, Scotland, the Hebrides, Bristol, London and more, all waiting to perform a local song, tune or custom. Such a thing hadn't been attempted before on such a scale. Alan was in the Birmingham studio masterminding and compering the whole thing, almost through the strength of his will making it come together.

It was a mammoth broadcast for its time, made more difficult and nerve-racking for the performers by the fact that none of the studios could hear what was going on elsewhere. Yes, we'd got a printed outline of the show that we could follow, but we all had to wait until the green studio light came on after an over-excited Alan yelled, 'Come in, London', or wherever, and you then had to do your piece immediately. The tension in the London studio was quite intense, I remember, the only relaxed person being Fitzroy Coleman who was there to sing a calypso. I think I sang 'This is the Truth Sent From Above' and 'The Cherry Tree Carol'.*

That was quite a nerve-racking experience, but possibly a worse one for me was a week's booking to sing in the interval at Theatre Royal Stratford East in the Theatre Workshop's production of Tennessee Williams's *The Glass Menagerie* in 1958. Alan, Elizabeth, Herb and Anne had all cleared off to Crete for a holiday at the invitation of Alan's previous girlfriend, the tall, beautiful, sophisticated Susan Mills, a painter, photographer and model, and incidentally, a really nice woman. It was she who took these 'glamorous' photographs of me (pages 95, and opposite).

But back to the theatre: I had to sing six Appalachian songs in the interval and introduce each one with a brief story. Alan said it would be a useful experience, and suggested what I should say, for example, when I sang 'Single Girl': 'When a young mountain girl, about to marry, asked her granny for advice, she was told, "Don't do hit, honey, don't never do hit."' I couldn't bring myself to say 'hit' instead of 'it' and always thought up my own lines after that. The whole experience was embarrassing, and I would imagine a dismal failure. Audiences don't want extra 'entertainment' during the interval; they either want to dash off for a drink, or stay in their seats and chat. Still, it toughened me up a bit and I got paid, but I

---

*You can still hear the programme on Radio 4 Archives, but I'm not sure that you'd want to.

had to make my way home from Stratford East to Highgate and an empty flat. Alan brought me a present from Crete, a turquoise ring, but even as I thanked him, I could tell that it was rather cheap. He told me that I wouldn't have enjoyed the holiday anyway, as Crete was full of large wasps!

The big event of 1958 was the completion of Alan's book, the one that Peggy and I had been working on: *The Folk Songs of North America*, published in England by Cassell in 1960. It contained 317 songs from all over the United States, with comprehensive notes for each section and for every song. Peggy transcribed the tunes and provided guitar chords; Mátyás Seiber and Don Banks wrote a hundred piano arrangements; Michael Leonard was the illustrator, and I was editorial assistant. Perhaps it was this work that turned Alan's mind towards America and made him decide to return home. It was also the last time he recorded my singing, and I wonder now if this was a gift he made me as an apology, perhaps, for deciding to leave me behind. He and Peter Kennedy recorded some thirty-eight songs from my repertoire in just two days, one day in Peter Kennedy's home, and the second in the basement room at Cecil Sharp House. They became my first two LPs, *Sweet England*, on Argo, Decca's subsidiary label, and *False True Lovers*, released on the Folkways label in the States. I still have that first contract. To make it legal I had to sign my name across a postage stamp, and I received seven guineas; how wonderfully old-fashioned that sounds. You have to take those first steps at some point, and faltering as I think those early recordings are, I can hear in some of the songs a glimpse of what I would become. Alan wrote in his notes:

> During the whole time I knew her, her command of her songs and her grasp of singing style grew stronger... Picking her way back across almost a century finding for herself the traditional heart of each song and making it come alive again. What comes through is sincerity, purity of instinct and a tremendous delicacy of feeling. Here one occasionally has that rarest of

musical experiences, hearing a young girl singing alone
in the house or garden, dreaming of love. This is a
quality she is bound to lose as time passes…

Alan left to return to the States in July 1958. My mum had
volunteered to come to Highgate to help with packing up the books,
tapes, papers, albums and clothes that all went into cardboard boxes
for the sea voyage back across the Atlantic, and for me and my
possessions to go to Kentish Town where by now, she, Dolly and
Jonathan were living in a council flat, having moved to London.
In the pile of books that were going to America, I found the two
volumes of Sharp's *English Folk Songs from the Southern Appalachians*,
which had cost me two weeks' wages when I first came to London.
They'd got my name in them, but crossed through with pencil, and
the name 'Lomax' written under it. Oh no you don't, I thought, and
quietly rescued them.

I'm not sure whether Mum was glad or not that Alan and I would
no longer be together. I don't think she ever really approved of our
relationship, he being twice as old as me, and about the same age as her.
True to form, Alan criticised Mum's packing abilities and her replies
were caustic. It wasn't quite the fond farewell I'd hoped for. Eventually
though, it was all completed, and away we went down to Waterloo
Station where Alan was to board the boat-train for Southampton. I
stood on the platform and waved a heartbroken goodbye until the
train was out of sight. I didn't expect to see him again.

To cheer me up, Mum brought a box of chocolates and took
me to a cinema in Leicester Square to see *Attila the Hun*, starring
Anthony Quinn and Sophia Loren.

I spent the next few months listening to Peter Kennedy's
collection of field recordings, learning more songs, trying to improve
my rather basic banjo playing, and doing the occasional folk club
booking. I was starting to introduce the songs, following Alan's
advice that I should find something interesting, amusing or relevant
to relate, but above all, to acknowledge the source singer.

Some six months later, early in 1959, quite out of the blue, a letter
arrived from Alan saying that he was planning a field recording trip

in the Deep South. He needed an assistant. Would I like to join him? I didn't hesitate. A ticket arrived for my voyage to New York on the SS United States, that being the cheaper option – in those days only film-stars and the wealthy flew. In April 1959 I was on my way to join the man I admired and loved, and to have the biggest adventure of my life.

I wrote my first book *America Over the Water* in 2005, detailing, as best I could, my memories of that field recording trip with Alan Lomax in the deep South of America in the autumn of 1959.

The Southern Journey was such a shock for a 23-year-old from Hastings, plunged into a foreign society that, shaped by extreme poverty, religious fundamentalism and racial segregation, felt completely alien, even though we shared a common tongue. Yet the universal language of folk music allowed me to form strong personal connections and friendships with many of the musicians I met along the way; and I relished every one. To name just a few: Texas Gladden and her brother Hobart Smith in Virginia, Fred McDowell and his wife Annie Mae, Lonnie and Ed Young in Northern Mississippi, Jimmie Driftwood, Ollie Gilbert and Almeda Riddle in the Ozark Mountains of Arkansas, Bessie Jones and Big John Davis in the Georgia Sea Islands.

I am sometimes asked why, given that 1959 was just on the cusp of the Civil Rights Movement, we weren't more actively and openly involved in that. There had been incidents prior to our journey, notably the arrest, on 1 December 1955, of Rosa Parks, a black seamstress and member of the NAACP (National Association for the Advancement of Coloured People), who had refused to give up her seat on a segregated bus to a white man – as was the law at that time. She was tried, found guilty and fined. The Montgomery NAACP and their leader, a young reverend, Martin Luther King, took up her cause, leading to the year-long Montgomery Alabama Bus Boycott that caused a huge loss of income to the Montgomery Bus Company. It was almost a year later that The US Supreme Court ruled that the Segregation Law was unconstitutional and the buses were integrated.

However, this didn't change the mindset of a great many white supremacists, and the Deep South was still a dangerous and charged place in 1959. Alan was arrested one time – and held overnight – for recording in the black community of Hughes, Arkansas; we were threatened by guards with raised guns at a roadside chain-gang in Georgia; we drove into many towns where Ku Klux Klan signs were highly visible and saw that many diners still had 'Whites Only' signs in their windows. And, most chillingly for me, an old white farmer attending a Sacred Harp all-day sing that we'd been recording in Fyffe, Alabama, said to me as he thumped his beautiful Sacred Harp hymnbook with his palm, 'This book makes me love my enemies'. But then, when I told him that we were heading into Mississippi next to record black musicians, he said 'Don't want no niggers here. Nigger come here last year and the boys run him to death with their guns. No sir, don't want no niggers here.' It was – and still is – the most chilling thing I'd heard in my entire life.

There was often a sense of real unease in various parts of the South, a feeling of being watched. I sometimes think that if we'd been more open about where our sympathies lay, we'd have been in real trouble, and I might have ended up as a pile of bones lying buried under the Mississippi mud.

In any case, a lasting way for us to help was to bring the culture of oppressed black people to the attention of the world. Alan best expressed it in his 1993 book *The Land Where The Blues Began*:

> Thus the portable recorder put neglected cultures and silenced people into the communication chain. Never before had the black people, kept almost incommunicado in the Deep South, a chance to tell their story in their own way… It gave a voice to the voiceless.

SIX: *And Thank God I Was Back In Sweet England Again*

When I returned home from America in early winter of 1960, I joined my mother, sister and Jonathan – who had left Hastings to find work in London – in a council flat in Torriano Avenue, Kentish Town. The estate's name, Long Meadow, must surely have been a reminder of the place it had been in earlier times, before London began to sprawl. How mundane, grey and flat things felt. America and Alan Lomax were behind me; but I knew I had been enriched by the experience. And although I hadn't had the option to stay in the States, I did feel something of a sense of relief at being back in England. Had I stayed with Alan, I would be living his life, not mine.

Realistically I couldn't ever expect to find a life as eventful as the one I'd experienced in America, yet much as I'd enjoyed that unique and remarkable experience, and as greatly as I'd loved the people I met there, deep down I realised that I belonged to England, that I wanted to be an *English* singer of *English* songs. Whatever it was, it would have to involve folk music. So I believe, truly, that, had Alan offered me the choice of staying, the outcome would probably have been the same. I refused to let the words 'mundane, grey and flat' get the upper hand, but allowed a youthful surge of optimism to wonder what might turn up next.

The folk scene had burgeoned while I was away; not only were singers coming down to London from all over the country, but folk clubs were opening everywhere. I must have picked up singing straight away – places as far apart as Newcastle, Brighton, Oxford, Bradford, Nottingham, Cornwall, Wales and Scotland. I was playing five-string banjo in my 'English' style, as well as guitar, and now I also had an Appalachian dulcimer that Alan had given me, handmade in North Carolina from cherry wood. I made good friends; one special one was Louis Killen in Gateshead – I'd stay with Louis and his mother in her flat when I was up there singing at his folk club. Some years later as we were reminiscing he laughed as he remembered the time I swapped giving him banjo lessons – although he didn't have a banjo – for him giving me a cigarette holder – although I didn't smoke! Such little things to remember for years, especially as Louis, or Louisa as he became years later, died in 2013.

In the late spring of 1960 Jean Ritchie, the Kentucky singer who I had long admired, came to London with her husband, the photographer George Pickow. He offered me a few days' paid work as his assistant, one of which was to cover Princess Margaret's wedding on 6 May, 1960. We stood in the crowds massed at the Mall in front of Buckingham Palace. I couldn't see a thing, but George gave me a camera, told me to stand with my back to the procession, lift the camera above my head and snap away. He had also been given permission to photograph inside Big Ben on the strict understanding that he was not to touch or move anything. But George moved a ladder, and stopped Big Ben! How many people can say that?

I was adding to my repertoire of songs, focussing on my own country's tradition, although still singing some Appalachian songs. My friendship with Peter Kennedy and his wife Eirlys (Tommy) had grown even closer. I'd written to them constantly while I was away, often duplicating the letters that I sent to Mum and Dolly. I'd brought back for their boys, David and Jonathan, a leather wallet each with a horse embossed on the front, made by convicts in the Mississippi State Penitentiary. And I was listening regularly to Peter's and Alan's field recordings of English songs and learning many of them. Peter was always endeavouring to promote traditional song, and he'd succeeded in convincing HMV to release three more ten-inch records – *Rocket Along*, *A Jug of Punch* and *A Pinch of Salt*, mixing field recordings of the older generation of singers with us young 'uns. I had a couple of tracks on all three which I had recorded before I went to the States. Peter invited me to meet the young artist he'd found to design the sleeves: charming, light-hearted illustrations of beatnik folkies, very much of the period.

His name was Austin John Marshall, a graphic designer working for Vogue. He was tall, slender, elegantly dressed – a far cry from the average folkie, who was mostly casually, even scruffily dressed and invariably bearded (a generalisation, I know, but not entirely inaccurate). AJ had a more sophisticated air about him, and I was quite intrigued. He was well-spoken and talked about art, music, literature and films. He'd been educated at Christ's Hospital, Horsham, his fees paid by the tobacco company Carreras for whom his father had worked in the years leading up to World War II when he became an RAF pilot. He had lost his life while returning from a bombing raid when his plane came down in the North Sea. Carreras looked after his widow and her two children, Austin John (known as John) and Diana. After Christ's Hospital, John studied at The Slade School of Fine Art.

I started to go out with him; this news reached Alan, and he came to London and asked me to marry him and return to the States. I was sensible enough to believe this was just a reaction on his part. How could I be sure he wouldn't send me away again?

After a few months more I moved in with John at his flat on Maida Avenue, in the area known as Little Venice. The flat, 2A, was on the slightly less affluent side of the canal that ran down the middle of the avenue. It was a rented basement, a long room divided by a large bookcase into a sitting room and a bedroom, and the concrete floor was covered throughout with dusty coconut matting. We had a small table, a couple of chairs, and an Edwardian wicker armchair that was falling apart and whose sharp ends snagged my tights. The one redeeming feature was the French door at the far end of the room that opened onto a walled garden, with a beautiful, crooked old mulberry tree propped up by a time-bleached wooden crutch. Our small kitchen had an exploding water-heater – I learned to be very wary of its temperamental pilot light. There was a shared bathroom out in a cold corridor that had a 'geyser' water heater that made a loud *whoomph* when you lit it, followed by a very thin trickle of water. A breeze-block wall separated us from the flat next door.

It was from this flat that we married, on 13 March 1961, with Peter and Tommy Kennedy as our witnesses. (Alan married Antoinette Marchand on 26 August that same year, although they separated a year later.) Before we set off for the Paddington Registry

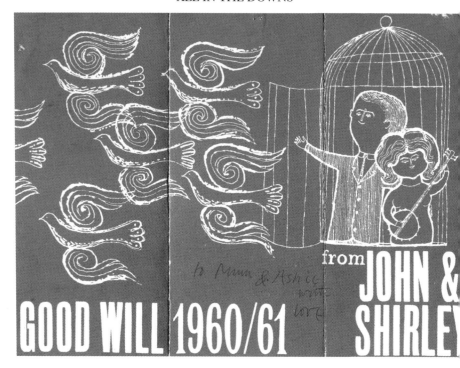

GOOD WILL 1960/61 from JOHN & SHIRLE

Office I put a chicken in the oven to roast, so that we could have a celebratory lunch on our return. But when I started to carve the bird, I found I'd left the plastic-wrapped giblets inside, and the plastic had melted… Did I laugh or cry? I don't remember.

I was pregnant; my craving fortunately was ice-cream, not the lumps of coal that my mother told me she nibbled. That craving never quite left me; my *Desert Island Discs* luxury would be a self-replenishing fridge full of ice-cream, with a couple of lipsticks thrown in. My daughter Polly was born on 17 August 1961 in Queen Mary's Nursing Home in Hampstead. I didn't want her born in Paddington – that felt too brutally urban. I had persuaded Tommy, whose boys had been born in Hampstead, to let me put her address down on all my medical forms so that I'd be accepted there.

Late in the evening of 16 August, after a few hours of labour, I was in an ambulance on my way to Hampstead. Polly was born at

6.50pm the following evening, a labour of twenty-seven hours. When the midwife said 'Mrs Marshall, you have a beautiful daughter', I immediately replied, 'That's Polly.' Over the next couple of days I noticed that her left leg was a little twisted. The doctor thought it was most likely caused by the way she had been lying in the womb, but for safety's sake he thought that her leg should be looked at by a specialist in the hospital down the road, as it couldn't be done in the nursing home. In those days, you spent ten days in hospital after giving birth, so I wasn't allowed to go with her. She was taken down to Hampstead General in a thunderstorm. I stood at the window of the ward, beside myself with anxiety, watching a nurse with my precious baby under her cloak; when Polly was brought back to me, her tiny leg was in a splint.

The care given in those days was exemplary for both mother and baby, with regular home visits from a nurse; how reassuring that was. I breast fed Polly, but was told to give her boiled water in a bottle as well – but to make sure the bottle was sterilised. So I boiled a small saucepan in a large one, then boiled the bottle in the small one, filling the kitchen with steam. What a palaver! What a responsibility! I eventually became more relaxed about the whole business, but it was a bit of a struggle in that small kitchen. I bathed Polly in a large washing up bowl on the kitchen table, having to be really careful not to get the splint wet. Tommy had given me her large Silver Cross pram, but it was too big to go in our front door and our landlord who lived above us refused to let me put it in the main hall. So I had to leave it outside at night, at the bottom of our basement steps. I covered it with a tarpaulin, then the next morning put hot water bottles and warm blankets into it, to make sure it was warm and dry.

My second child, Robert Austin Frederick, named after John's father and my grandfather, was born at home on 25 September 1962; the children worked out years later that there was exactly one year, one month, one week and one day between them! While I was lying on the bed in labour, John was in the kitchen, deep in conversation with the student midwife who'd arrived earlier. When I realised the birth was imminent I yelled for help. The poor student was shocked and scared, and phoned for the actual midwife, who arrived just in the nick of time to bring Robert into the world. Polly had been taken by her grandmother down to Hastings, and while there, took her first steps; I was so upset at missing them.

London in the early 1960s was a city of smog so thick that traffic was often at a standstill, at best a crawl. I remember one earlier Christmas Mum insisting that Dolly and I go with her to a *Daily Worker* Christmas Fair at King's Cross, even though there was such a thick fog that we could scarcely see a yard in front of us. And yet, so determined was Mum that we got there and back from Kentish Town, and I still have the Russian stainless steel long-handled jam spoon that I bought that day. The official 'smog' advice was that you should burn ammonia in saucers to clear the air inside your home, so we did. Then there was the winter of 1962–3, the Big Freeze. The snow had piled so high against our basement door that we couldn't open it, and were housebound for three days with two infants. How on earth did we stay warm with no central heating? We only had a one-bar electric fire and an oil-stove… We were simply used to it, I suppose, and we wore thick jumpers!

By the time we married John had left *Vogue* and was working as a graphic designer for *The Observer* colour supplement. I now had two quite separate groups of friends, my folkies, and those I had acquired through John, most of whom worked in the arts. Among them was Len Deighton, *The Observer*'s food editor and John's boss. Len had come up with the brilliant, innovative idea of The 'Cook-Strip' – recipes presented in a cartoon-like form. They were immensely popular and opened people's eyes as to how good, how interesting, food could be. Nowadays we take the variety of recipes and cooking for granted, but Len really made a difference then. He was also writing his first novel, *The Ipcress File* – published in 1962, and made into a film starring Michael Caine in 1965 – and he asked me if I could type the manuscript for him. Even though John was reasonably well-paid, we were short of money, so I took it on. My earnings were part cash, part Len's old TV set – the first one we had.

During these years I was singing occasionally, though not

travelling far, and I recorded five EPs, the first of which was *Heroes in Love* for Topic Records in 1963. It was the first time I felt I'd made something worthy and it contained four good songs: 'The False Bride' (from Bob Copper), 'Locks and Bolts' (from Sharp's *English Folk Songs from the Southern Appalachians*), 'Rambleaway', and 'The Blacksmith' (from the English gypsy Phoebe Smith).

We stayed in Maida Avenue for three years or so, but it wasn't the easiest place to raise two infants and we needed to move. One day while at work at *The Observer*, John bumped into John Wain, the novelist and critic, who mentioned that he was selling his little Span house in Blackheath. Designed by the architect Eric Lyons, the Span estates were popular and affordable homes. This house had an open-plan living room and kitchen, three bedrooms and a small back garden. They were new, they were clean and they were in fresher, greener surroundings. At the front of the house was a lawn with a laburnum tree, and beyond that a rambling orchard. It was almost like being in the country with space for the children to run and climb trees.

We got a mortgage, bought 15 The Keep for £5000, and moved there on Polly's third birthday, 17 August 1964. We were going up in the world! We treated ourselves to a settee from Heal's, we had William Morris curtains, and we wanted William Morris wallpaper on one wall. This brought a scathing remark from the decorator who pasted it for us – he thought us Span house owners were being pretentious decorating our rather small homes in a style more suitable for Blackheath mansions. In a local antique shop we found what we believed to be a genuine Arts & Crafts black varnished chest painted with four figures representing the seasons. It was signed Hassam, a name that no one recognised, but that many years later was a signature I would see on a stained glass window at Standen House, an Arts and Crafts house in West Sussex. Finally we were vindicated!

The Keep was only a short walk away from Blackheath Village and the Heath itself, where twice a year circuses and funfairs set up. One memorable Christmas the circus performance opened with two trapeze artists dressed as Batman and Robin, Robert's two TV heroes. His face lit up, and his wide blue eyes wandered from mine to theirs to make sure it was true. One time I called him in for tea saying '*Batman*'s on!' and he simply let go of the branch he was climbing half-way up the big old oak tree opposite the house. He fell straight to the ground, winded but not wounded. There was a pond on the Heath where we could sail toy yachts, and shallow enough that it didn't matter too much when Rob fell in. It was a short walk down to Greenwich and the River Thames from where, on New Year's Eve, all the ships sounded their hooters to welcome the New Year in; a thrilling sound. And the district felt so safe that in the run-up to Guy Fawkes' night we young parents would allow our children out alone with their home-made guys to stand on Corner Green and The Keep, collecting pennies from passers-by to buy fireworks.

I was now gigging a fair bit, and as John's hours at *The Observer* were irregular, I had to find childminders. One was a plump, Irish retired nurse, but the main one was my mother who came to stay while I was working away for more than one night. Polly and Rob loved her coming as she played inventive games with them, games that always seemed to involve moving the furniture about to make cars and castles, and dressing up; and of course, I knew the children felt happy, so I was reassured. Otherwise, I occasionally swapped childminding with friends, the husband-and-wife folk duo Dave and Toni Arthur who lived close by and also had two young children – a mutually handy set-up.

But gig days were a strain, first making sure that everything was organised at home, kids settled, me ready; mostly I remember always leaving at the last minute, running along Blackheath Park with my banjo, and falling breathless onto the train at Blackheath station. I travelled everywhere by train, and I enjoyed it. I loved gazing out at the landscapes, and as mobile phones hadn't been invented then, the journeys were relatively quiet and relaxed. I learned a lot about the geography of England, too.

I'd always try to get home overnight from clubs and concerts if I could, so that I could be with the children in the mornings, and rather resented the men who could leave the responsibility of their families to their wives, and doubtless rest when they got home, too.

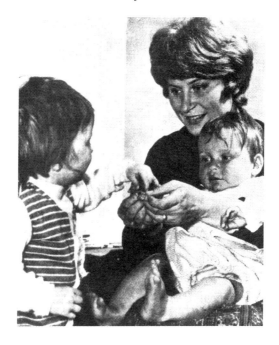

I had a regular mini-cab driver who would pick me up at mainline stations in the very early hours. Sometimes the late-night journeys threw up problems – if you were picking up a train en route from Glasgow, there were inevitably a few drunks on the train. If it got too alarming, a friendly guard would move me to a first-class carriage. One time, after playing at a concert in Birmingham, I stayed on for a Chinese meal with the Ian Campbell Folk Group. I made the late train, but felt rather queasy, putting it down to the prawn toasts. I made it over to Charing Cross before throwing up in a litter bin; it was 5am, so fortunately not many people were around! Then there was the night when, as I sat on Bradford Station at close to 2am waiting for an overnight train, I was approached by two towering policemen who accused me of being a prostitute. I showed them my return ticket and contract for the gig, so they accepted my explanation that I was waiting for a train. How many banjo-playing prostitutes were there, I wondered.

Of course there were times if I was on a short tour that I'd stay with hospitable organisers of clubs, becoming friends with many of them. But there were exceptions… I had a booking at The Blue Parrot Night Club in Birmingham – the agent had persuaded me that every Wednesday was a 'folk night', but it turned out to be a disaster. After I'd finished my first set to an almost hostile audience, the manager came up and said 'I don't think you need do your second set.' He handed over my £15 fee and took me to my accommodation, a run-down hotel close by; I was left in a dark basement room with a door that didn't lock, and an Alsatian prowling around. Another time, the organiser of a club in Liverpool insisted on putting me up for the night at his home. The front door of the house wasn't even attached; there was a plank propping it up outside. When we got in, there was an (understandably) angry and resentful wife who had turned her toddler out of his camp bed and put the bed downstairs for me in their one living room, still with the damp sheets of their equally damp infant. They too had an Alsatian on the loose downstairs. During the night, I needed to use the lavatory, which was outside the back door, but every time I moved, the dog growled. It was probably the most uncomfortable night of my life – even compared to the night spent in the attic room of a hotel that was so cold I slept with my clothes on and my feet in my fur hat in a vain attempt to keep warm. What fun life could be on the road!

Even gigs at more established institutions could frequently be difficult – or even demeaning – but all you can do is laugh at the memory. At a Nottingham University May Ball, I was booked as 'Folk Singer' and put in a room with a notice on the door that said 'Folk Room'. I sat in isolation for well over an hour before a student, a young man, came in and asked if I knew 'Where Have All the Flowers Gone', a song written by Pete Seeger, recorded by Peter, Paul and Mary and Joan Baez. It was ubiquitous in the '60s so of course I *knew* it, but scorned to have it in my repertoire. Still, I sang it for him. He thanked me and sloped off. After another couple of hours on my own, he came back and asked if I'd sing it again. So I did – and that was it for the whole evening. I waited over six months to be paid – the booking had come through a big, reputable (ha!) London agent, and I wanted to get my train fare back at least.

At another University gig, at a concert with Dolly, during the interval after we'd played our first set, a student interviewed us for the University newspaper. I couldn't really make much sense of the questions he was putting to us until he said, 'Oh, Miss Collins, are you going to sing "Amazing Grace" in the second half?' It was then I realised he thought I was Judy Collins, who'd had a big hit with the hymn. I set him straight, and we continued with the interview. He asked Dolly if she wrote all the songs herself, and this in spite of the fact that I'd introduced them as I always did, as traditional songs, giving my sources for them. We still soldiered on. He asked what sort of music I listened to. I replied that I had fairly catholic tastes. 'Oh I like religious songs, too!' he said. I gave up at that point. I think it was also the University that had issued our contract in the names of 'Shortlegs and Dolly Collins.'

Singing English traditional songs as I did was never the easiest, and certainly not the most popular, option. Irish and Scottish music was what most people preferred, and it was loved worldwide: The Dubliners, The Chieftains, The Corries and the Clancy Brothers were crowd-pleasers. I knew I could never achieve that, nor did I want to; it wasn't what I'd set out to accomplish. The downside of their popularity was that it spawned so many second-rate singers and musicians who copied their repertoires; the music was everywhere, you couldn't get away from it and it became commonplace. A general laziness pervaded the scene, and audiences seemed quite content to sing the same old chorus songs and to listen to the same, often second-rate, material being churned out night after weary night.

I was certainly outside the mainstream; but I'd chosen that, and carried on with my English repertoire, as of course did others such as Martin Carthy, Nic Jones, Louis Killen, Anne Briggs and Frankie Armstrong. Even so, when The Young Tradition burst on the scene it was a breath of fresh air. The YT had a great repertoire of songs, several from the Copper Family of Sussex, and they sang bold and brilliant harmonies. They dressed – not outrageously, but certainly noticeably

– almost in costume. Royston Wood was a bit of a dandy, a dignified figure in rather dark and formal long jackets, their sombre aspect lifted by the frilled white collars that framed his handsome face with its generous sideburns. Peter Bellamy wore exuberant hippy clothes; he had a fall of fine flaxen hair and long, elegant features, while Heather Wood (no relation to Royston) had long wavy golden hair and wore long wavy frocks. Their singing was a revelation, charged with energy: Royston's deep voice lending gravitas to a song, the amazing timbre of Peter's shrill voice, almost a bleat – although that does him an injustice; while Heather soared away over both their voices, providing sweet and beautiful harmonies. It was brave, passionate and compelling and they were powerful and fun and unique.

After one gig I did with them in Wales, we decided to travel back to London that same night. As we drove through Gloucester at around one in the morning, the windows closed and the car full of the fug from the pot they were smoking, a policeman pushing a bicycle appeared in the middle of the road and signalled us to stop. 'Oh God,' I thought, 'Now we're for it!' Royston wound down his window and calmly said 'Good evening, Officer,' in that beautifully modulated voice of his. The fumes must have been wafting out of the window, but the policeman merely greeted us with a 'Good evening,' back, and apologised, but said we'd have to make a detour as the road ahead was closed. He waved us on and off we drove. Either he was being lenient or he simply didn't recognise the smell of pot – it might have been a still-innocent time in Gloucester. Or perhaps he didn't want to tackle a car with four people in it, alone in the middle of the night…

Dolly and I recorded one album with The Young Tradition in 1969, *The Holly Bears The Crown* for Argo, produced by John Gilbert. We went into the studio; I had a heavy cold and the YT were under-prepared. Some weeks later they broke up, and the album didn't see the light of day until David Suff put it out on his Fledg'ling label in 1995, a quarter of a century later. Dolly had worked with the YT on other albums, but it was on Peter Bellamy's masterpiece, his ballad opera *The Transports*, that she was in full flight again as the arranger; it was acknowledged as a major work.

Sadly, both Peter and Royston are dead. In 1990, Royston, ever chivalrous, had stopped on a motorway to assist a woman whose car had broken down and was hit and killed by another vehicle. Peter died by his own hand a year later. The shock and disbelief was extreme, and yet even as I heard the news I recalled something that had happened when he and I were on an Australian tour together in 1980. We were in Tasmania at The Hobart Folk Festival, and had a free day and were taken for a drive across the island. On the way back we came to a point where the land fell away, an incredibly beautiful vista set in front of us. The driver and I got out of the car to take in the scene, but Peter refused; he sat in the car and continued chain-smoking. I was so disturbed: that is a man who has lost interest I thought, who is tired of life. One thing consoled me after his suicide, and that was the knowledge that he and Bob Copper had a great regard for each other, and had forged such a good, deep friendship.

Not only was Austin John a great supporter of my singing, he was always aware of what was going on elsewhere musically and, apart from jazz, he had a fine ear for what was good and interesting. It was his suggestion that I should collaborate with Davy Graham, a young guitarist that he'd heard play in one of the jazz clubs he frequented. Davy was making a name for himself with a revolutionary style that combined folk, blues, and jazz, with Middle Eastern, North African and Indian overtones. The word 'jazz' rang alarm bells, but I agreed to listen to Davy. He came out to Blackheath one day; a handsome, gentle and charming young man. He sat down, tuned up his guitar and said that he'd like to play his arrangement of 'She Moves Through the Fair' – a song I knew well from the singing of Margaret Barry. What, I wondered, would Davy do with this classic song? Well, he played it like an Indian raga – it worked, and somehow he enhanced its Irish quality at the same time. I was both impressed and captivated, and decided there and then that it could be a worthwhile and workable experiment.

An unused promotional photograph of Shirley and Davy Graham.

John proposed a collaborative album to Decca Records, and in 1964 *Folk Roots, New Routes* was recorded and released. Davy played three of his own compositions, 'Rif Mountain', 'Grooveyard' and 'Blue Monk'. His most famous piece, 'Angi', had already been recorded on his first EP *3/4 AD* with Alexis Korner in 1962. Every guitarist worth his salt played 'Angi'; it was even covered by Simon & Garfunkel on their 1966 album *Sounds of Silence*.

I chose three English songs, two Scottish, two Irish and seven American songs, two of which, 'Dearest Dear' and 'Pretty Saro' (for which I wrote the tune) came from Sharp's Appalachian book. 'Saro' was one of Davy's most radical arrangements, pushing and whining the notes, taking off between verses with Indian and North African riffs, then settling back down to a long deep chord to open the next verse. It was powerful stuff, and it strengthened my singing. Two of the songs I'd learned on my American field trip with Alan Lomax, 'The Bad Girl' from the noted Virginia singer Texas Gladden, and 'The Boll Weevil', from Vera Hall, a black washerwoman of Alabama, who was one of the most simply beautiful singers I'd heard – she sang so lightly, and so gracefully. I tried to capture her spirit, and I hope I didn't do too badly. Davy enhanced all the songs with his distinctive arrangements, while never losing their original identities, understanding how essential that was. He played with such strength, allure and depth, the like of which none of us had heard before. Everything, everyone paled beside him.

The recording process was quite straightforward; neither of us being temperamental. We were, however, quite widely separated from each other across the studio floor, perched on stools, my least favourite position for singing. There's a photo of us from that session looking quite forlorn! It was here that I learned the importance of a great recording engineer – and ours was Gus Dudgeon, one of the very best. And a very fine producer, too, Ray Horricks.

I was pleased with the album – and still am; I sang well, and there was a certain poise about it. There's only one song I wish I hadn't included – 'Jane, Jane', which I'd learned from Peggy Seeger and was totally unsuitable. I think I felt that I needed one lighter song, but why I chose that one, I don't know, agreeing with one reviewer who wrote 'What on earth made her sing that?' Was the album well received? In some quarters yes, in others not. Hackles rose; the knives were out from the MacColl gang.

In one of the folk magazines this verse was printed, the writer hiding behind the pseudonym of Speedwell… but we all knew who it was.

> *The words form in her mouth like jellied eels,*
> *Sloppy, slithering half-formed words*
> *that fall to earth like wing-less birds*
> *like half-chewed ju-jubes, consonants congeal*
> *But nimble fingered Davy carries her along*
> *The Lady Baden-Powell of English song…*

There was also something about me being bucolic, lumbering like a Jersey cow…

But apart from that, it was generally agreed that it was a defining moment in the world of folk song; that could hardly be denied. Karl Dallas later wrote in his book *The Electric Muse*: 'It was there at that instant that Electric Folk was born; Folk-Rock, call it what you will'. Even though it was an entirely acoustic album!

I never liked the original album sleeve, and was happy when it was reissued in 1980 by John on his and Gill Cook's label, Righteous Records, with a new cover, a lovely, sensitive drawing that he did of Davy and me, our two heads together. John was delighted that he was able to release it in stereo; the original, although recorded in stereo, was released in mono.

The whole experience made me aware that there were ways to accompany songs that, while still respecting their source, breathed new life into them; the songs deserved that. At the same time, I was still Shirley Collins, from Sussex, singing in her own natural voice; I wouldn't, couldn't, change that – ever.

Davy and I gave just four concerts together. One was at the Mercury Theatre, another I think was at The Lyric Hammersmith, which we shared with The Youth Jazz Orchestra. I wonder what the audience made of that one! And, in January 1965, we played Cecil Sharp House, a troubling evening for me. John suggested that I bring my 'look' (I didn't think I had one!) up to date, and had bought me a corduroy shift with a lace-up collar in the style of Robin Hood. It was a dress I loved, but John insisted that I team it with knee-high black leather boots. These were very slowly becoming fashionable, but I still associated them with Nazi jackboots, a long memory from wartime, and from films; only villains wore long boots! I was very uneasy about appearing in public wearing them, and I was anxious as to how Davy and I would be received in the home of the English Folk Dance & Song Society – how challenging might our music be, and how outrageous and masculine my appearance! I needn't have worried; the concert was well-received, and nobody made any comment at all about my boots! I know it sounds far-fetched nowadays, when anything goes in the world of fashion. Then there was the time that John had persuaded me to buy my first black maxi-coat, the style doubtless encouraged by fabric manufacturers as an antidote to the ubiquitous mini-skirt which didn't use much material. The first time I wore it was to a gig at The Fo'c's'le Club in Southampton, and it even attracted attention on the train. When I walked into the folk club in the pub, a group of men actually booed – then cheered when I took the coat off and was seen in my mini-dress! I can scarcely now believe that there was such a fuss about a garment being too *long*! Just to reinforce the truth of this, there was an incident at Polly's primary school. Virtually all the little girls wore the current fashion for very short skirts, almost like pelmets, and often strips of vinyl. I had bought Polly a mid-calf-length denim pinafore, and the first day she wore it to school she was called into the headmaster's office and instructed to tell her mother that she was NOT to wear 'that disgusting garment' to school. Poor child – she felt so humiliated, and she was only seven years old.

But back to Davy. Our musical partnership wasn't to last. I was often nervous in his company; he was occasionally unreliable, or behaved strangely, due to the drugs he took, I suppose. One evening we had a concert together just north of London and had arranged to link up at King's Cross Station, but when we met he said we couldn't travel on the same train, and wouldn't give a reason. So, baffled and a little humiliated, I caught one train, he another, a very unsettling start to a concert. He was highly intelligent, intellectual, and with wide-ranging interests. He always carried a book and would read passages to me, mostly about Eastern religions. I didn't understand it, and anyway it simply didn't hold any appeal for me; but the outcome was that I felt somehow superficial and trivial. Davy was exquisitely courteous, but often stern and aloof; a man you couldn't always feel at ease with, but one that you were bound to admire.

Overleaf: Unused photograph from *The Power of The True Love Knot* sessions, 1968 (David Montgomery).

SEVEN: *The Whitsun Dance*

The experiment with Davy was over, but I couldn't bear the thought of going to back to singing or recording with just my own five-string banjo or guitar accompaniments. I had always believed that English folk songs were so beautiful, the melodies so exquisite that they merited the best of arrangements – more than the standard everyday ones that were the norm. Of course, Nic Jones and Martin Carthy were streets ahead of everyone with their accompaniments, but I knew I could never reach that level with my own playing. Mine was minimal; it worked in its gentle, untaxing way, but it was no longer sufficient.

I was sitting one day in the living room at Blackheath mulling over this problem, when the thought floated into my mind that back in the Highgate days, when Alan Lomax was planning his book *The Folk Songs of North America*, he had commissioned two composers, Mátyás Seiber and Don Banks, to write keyboard arrangements. I hadn't ever heard them played, and suggested to John that we take the book to Dolly and get her to play them to see what they were like. She played the two songs I wanted to hear – 'When A Man's in Love' from Nova Scotia, and a stately Sacred Harp hymn 'Through All the World Below'.* Neither Dolly, John nor I were convinced by the arrangements; they sounded banal, lacking an understanding of the songs. I don't know why it hadn't occurred to the three of us that Dolly should try her hand at writing some arrangements – after all, she was both a composer and a pianist. She agreed to give it a try, and turned up a week or so later with her first attempt – a song set for three French horns! It was impossible to sing against, and I thought a baffling choice on her part, although she always was keen

* Just for interest, John recorded the session and both tracks were included, some forty years later, on *Within Sound*.

on pushing the boundaries! She took the rejection very well and promised to write for the piano. Meanwhile a miracle was waiting in the wings.

It was around this time that we discovered the portative pipe-organ, the beautiful flute-organ, a faithful reproduction built by the master organ maker Noel Mander of an instrument made in Bucharest in 1689. Dolly, John and I used to go along to the Early Music Centre in West London to sit and listen to the music, and the rehearsals. We'd had a love of Early and Renaissance music since we were teenagers, when Uncle Fred had introduced us to Monteverdi through his wind-up gramophone; and Mum, Dolly and I used to sing madrigals at home. One of them, Orlando Gibbons's 'The Silver Swan' had five parts, but as there were only three of us, Mum sang the soprano, Dolly the alto, while I had the bass!* The minute we heard those first few notes of the little organ, we knew straightaway this was the instrument we'd been looking for. It would inspire us: Dolly to write *for*, and me to sing *with*. Not only was it beautiful to look at with its slender, squared wooden pipes, it also produced the sweetest, breathiest fluting notes. We never owned the flute-organ, it was far too expensive to buy, so we hired it from Noel Mander every time we recorded or were out gigging. Either Dolly's husband Dave Busby drove us, or later, her second husband Stuart Hollyer. It was slightly too large to fit into Stuart's estate car, and Noel Mander obligingly trimmed a tiny corner off. I've often wished I had that piece of wood as a souvenir. And it was there at The Early Music Centre that we first met David Munrow, the genius of Early Music. At that time he was playing in Michael Morrow's consort, Musica Reservata, from whom he would soon split to form his own Early Music Consort, but it proved to be a crucial meeting for us.

From then on, Dolly wrote for the flute-organ. To work with written arrangements was going to be new to me as a singer, but not a problem; Dolly was such a sympathetic musician, and she knew and felt the importance of my wanting an 'English' sound. She had a

---

*It's the final track on *Lodestar* – just my voice, with the other parts played on harmonium and viola, capturing the entire song.

sublime sense of harmony and wrote such beautiful introductions to the songs that I could simply launch myself into the singing. When a song needed to be subtle or understated, that's what she wrote; or she could be triumphal and regal, or tender or full of sprightly joy. One of her loveliest arrangements was 'The Streets of Derry' that I'd learned from the singing of Irish singer Mrs Sarah Makem; Dolly making the flute-organ sound like uilleann pipes.

It was really pleasing that Dolly was now writing and arranging professionally. And she was wonderful to work with, both as a sister and an accompanist. I didn't have to change the way I sang; it was still my voice. Our first outing together was in 1967, recording *The Sweet Primeroses*, produced by John for Topic Records. The one downside to making this was that I'd had my tonsils out shortly before, and when I play the album now, I can hear a tentative quality to my singing (or perhaps I'm listening for it). We brought three people in to sing chorus, called for contractual reasons The Heathwood Friends. They were in fact The Young Tradition, *Heath*er Wood, Royston *Wood*, Peter Bell*amy* (a bit of licence there for the French *ami*!).

On the fashion front, I was photographed by Brian Shuel for the cover wearing a sage-green corduroy trouser suit, very dashing with its high collar and brass buttons. It was made by Jeff Banks, the fashion designer, who was married to the singer Sandie Shaw at the time, at Clobber, his boutique in Blackheath Village.

My next task was to persuade Dolly to accompany me on gigs; I wanted audiences to hear the flute-organ and Dolly's transforming arrangements live. She was reluctant at first, nervous and shy of appearing in public, pointing out that she wasn't really a pianist, and certainly hadn't trained to actually perform on stage. But I said I'd do all the talking and singing – all she had to do was play.

By now Dolly had left Hastings and was living in Chingford with her husband Dave Busby, an art teacher and Morris dancer. They had married on 12 November, 1968 at Battle, in East Sussex, a memorable ceremony where the wedding party processed the length of the High Street behind a side of Morris Men dancing down through the town.

She was reluctant at first but, begged by me and persuaded by her husband, gave it a try. And so we became Shirley & Dolly Collins. I loved working with Dolly, having her there on stage with me. There was such sympathy between us, and as well as the beautiful music, lots of laughter.

Dolly began to enjoy the experience of gigging; after all, you never knew what might happen. One night we were interrupted mid-song by a shout from a chap in the audience, 'Excuse me, miss – your organ's on fire!' The audience laughed and gasped in turn. I turned to Dolly and sure enough there was smoke billowing lightly out from the back of the wooden base, from the electric motor that powered it. But soon both the organ and the audience were back under control and we continued.

Our next album was *The Power of the True Love Knot*, recorded in 1968 for Polydor Records, with Joe Boyd as producer. Joe managed Sandy Denny, Fairport Convention and The Incredible String Band. Poor Joe – he didn't quite know what to make of me. He thought my singing was too plain and urged me to *sell* the song a bit more, put

a bit of life into it! 'Can you give it a bit more go?' he asked at some point. I think he wanted me to be Sandy Denny! But I wasn't and never could be. I was pretty annoyed, and I certainly wasn't going to change what I did, what I was, just to please this young American, even though he was a powerful person in the music industry.

To add some lustre and fun to the album, Joe brought in Robin Williamson and Mike Heron of The Incredible String Band. They played percussion on Indian finger cymbals, African drum, Japanese finger sticks, and Robin on whistle and chanter. And as if that wasn't enough, they hand-clapped through 'The Seven Yellow Gypsies'. Mind you, they *did* enhance a couple of tracks, it was fun, and they were – still are – the most charming of men, and uniquely talented, too. We became good friends from the very first; you couldn't help but love them and their music; beautiful, fey, Celtic, funny, and perhaps above all, wise.*

---

* Joe didn't even give the album a mention in his book *White Bicycles*…

The Incredibles invited Dolly to arrange and play two or three songs on their 1968 album *The Hangman's Beautiful Daughter*. The only time I saw her angry with them was the occasion when Robin tried to persuade her to take some LSD, telling her that she couldn't see trees properly until she took the drug. She was enraged! It was quite the wrong thing to say to my sister whose knowledge of all things in nature was quite exceptional, and whose contempt (and fear) of people who took drugs was as strong as mine.

In October of that year we had a joint concert, *October Songs*, with The Incredibles at The Queen Elizabeth Hall. I still have a copy of the poster that Austin John designed. And Robin sent me a song, 'God Dog'. In an interview for *Swing 51* magazine he said:

> I thought it would be a very suitable song for Shirley
> to sing because I'd always liked her voice. To me it's a
> very natural voice and because 'God Dog' is such an
> innocent song, – it's a child's song really, I didn't know
> anyone else who would be able to sing it. In the end, I
> guess I more or less wrote it for her.

Those are such precious words to me, and one of the best gifts I ever received, an honour. It would have to be sung on the next album, whenever and whatever that might be.

Nowadays, when people talk to me about our 1968 album *The Power of the True Love Knot*, they mostly remember the exquisite cello on the first track 'The Bonnie Boy' played by Bram Martin on his 1740 Testuri cello. As it says in the original sleeve-notes:

> Mr Martin was able to grasp very quickly the idiom we
> were after: even, discreet and 'wonderful warm', two
> words from the second verse of the song.

On the original cover, I'm photographed by David Montgomery sitting in a meadow at the foot of the South Downs. I'm wearing a long dress made for me by my cousin Mary Ball, from a Liberty William Morris blue and green velvet, holding a beautiful instrument which I play on the album. I had commissioned it in 1967 from John Bailey; its body is shaped like a half of a mountain dulcimer, which is attached to a Victorian 5-string banjo neck. I could never think of a name for it – should it be a banjimer? A dulcimo? It is now called This Instrument after the heart-shaped label that John Bailey put inside it, that read 'This instrument was made for Shirley Collins', although I no longer have it. I sold it to musician and long-time friend Ian Kearey in the 1980s when I needed money and was no longer singing. Decades later Ian would be the musical director of my album *Lodestar*, on which he plays This Instrument, so in that sense it is still with me.

There are some things I've said, perhaps to get a cheap laugh that I am now ashamed of. One of these was to mock the elderly ladies who danced in such a genteel manner with each other at the country dances at Cecil Sharp House. That is until Austin John chided me one day and rightly so, pointing out that they were most likely women who had lost their husbands or sweethearts in the Great War. So he wrote 'The Whitsun Dance': 'The feet that were nimble tread carefully now, As gentle a measure as age do allow'. The one redeeming feature of my insensitivity at that point was that had I not been so derisive, the song might never have been written… And what a loss that would be.

In my defence, the atmosphere at Cecil Sharp House for many years was so middle-class, so middle-aged, so lacking in energy. Outside the House was a stone bearing the words: 'This building is erected in memory of Cecil Sharp who restored to the English people the songs and dances of their country.' But remembering the difficulties I'd had trying to get into the library, it seemed to me that the English Folk Dance & Song Society was trying to keep the people *away* from their heritage. In 1960 Princess Margaret was made President of the Society; there are some illuminating photographs of her arriving at Cecil Sharp House one Christmas in evening dress, with her retinue all dressed formally. Dancers were so careful, toes were pointed daintily, skirts held up nicely. It all looked so polite, so joyless, rather as if dancing was more a duty than a pleasure. There was nothing about it that felt robust or of 'the people.' Thank heavens that was all to change in time.

I wanted to sing 'The Whitsun Dance', so I had to find a tune for it, one that would match the words. One tune persisted in my head, and that was the Copper Family song 'The Week Before Easter.' It fitted perfectly.

The Whitsun Dance

> 1: *It's fifty-one spring times since she was a bride*
> *But still you may see her at each Whitsuntide*
> *In a dress of white linen and ribbons of green*
> *As green as her memories of loving*

> 2: *The feet that were nimble tread carefully now*
> *As gentle a measure as age do allow*
> *Through groves of white blossom, through fields of young corn*
> *Where once she was pledged to her sweetheart*

> 3: *The fields they are empty, the hedges grow free*
> *No young men to tend them or pastures go see*
> *They've gone where the forest of oak trees before*
> *Had gone to be wasted in battle*

> 4: *Down from the green farmlands and from their loved ones*
> *Marched husbands and brothers and fathers and sons*
> *There's a fine roll of honour where the maypole once was*
> *And the ladies go dancing at Whitsun*

> 5: *There's a straight row of houses in these latter days*
> *Are covering the Downs where the sheep used to graze*
> *There's a field of red poppies and a wreath from the Queen*
> *And the ladies remember at Whitsun*
> *And the ladies go dancing at Whitsun*

Shirley and Alan Lomax in Majorca, 1960.
(Photographs by Alan Lomax and Shirley Collins).

Top: Shirley photographed by Brian Shuel for *The Sweet Primeroses* (1967).
Bottom: The inscription inside This Instrument (Ian Kearey).

Top: Shirley and Ashley Hutchings with the Etchingham Steam Band at Lewes Folk Day 1974/75. *Bottom:* Shirley with Julie Carter and Dan Quinn, circa 1980.

Top: Shirley and Dolly photographed by Brian Shuel on Bexhill beach, for *As Many As Will*, 1978. *Bottom:* Shirley and Dolly, family photo, circa 1993. *Opposite:* Shirley and Dolly at Cecil Sharp House, 1978.

Top: Lodestar at the Barbican (Keith Bache).
Bottom: Shirley and friends celebrate her 80th birthday at the
South Bank Centre (Ruth Bayer).

This Page: Lodestar live, 2017. *Overleaf:* Shirley filming the video for *Death and the Lady*, at the ossuary in St Leonard's, Hythe (photos by Toby Amies).

When John wrote the poem he had in mind for the final verse the coastal town of Peacehaven, a few miles east of Brighton. It had been built after the Great War to house returning soldiers and their families, but of course the building encroached on the precious South Downs near to where the Copper family had lived for centuries. Bob Copper told the story of the time that he and his Dad, James Copper, were looking at the rash of new buildings 'where the sheep used to graze'. James said 'I don't know what your old grand-daddy would say, boy, if he could see this lot. "'Ouses, 'ouses 'ouses. Y'know, my boy, that makes me prostrate with dismal"' (*Bob Copper's Sussex*, 1997.)

Whenever I sang 'The Whitsun Dance' I introduced it with the fact of the women's losses in The Great War, that they were left to dance alone. I told, too, of the maypoles, once the centre of so many village greens that were replaced by the war memorials.* This song, which in its gentle way made such an impact, inspired our next album *Anthems in Eden*. The first side was a suite of traditional songs, the innocent Eden of England before 'The Fall' of the Great War. Yes, it could be held to be a romantic notion; was there ever a peaceful or innocent England? How could there be with such a dark and violent history as ours? The lives of the rural population had been torn apart in earlier times by the Enclosure Acts of the eighteenth and nineteenth centuries, depriving small farmers and peasants of their rights to graze their animals and grow crops on the common land, forcing people to leave to earn a living, splitting up rural communities throughout the land.

> *They hang the man and flog the woman*
> *Who steal the goose from off the common*
> *But leave the greater villains loose*
> *Who steal the common from the goose*

Anonymous; seventeeth-eighteenth century.

---

*This introduction was to make a profound change to my life in a future year.

There was a further drift from the land with the coming of the Industrial Revolution, the rural population moving away from the land and into mill and factory towns to earn their livings. And then came the introduction of mechanisation into farming, more jobs and livings gone, people no longer needed.

And yes, I know that life wasn't a bed of roses in the countryside, and that there was dreadful hardship and poverty… and yet, so many of the songs are full of the pleasure of the landscape, the delight of birdsong, of the seasons, the freedom to walk out 'on a May morning', the pride in your work. To exchange that for life in 'those dark Satanic mills', still living in poverty, but now in cramped, crowded and unhealthy conditions, with very little beauty to see or fresh air to breathe, must have broken many hearts and spirits. Now, instead of being under the heel of landowners, they were up against the mill and factory owners.

The *Anthems* suite told of yet another event that tore apart people all across the land – The Great War. It was made up of seven traditional songs depicting A Meeting, A Courtship, A Denying, A Forsaking, A Leave-Taking, An Awakening and a

New Beginning, with 'The Whitsun Dance' and the powerful, primitive 'Staines Morris' ending the set.

John took *Anthems* to the BBC, and there we received encouragement from two people: John Peel, who played some of it on his *Night Ride* programme, and from a producer for Radio 1, Frances Line, who broadcast the whole suite on Radio 1 in August 1968. She later became Controller of Radio 2.

From that point, Austin John took the concept to Malcolm Jones who was masterminding EMI's new 'underground' label, Harvest, and Dolly and I were signed. Harvest existed to put out 'progressive' music that didn't fit either 'mainstream' or 'popular' styles. We were on the same listing as Deep Purple, The Edgar Broughton Band, Pink Floyd and Kevin Ayers. Dolly and I didn't exactly fit *that* list either, but it amused us that we were considered 'underground'.

We played in the Harvest launch concert at The Roundhouse alongside these groups; I think the audience was a bit bemused at first. Someone heckled us, so I heckled back, and things got more appreciative after that.

Anthems was recorded at EMI's famed Abbey Road Studios, engineered by Peter Mew, produced by Austin John Marshall, with David Munrow as musical director; it was played by David and musicians from his Early Music Consort, and all the music was arranged and scored by Dolly. Those early instruments, rebec, viol, sackbut, racket, cornett, harpsichord, crumhorn, sordun, recorders and bells, and not forgetting the flute-organ, provided the perfect sound – natural, earthy and sympathetic. The musicians were Dolly, Christopher Hogwood, Oliver Brooks, Alan Lumsden, Roderick and Adam Skeaping, Michael Laird, Richard Lee and Gillian Reid, and for this album they were called 'The Dolly Collins Sweet England Harmonious Band'. The chorus were folk friends Royston Wood of The Young Tradition, Steve Ashley and Home Brew (Mike Clifton, Ray Worman and John Fordham). Dolly was in her element; she had a proper commission, professional musicians of the utmost quality to write for and an association with David Munrow, who gave her his complete approval for her scores.

Working with David was an unforgettable experience; he was the most talented, energetic, enthusiastic and kind man, and the resulting music had great integrity, strength and beauty. I was keenly aware, though, in the studio, that everyone was working from a written score – except for me; I had never learned to read music as I had all the songs by heart. So when there was a point when there was a discussion about which bar they were working on and which bar I was to come in singing, I felt at an embarrassing disadvantage. It seemed pointless trying to keep this to myself, so I confessed to David that I couldn't read music. 'That's OK – that's probably the right thing – the best thing for you,' he said airily. 'You know when to come in, anyway.' He then went on to tell me that, as a young man, he had learned a great deal of his wind instrument technique and knowledge from folk musicians he'd met in South America, who naturally continued a handed-down tradition.

Mike Clifton, as well as being a singer, was also a Morris dancer with the Chingford Morris, and a talented potter, and it was he who made the beautiful slipware ceramic depicting Adam and Eve before 'the Fall'. He had modelled the couple on Dolly and

Shirley Collins

her husband Dave Busby – also a Chingford Morris man. Austin
John designed the entire sleeve and used the ceramic on the front
cover of *Anthems*. The centrefold was another of Mike's creations,
a huge ram's head with curving gilded horns; there's a photograph
of Dolly and me on either side of the ram that was taken at The
Woburn Festival in 1968, where we were on the same bill as T.Rex
and Jimi Hendrix!

Mike had also made a large, regal golden lion's head for
Chingford Morris, and he amused us with his tale of the time he was
stopped by police late at night after a Morris practice. He had driven
over the newly opened (in 1967) Bow Flyover across the Thames,
and was heading home when he was pulled over. One officer asked
him where he had come from, and Mike, tetchy at being stopped,
got muddled and said rather crossly 'I've just come across the fly
bow-over'. 'Oh yes – and have you been drinking? What's in your
boot?' 'No, I haven't been drinking,' replied Mike, 'and I've got a
lion's head in my boot!' And, of course, when he opened the boot
of his car, there was… a lion's head. The cops simply had to let him
go on his way.

We had a short tour of *Anthems*, taking with us a full complement
of the early musicians as well as The Chingford Morris Men who
danced for the finale, 'The Whitsun Dance' and 'Staines Morris'. It
was the start of a long working relationship with them… and they
eventually became Albion Morris, dancing with the original Albion
Band, the Albion Country Band, and The Albion Dance Band.

While the music was flowing freely for Dolly and me, this period
was also the beginning of the breakdown of my marriage to Austin
John. In so many ways we were unsuited, right from the start. I
remember a rather telling moment early on in our marriage, in
1963, while we were still living in Maida Avenue, when I was being
photographed by a rather eminent Czech for the cover of the Topic
EP *Heroes in Love*. As he walked around the room taking pictures, I
heard him mutter to himself 'Who chose who here?' It didn't seem
significant at the time, but it stayed with me.

Our life together was floundering and foundering over a thing
that might appear petty: John loved jazz and I hated it. You

wouldn't think that this could cause such a difference between us, but it did, and it was a crucial one. At first I tolerated Charlie Mingus, Ornette Coleman, Charlie Parker on the gramophone so much of the time... too much of the time. It simply wasn't music that I could understand, let alone enjoy, and I grew more and more intolerant simply *watching* John listen to it – the snapping fingers, the nodding head, the twitching legs and feet, the almost religious fervour of the light in his eyes. I'd always felt that jazz was alien to me; it belonged in dark clubs in the night-time, nothing of sunlight or fresh air or the outdoors. I minded the way jazz musicians dressed – silly pork-pie hats, and the way bass players leaned over their instruments, chewing their lips in rhythm to their playing; it made me squirm.

There were two occasions when I became so angry that I threw two full cups of coffee against the kitchen wall, and worse, when I dragged down the two heavy William Morris curtains from the big picture windows in the sitting room. Such acts leave you with far more clearing up and repairing than warrants the act in the first place – but I was enraged!

Looking back, it seems ungrateful. John was such a supporter and promoter of music – not only of Dolly's and mine, but of Steve Ashley's too, who he worked with for years, producing Steve's 1974 album *Stroll On*. Steve and I recorded John's song 'Honour Bright' (available on *Within Sound*), from a ballad opera that John was writing, *The Anonymous Smudge*, who stood as 'the everyman soldier'. Sadly, *Smudge* never had a performance in England, but years later in 1981, when John had moved to New York, it was broadcast on the radio station WBAI. In 1978 he wrote *The Blackbirds of Brittany* with Bert Jansch, a protest in song following the catastrophic oil spill off the coast of Brittany which killed untold thousands of seabirds. His heart was always in the right place.

John was also filming Jimi Hendrix. He had interviewed Jimi shortly after his arrival in England in August 1967; the article was published in *The Observer* that December. One unforgettable summer's day (in 1968 or '69) Jimi visited us in Blackheath. We had been to see him in concert; he had such presence and his songs were original and great and his performance beautiful, exciting and charged with danger. I sat gasping at the sounds he produced from his guitar and anxious about his teeth when he used them on the strings! For Jimi to come to our home was a thrill and a pleasure; he was handsome, playful, teasing, sweet and graceful. He sat Polly on his knee; she'd have been about six or seven years old and was enchanted by him, gazing raptly into his face. I have no photographs of this occasion (we didn't own a camera, can you believe) – just the memory of him touching my bare arm and whispering close in my ear, 'I can see why John married you.' I felt a little guilty about being so thrilled, but it's a memory I still cherish!

But I was angry a lot of the time, and despondent that John spent so much time out in the evenings; domestic life wasn't of great interest to him, and I felt he neglected the children. And when he was home, he spent what seemed like endless hours on the phone, reading *The Anonymous Smudge* to people. There must have been some happy times, but they were overshadowed.

The breaking point came when, late one night, John brought a young drug-addicted jazz player that he'd befriended back with him, and insisted that he stay for a few days, very much against my will. He moved Polly out of her little bedroom and made her share with Rob. This 'guest' would often come back in the early hours of the morning, then sleep throughout the day. One night around ten o'clock, when he and John were out at a jazz club together, and I was alone in the house with the children, there was a loud knock on the door, and there stood two South London heavies. They were from a mini-cab firm and wanted the money there and then that our guest owed them for several late-night fares. It was a sizeable amount. I apologised to them, wrote out a cheque and handed it over. When they'd gone, my knees buckled and I started to shake with fright and anger. I didn't wait up for John and the young man. I'd had enough. The next day, I threw the jazz musician out. John apologised to him… But not to me.

Go from my window, my love, my dove, go from my window,
my dear
For the wind is in the west and the cuckoo's in his nest
And you can't have a lodging here

Go from my window, my love, my dove, go from my window,
my dear
Oh the weather it is warm it will never do thee harm
And you can't have a lodging here

Go from my window, my love, my dove, go from my window
my dear
For the wind is blowing high and the ship is lying by
And you can't have a harbouring here

Go from my window my love, my dove, go from my window
my dear
The wind and the rain have brought him back again
But he can't have a harbouring here

Go from my window, my love, my dove, go from my window
my dear
O the devil's in the man that he will not understand
He can't have a harbouring here

From John Stokoe's *Songs of the North.*

We still had one album left to record while we were together, again for EMI's Harvest label: *Love, Death & the Lady.* Reflected in it, running through it, are all the difficulties, the sadness, the despair and, perhaps, also the relief of our marriage breaking up. There were some fine songs on the album including 'Death & The Lady', 'The Oxford Girl' and 'Six Dukes'. But perhaps the finest was 'The Plains of Waterloo', dating from the Napoleonic Wars, true lovers eventually re-united after being tested for their fidelity – a broken-token song. Dolly's arrangement was steady, stately, beautiful. There are a couple of verses where the story moves to the battlefield, and John suggested that we use percussion there. I wasn't keen at first, drums meant jazz, but agreed to give it a go, and it became a most telling moment, powerful and right, and so subtle in Terry Cox's hands.

If Willy Smith's your true love's name then he's a hero of great fame
He and I have fought in battle through many's the long campaign
Through Italy and Russia, through Germany and Prussia
He was my loyal comrade through France and through Spain
Till at last by the French oh then we were surrounded
And like heroes of old then we did them subdue
We fought for three days till at length we did defeat him
That bold Napoleon Boney on the Plains of Waterloo

And on the fifteenth day of June it is ended the battle
Leaving many's the bold hero in sorrow to mourn
Where the war drums they do beat and the cannons loud do rattle
It was by a French soldier your William was slain
And as I passed by, oh to where he lay a-bleeding
I scarcely had time for to bid him adieu
With a faint faltering voice these words he kept repeating
Fare-thee-well my lovely Annie, you are far from Waterloo…

It was certainly a less happy experience than *Anthems* had been; the unravelling of the marriage was present all the time, although I was grateful to John for producing a good album and art work. This time, the mood was bleak, Dolly and I photographed in black cloaks, with very serious, severe expressions. Dolly's arrangements were more spare, stark often, fitting the mood of the songs. Again she wrote her score for early instruments and the same musicians, with the addition of Eleanor Sloane on rebec, with only one folk musician, Peter Wood, on concertina. Dolly said, years later in an interview, that these arrangements had 'a more classic approach, more modern chords. I was trying things out, pushing ahead, experimenting all the time.'

One reviewer wrote: 'Shirley Collins comes of age', and that was probably true. Later, Karl Dallas wrote of John that he was 'one of the great unsung pioneers of contemporary British folksong' and that was certainly true. *Love, Death & the Lady* was released in 1969, by which time John and I had separated. He had moved back to central London, and I was relieved and happy for him that he'd formed a new relationship. As, a little while after, had I. I stayed in Blackheath with Polly and Rob until my divorce came through. I remember that day – I had a booking at Exeter University that evening, and wished I could stay home, but duty prevailed. At the gig I mentioned that I was now officially divorced. A small cheer went up from the audience!

The little Span house was put up for sale, and I started packing, preparing to escape back to Sussex. I'd been away too long.

EIGHT: *All In The Downs*

When I was but thirteen or so
I went into a golden land
Chimborazo, Cotopaxi took me by the hand

I learned these words at school, a poem written by WJ Turner, about a boy entranced by Eldorado. I stored them in my memory, hoping that one day I too would find a place that took me by the hand. I didn't have to travel too far: I would find it in the South Downs.

It wasn't until some time in the 1970s that my love affair with the Downs began. For one of my birthdays, a 30-something one, I had requested that Ashley, Polly, Rob and I should go for a walk on the Downs; they were starting to call to me. I didn't know them well at all then. I have photographs – but no actual memory – of having been taken there as a toddler for outings and picnics with Mum and Dad, and Granny and Grandad, those weekends before the War when Dad had use of his employer's car.

When Ashley and I lived in Etchingham, we'd go for walks locally, across the fields and through the woods, and cycle along quiet lanes. But on this birthday walk, on a hot July day, we set off with a picnic but no map. We went by train to Eastbourne, caught the bus up to Beachy Head, then onto the Downs. We walked long stretches until the children grew hot and tired, and at last, late in the afternoon, we had wound our way down to the tiny village of Litlington. We sat outside The Plough and Harrow drinking lemonade and munching crisps, trying to work out how we'd get home. We were in luck; a man at the next table, overhearing our plight, offered us a lift to Polegate. From there, we could catch a train to St Leonards, and change for the Etchingham line. Quite a while later, after we'd stopped for celebratory birthday fish and chips in Polegate, we made our way home, the sleepy children drowsing on the train. At last we were walking down Borders Lane to the cottage. Although it was evening, the heat was increasing, the air filled with electricity. Ahead of us, huge dark thunder clouds were amassing; we quickened our steps on very tired legs, and got through the door of Red Rose just as the storm broke. There were great flashes of lightning; we counted the seconds to see how far away the storm was, and then before we'd got to three, there was an enormous, sharp clap of thunder, and our telephone shattered into many pieces. The lightning had come down the line. It was a memorable birthday!

I had loved being up there on those long stretches of Downland in such clear light, breathing air off the sea, wondering what was over the next hill brow topped by huge white clouds. I loved the feel of the springy turf beneath my feet, and the chalk and flints kicking up on the paths. And all the while, the sound of skylarks, those elusive songsters who you could hear, but rarely see, so high in the sky were they.

I felt too that those long, serene lines of the Downs were there in the songs of Sussex, whose anthemic tunes flow with such strength and grace. And the hawthorns, their bark covered in rusty lichen, blown and shaped by the prevailing south-westerly winds, were like the songs, shaped by the many voices that have sung them, changing gradually over the years.

Folk music reflects the landscape it's written in. Certainly it is true that the land necessarily once governed the occupation of its inhabitants, whether as shepherds, farm labourers, carters, fishermen, poachers, blacksmiths, or in times of war, soldiers and sailors, pressed away to join the armies and navies – all of which gave rise to hundreds of folk songs.

Many of the stories of the songs take place in a familiar landscape, opening with the lines 'As I roved out one May morning', setting the scene for whatever story is going to unfold and preparing the listener for an encounter. There were love songs and ballads, songs about work – carting, harvesting, shepherding and sheep shearing, poaching and hunting; others celebrated various high points of the year – old May carols, Harvest Homes, Christmas and New Year carols and Wassails.

Hundreds of these were sung across Sussex, and noted down by collectors from the mid-1850s up to the 1970s. The earlier collections are in books; the more recent ones are, happily, on sound recordings, allowing us to hear the authentic voices of the singers themselves, their personalities and their accents.

Using even a tiny selection of these genuine folk songs, a path can be traced across Sussex. We can set off on the journey well over a hundred years back with two songs whose melodies have become part of our national consciousness. The first was sung by Harriet and her husband Peter Verral, an agricultural labourer who was born in Lewes in 1854, although when Ralph Vaughan Williams met them in 1904 on one of his folk-song hunting expeditions, they were living in Monksgate, near Horsham. One of their songs, 'Our Captain Calls', dates from the Napoleonic Wars, and its tune so impressed Vaughan Williams that he later set the John Bunyan hymn 'He Who Would Valiant Be' to it. Next to the title in the New English Hymnal which Vaughan Williams edited are the words 'Tune – *Monksgate*'.

The second collected song was 'The Banks of Green Willow', which Mr and Mrs Cranstone sang to the composer George Butterworth, in Billingshurst in 1907; he later used it as inspiration for his orchestral idyll of the same name.

Also living in Horsham was the remarkable Henry Burstow, a shoemaker and a radical free-thinker, who knew over 400 songs by heart. His songs were noted down by Lucy Broadwood and Ralph Vaughan Williams at the turn of the nineteenth and twentieth centuries. One of his most beautiful songs is 'Gilderoy', which dates back to the late seventeenth century.

In the 1970s Mabs Hall and her son Gordon lived in Horsham, next door to Henry Burstow's home on Spencers Road. Their repertoire of songs and, especially, ballads seemed boundless – as was Gordon's voice. Gordon invariably lit up a cigarette when he started a song, and judged the length of a ballad not by its number of verses, but by how many cigarettes he got through while singing it!

In Lodsworth the songs of another fine Sussex singer, Henry Hills, were noted down by W Percy Merrick in 1899. His 'A Sailor's Life' was recorded by Fairport Convention on their 1969 album *Unhalfbricking*. Then in Lower Beeding, 'All Things Are Quite Silent' was noted down from Ted Baines by Vaughan Williams in 1904. This story of a man snatched away from his sweetheart by a press-gang is one of the loveliest and most poignant songs ever found in England.

But from now on we'll stay with material recorded as recently as the 1950s by Peter Kennedy and Bob Copper and broadcast on *Country Magazine* (see Chapter 5). With these sound recordings we could get a full sense of the character of the singers.

The singers, of course, knew more than one song, but I'll choose just one from each, and we start at Fittleworth in November 1954, where Bob Copper recorded a beautiful 'Deep in Love' from a housewife, Mrs Gladys Stone. And it was there that Bob also met George Attrill, a road maintenance worker, as he was cutting back grass at the roadside with a swop-hook. He sang 'The Broken-Down Gentleman' to Bob that same evening in his cottage, as they sat sipping George's homemade parsnip wine.

On to Copthorne, home to George 'Pop' Maynard. His dignity and the sweetness of his nature were clearly there in his singing which, in spite of his old age when he was recorded, was still beautiful and had a rare grace. His 'Polly on the Shore', recorded by Peter Kennedy in George's cottage in 1955, dates from the Napoleonic Wars, and gives a graphic and bloody account of a sea-battle, while at the same time being a love song with a noble tune. It would touch any heart.

Heading away towards Balcombe, where in 1963 Peter recorded Harry Upton singing 'Canadee-i-o', the song that was always sung on the last day of shearing in the barn known as Toad's Hall at Blatchington. The song had been handed down from Harry's father Frank, who was a shepherd all his life. His sister Mrs Wheatland told how they sang all around the villages at Christmas and added: "We're living in the same place now, Blatchington, but instead of it being the country place it was, it's now a large council estate, and ours was the last farm cottage to be pulled down. Before that, it was all farming land, a thousand acres of cornfields and sheep grazing".

A few miles away, and nearly ten years earlier, Bob had met Lily Cook, in September 1954 in North Chailey; in her kitchen she sang 'The Lark in the Morning'. It was his very first recording for the BBC, and he felt it was a most reassuring start to his journey.

A couple of months later, down towards the coast at Hammerpot, near Angmering, Bob found Jim Swain, a carter, and recorded 'The Banks of Sweet Mossen', which Jim had learned from an old shepherd at Felpham. It was unique – no other version of this song had ever been heard before or since.

Heading along the coast to Hastings, in November 1954 Bob recorded Ned Adams, the cox'n of the Hastings lifeboat, singing 'The Bold Princess Royal'. 'When Ned sang,' wrote Bob, 'you could smell the sea'. From Noah Gillette, a retired, illiterate fisherman in St Leonards, Bob heard the remarkable ballad about Napoleon's demise 'The Bonny Bunch of Roses'. Noah had learned it by heart from his grandmother, who Bob reckoned was alive at the time that the ballad was written and sold on the streets following Napoleon's death, creating a direct link to an historic event.

Inland now to East Dean, where in 1952 Peter Kennedy met the blacksmith Luther Hills who sang 'The Foggy Dew', the recording made in Luther's smithy. And not far from there, in November 1952, Peter came across a group of gypsies camped on a grass verge outside the village of Laughton. He recorded many songs from them, but the jewel, the most precious, was 'Come Father, Build Me A Boat', sung in true gypsy style by six-year-old Sheila Smith. With this recording, this little girl memorably and so sweetly sang her way into the history of English folk song.

A trip to Brighton now, where gypsy Mary Ann Haynes had settled, and earned a living as a flower seller. Mike Yates recorded her in 1974, and one of her songs, 'The Female Drummer', mirrors to a great extent the life of Phoebe Hessel, a female soldier who lived out the end of her life in Regency Brighton on a pension of half a guinea a week from the Prince Regent himself. She is buried there in St Nicholas Churchyard, her memorial stone cared for by admirers. Oh yes, and there's a Brighton bus named after her.

And finally, to the Copper Family of Rottingdean. When we get to them and their unique centuries-long history of singing, I *am* persuaded that the landscape shapes the melodies. The Copper tunes sound like anthems; they are beautiful, and with such a noble strength and sweep that they do truly resemble the Downs and make you feel grounded, safe and home. 'The Bold Fisherman' has all these qualities, and opens with the line

'As I roved out one May morning...'

Of the many wonderful singers that the Sussex landscape inspired, three in particular have remained heroes to me.

George Maynard was England's finest English traditional singer (matched only by Harry Cox of Norfolk). His large repertoire was crammed with wonderful songs that, of course, he knew by heart. Perhaps the best-known was 'Polly on the Shore'. Martin Carthy included it on his 1969 album *Prince Heathen* (1969), I sang it on *Love, Death & the Lady* (1970), and surprisingly, the comedian Stewart Lee (author of this book's introduction) sings it, too. When I first heard Stewart sing it live, I was quite overcome and on my feet applauding.

George was a countryman through and through. Born on Old Christmas Day (7 January) in 1872, he left school at the age of twelve and was apprenticed to his father, earning his living woodcutting, hedging and ditching. He'd travel to harvesting and hop-picking, with the occasional bit of defiantly unapologetic poaching when times were hard, to feed his wife and six children.

'Poaching?' he said. 'I should go out again if I had my time over again before I should let my family go short of anything. I'd rode my old penny-farthing over to Langshot, came home and had my tea... And I heard the wind a-blowing hard, and there was Arthur and Nelly wanted a pair of shoes bad, so I said to my wife, "After I've had my tea, Polly, I'll go out and see if I can catch a few rabbits, to see if I can earn they youngsters a pair of shoes." I hold any man a coward who would not poach to feed his family.'

George was also a marbles champion, and captain of The Copthorne Spitfires, beating their rivals The Tinsley Green Tigers at the marbles tournament which still takes place on Good Friday at Tinsley Green in Sussex. He was given his nickname Pop because he was such a good marbles popper.

The most graceful and gentle of singers, he sang naturally in his local Sussex style, with integrity and dignity. You can hear him on *Ye Subjects of England* (Topic LP 1976) and on various CDs of the Topic series *The Voice of the People*.

'Down by the Seaside' is another song of his, most likely also dating from the Napoleonic Wars. With its beautiful tune and a touch of sweet gentility in the use of the word 'opera-glass' (very rarely heard in English folk song!), this tender song is another of my favourites from George's extensive repertoire, and can be heard on my album *Adieu to Old England* (Topic 1974).

Down by The Seaside

As I was a-walking down by the seaside
I gazed on a young damsel, put her in surprise
I stepp-ed up to her, these words I did say
Well my pretty fair maid, well my pretty fair maid
Are you going my way?

O no, O no this young damsel replied
I'm seeking for my true love who's gone far and wide
And if I don't find him, it's here I'll remain
I hope that my true love,
I hope that my true-love will return safe again

As she was lamenting and could not prevail
She looked through her opera-glass and saw the ships sail
May the heavens protect our lads on the main
I hope that my true love
I hope that my true love will return safe again

As she was a-standing all on the same spot
The news it came to her, her true love was shot
Now since it's been so I will go to some grove
And if he died for honour, if he died for honour
Then I'll die for love

Bob Copper was the outstanding figure in the recent history of Southern English traditional music. An author and poet, an artist, a raconteur and broadcaster, and parish historian, as well as a singer, he was employed by the BBC throughout the 1950s to work in Sussex and Hampshire, recording what remained of traditional song in the field, making a remarkable collection. In his book *Songs and Southern Breezes*, he told of that experience with humour, compassion and understanding. Like Alan Lomax, he wrote with a romantic passion, but always truthfully. And both men had a great respect, admiration and affection for the singers.

I first met Bob when I was a teenager in Hastings. I listened to the BBC's Home Service broadcasts of the programmes *Country Magazine* and *As I Roved Out* on the radio, or wireless as we knew it, and often a folk song would be played, sometimes sung by a trained singer with pianoforte accompaniment, which didn't sound quite right to me, or an unaccompanied song from a genuine traditional singer, which I felt much happier with. I had also seen a film *Night Club Girl* at the Gaiety cinema in Hastings, the story of a girl from the mountains of Tennessee taken to New York by a talent scout to sing in a night club. (There was love interest as well, and she did seem to have a lot of pretty frocks at her disposal – something I envied in those post-war days of austerity and rationing – you had even needed clothing coupons.)

So I thought I'd like to be a folk singer, and at 15 years old wrote to the BBC to let them know! By some miracle – and I truly believe the arc of my life would have been so different if this had not happened – the letter was passed to Bob Copper. One day, there was a knock on the door at 117 Athelstan Road, and there stood Bob Copper. He was in Hastings recording songs from fishermen in the Old Town. Naïvely, my sister Dolly and I tried to impress him with songs and a Scottish ballad we'd learned off the wireless – which I'm sure we tried to sing in a Scots accent, and of course that wasn't what he was looking or hoping for. But it was a first meeting with a man who was to influence me for the rest of my life. I learned songs from the Copper Family repertoire – songs that had been handed down in their family for many generations, forming the canon of the folk culture of Southern England – and which helped root me in it.

I became good friends with Bob over the years. My favourite personal memory of him? We had taken a walk together over the Downs from Peacehaven to Rodmell, to have lunch with the blacksmith there. Bob was the ideal walking companion, talking so knowledgeably about the landscape as we walked through it, loving the very air we breathed, and aware of so much that was there to see. At one point, he stopped and stood still, waiting until a shiny black beetle that was crawling across the chalk path in front of us had reached the other side safely. Unfailingly kind, this great but modest man was someone you always felt better after seeing. And these lines from an old Sussex gypsy carol sum up what I believe we owe Bob Copper:

> *Had we as many years to live as there are blades of grass*
> *We could never do for him all he has done for us*
>
> Bob & Ron Copper: *Traditional Songs from Rottingdean*
> (Fledgling 3097)

I first became aware of the name Henry Burstow in the 1970s when I was in the library at Cecil Sharp House. While looking in a *Journal of The English Folk-Song Society* of 1909, I came across a song that straightaway intrigued me when I saw that, of the eight lines of verse three, six had been substituted by asterisks. The song was 'Gilderoy' and it had been noted down from the singing of Henry Burstow of Horsham by Lucy Broadwood, the daughter of a wealthy Surrey family, who collected folk songs widely in Sussex and Surrey around the turn of the nineteenth and twentieth centuries. Lucy had added a note: 'Mr Burstow sang me one verse of Gilderoy and sent me the whole ballad a year later. I have omitted one stanza.' Obviously it was considered too frank for the delicate, albeit hypocritical sensibilities of Edwardian England.

I was determined to find the missing words, and got permission to look in the Lucy Broadwood files. To my horror and anger, I found that they were locked away in a little side room, books and loose sheets of paper scattered on the floor, covered in dust and with every sign of being nibbled by mice. (This was symptomatic of the way The English Folk Dance and Song Society was at that time – dance was king, song was by and large neglected).

I hunted for 'Gilderoy', and found it with its complete words, and I also came across a letter written by Henry to Lucy in 1902, couched in such gentle and courteous terms that it quite broke my heart. It read:

14 Spencers Road
Horsham

January 22nd 1902

Dear Madam

I cannot tell you how surprised and pleased I was with the beautiful song book you kindly sent to me. I shall always prize it and think of you and the times when I came and sung to you. I wish I had sung the 400 I knew. I think perhaps their [sic] was some if you had heard you would have liked. I sung all of them to an old gentleman one Christmas. It took me a month. I use to sing to him every night.

I should have wrote and thanked you before, but I have been waiting. A Warnham singer promised to write the song for me. He said he knew the Americans has stole my truelove away. I will send it to you, if I get it.

I think the song book you so kindly presented to me a most beautiful got up work. What a lot of trouble and expense it must have been to you. I am so sorry I cannot read music. I should have learnt a great many more songs. I am very much oblige [sic] to you for The Rival. I will learn that has I know the tune. I whent [sic] to Dunsfold with the Rusper ringers a few years ago there is six rather small new bells.

I shall be very pleased with a copy of the paper with the songs when it is printed.

Thinking [sic] you very much again for the book and kind rememberance of me.

Yours truly
Henry Burstow

P.S. I only know about half dozen songs in the book you gave me.

I resolved to save the letter from the dust and the mice, and popped it into my handbag. Yes, I stole it. But I had also rescued it, and it was my most treasured possession right up until recently when I gave it back to The English Folk Dance and Song Society, handing it over to Malcolm Taylor, the librarian of The Vaughan Williams Memorial Library. He put it into the safe with what I thought was rather indecent haste! I knew that it would now be taken proper care of, but I couldn't help feeling quite bereft.

Henry Burstow was born in Horsham in 1826, and lived there all his life, earning his living as a shoemaker. He lived through the reigns of four monarchs, George IV, William IV, Queen Victoria and Edward VII. He was well known locally as a church bell ringer, but he was much more than that; he was an atheist and a radical free-thinker. The story was told that he'd ring the bells at the Parish Church every Sunday, but, much to the annoyance of the Vicar, would never stay for the service. The Vicar collared him one Sunday and asked him why. Henry looked him full in the eye and replied, 'I brings 'em in, I leaves it to you to drive them away again.'

When he was a boy of twelve he and his friend Bill Etheridge, (a lad from such a poor family that he was dressed in rags and was barefoot) walked all the way from Horsham to Pease Pottage – a distance of a few miles – to join the huge crowd that had gathered to see the young Queen Victoria pass by in her carriage on her way to Bognor Regis. The crowd sang the national anthem, but Henry remarked later that instead of God sending her victorious, it might be better if he sent the Horsham boys something to eat, and a pair of boots for Billy to wear.

Henry wrote his own account of his life and times in a book *Reminiscences of a Horsham Shoemaker* which can still be found.

Gilderoy

Now Gilderoy was a bonny boy
And he would knots of ribbons wear
He pull-ed off his scarlet coat
He garter-ed below his knee
He was beloved by the ladies so gay
And he was such a rakish boy
He was my sovereign heart's delight
My handsome, bold young Gilderoy

Now Gilderoy and I was born
All in one town together
And at the age of seventeen
We courted one each other
Our dads and our mums they both did agree
And crowned with mirth and joy
To think that I should marry with
My handsome, bold young Gilderoy

Now Gilderoy and I walked out
All in the fields together
He took me round the waist so small
And down we went together
And when he had done all a man could do

He rose and kissed his joy
He is my sovereign heart's delight
My handsome bold young Gilderoy

What a pity it is a man should hang
For stealing of a woman where
He had neither robbed a house nor land
And he stole neither horse nor deer
For he was beloved by the old and the young
And he was such a rakish boy
He was my sovereign heart's delight
My handsome bold young Gilderoy

Now Gilderoy, they've hung him high
And a funeral for him we shall have
With a sword and a buckler by my side
I'll guard my true love to his grave
For he was beloved by the young and the old
And he was such a rakish boy
He was my sovereign heart's delight
My handsome bold young Gilderoy*

What is it in English folk song that holds me so, that gives me a sense of inhabiting the songs? Or is it that they inhabit me?

'The Oxford Girl' is such a one – perhaps the most extreme example: I learned it from Phoebe Smith, a gypsy, whose singing had command, power and nobility. It's a song about a brutal murder:

I fell in love with an Oxford girl,
She had a dark and a roving eye
But I feeled too ashamed for to marry her
Her being so young a maid

---

*On *For As Many As Will* (Topic 1978, Fledg'ling 1994). This was the last studio album Dolly and I recorded. 'Gilderoy' was the very finest of her arrangements.

That being established, he invites her out for a walk 'through the fields and meadows gay'. So far, so idyllic, but then the story changes gear... almost as if its events happen on a whim... or in a trance.

I took a stick from out the hedge
And I gently knocked her down
And the blood from that poor innocent girl
Come trinkling to the ground

I caught fast hold of her curly, curly locks
And I dragged her through the fields
Until I come to a deep river side
Where I gently flung her in

Look how she go, look how she floats
She's a-drowning on the tide
And instead of her having a watery grave
She should have been my bride

It was sometimes on my mind as I walked through the fields at the back of Red Rose in Etchingham. It's almost as though the murder happens in a trance – there's a terrifying tenderness in the brutality – heightened by that use of the word 'gently'. I felt that I understood the deed. I began to see corners of fields as seductive, beautiful but dangerous places where anything could happen, and in a curious way, I welcomed it. It was as though I had become the girl in the song. Such dark thoughts to have had, and indeed shaming ones, but they were there. I didn't normally view the Sussex countryside as dark and dangerous, quite the opposite. It was full of light and delight, the fresh sharp green scent of it in early spring; a place of beauty and safety; and it was home.

I've often felt that past generations of English singers are standing behind me when I sing, that I'm a conduit for them and their songs, a link in a mysterious chain, and that I'm responsible for maintaining their integrity. But where did this come from, this unbreakable hold on me? I think it's partly the age in which I was born, still in touch with and not too many years ahead of those singers, and partly the rural working-class family I was born into. And was it inherited memory that gave me recognition of the music? Or is that too fanciful? Most likely it's because of the songs and nursery rhymes that Granny and Grandad sang to us in their air-raid shelter, the songs we learned at school, the Playford tunes that we danced to, and the carols we sang at Christmas – those cadences and rhythms of the English tunes that I loved.

My first intimation of this recognition occurred when I was seven years old or so, at Primary School. We were learning a new song, a folk song, 'Turpin Hero', and as I sang it I thought – 'that sounds a bit like 'Greensleeves'.'* 'Turpin Hero' had that same familiar 'Englishness' about it that I liked. Much later I'd recognise that same quality in the music of Henry Purcell, Ralph Vaughan Williams and George Butterworth; but I didn't find it there in Benjamin Britten's or Percy Grainger's arrangements of English folk songs, which had too many uncomfortable harmonies, and were generally sung by trained voices, losing their identity and making them quite unsuitable. And yet I had a reason to be grateful to Percy Grainger, as he'd collected one of my favourite songs in 1907 from George Gouldthorpe, a lime burner who had ended up in the Brigg Union Workhouse, Lincolnshire.** And, incidentally, it was George Gouldthorpe who sang 'Horkstow Grange', with its chorus: 'Pity them what see him suffer, Pity Poor Old Steeleye Span…' thus providing the folk-rock group with its name.

The song was 'Six Dukes Went A-Fishing', an unlikely title for a noble and ancient song: it's another example of the seemingly miraculous mystery of the survival of songs and what they have to tell us. According to A. L. Lloyd, the best theory is that the corpse in the song was that of William de la Pole, first Duke of Suffolk, who

---

*We heard Vaughan Williams' orchestral *Fantasia on Greensleeves* played on the BBC radio's *Family Favourites* programme almost every Sunday dinnertime – what we'd call lunchtime now.

**Folk song collectors found the inhabitants of these desolate places a great source for songs.

was murdered in 1450, and his body thrown into the sea off Dover. (See *Henry VI Part 2*, Act 4).

> *Six dukes went a-fishing down by the seaside*
> *They spied a dead body come floating on the tide*
>
> *And the one said to the other, these words I heard them say*
> *It's the royal Duke of Grantham that the tide has washed away*
>
> *And they took him up to London to the place where he was known*
> *From there back to Grantham, the place where he was born*
>
> *And they took out his bowels, and they bound up his feet*
> *And they 'balmed his body with roses so sweet*
>
> *Six Dukes went before him, nine raised him from the ground*
> *Twelve Lords followed after in their black mourning gowns*
>
> *So black was their mourning, so white were the wands*
> *So yellow were the flamboys they carried in their hands*
>
> *He now lies 'twixt two towers, he now lies in cold clay*
> *And the royal Queen of Grantham went weeping away*

The song surges like an inexorable tide on a wide sandy beach, long waves creeping in, leaving their marks of foam on the sand before they retreat and ebb away. Its tune is beautiful, spare, and the song has that heart-breaking last line – 'the royal Queen of Grantham went weeping away'. Can't you just picture her, grief-stricken, turning away from the cortege?

I wonder, too, as I do with so many songs, how it came to be on George Gouldthorpe's lips, and what journey it had taken over perhaps 500 years; it's remarkable that it was ever found at all. Its hold over singers even made it to the United States, a couple being noted in New England; and in the Southern Appalachians there are remnants of it attached to other old ballads such as 'The Brown

Girl', sung to Cecil Sharp and Maud Karpeles in Callaway, Virginia, in 1918.

> *O black was their mourning*
> *And yellow was the band...*
> *And white was poor Sally, poor Sally of time...*

They are little ghosts of songs, holding on... refusing to be entirely forgotten.

But back to why 'Englishness' should be so important? And what is it? I wonder why my family had such a deep feeling for England as a country. They weren't wearing rose-coloured spectacles: their lives had never been easy, my grandparents' especially had been harsh and unfair in so many ways. They loved England, but weren't ignorant of its dark history.

Consider my maternal grandparents, Frederick and Grace Ball. He was the head gardener on a small Sussex estate in Telham, just outside Battle, and she was the housewife raising their five children in a tiny isolated cottage surrounded by tall dark pines. She managed for five years without her husband, when he was sent as a soldier to India and Burma in 1916, not returning until 1920, and she nursed her family through the devastating flu epidemic of 1916. Her only relaxation and consolation was to read her beloved Dickens aloud to them in the evenings. In the final year of her husband's absence, the 'Old Gal', the owner of the estate, died; it was sold and with it went Grandad's job, but his family was allowed to stay in the cottage until his return. They then moved to Hastings where he'd found another gardening position. That lasted a few years, but came to a sudden end when one day he turned up at work to find that his employer had left, gone away for good without giving him notice or his final wages. So he took a job in a nursery, a bit of a come-down for him, but which had the advantage of it being just a short walk away from the home they had rented, 121 Athelstan Road. It had a small front garden full of Michaelmas daisies and California poppies in the autumn, and a long back garden where he grew fruit and vegetables to provide for his family throughout the year. Granny was happy to be away from the country at last and living in town, where she hoped her children would get a decent education. It must have been a bit of a sacrifice for Grandad though, as he loved the countryside, and had taken all his children as new-borns outside in his arms to show them the trees and the sky. To my mother the Sussex countryside was a refuge and a consolation during the war. My father celebrated it in the simple poems he wrote while serving in The Royal Artillery in WW2.

Sussex (September 1940)

A country mazed by winding lanes
Fields ever freshened by the rains
And rivers serving her as veins
Sussex

Her rolling Downs by Beachy Head
Where poets' footsteps always tread
And writers' thoughts are often led
Sussex

Her rivers, Arun, Rother, Ouse
Where fishing folk do sit and muse
Her autumn mists and sparkling dews
Sussex

Her ancient towns of Hastings, Rye
And Winchelsea; though times may try
To oust their names – They'll never die
Sussex

Her farming men, so bronzed and lean
Work harder now, and times are lean
They say 'For England' – But they mean
Sussex – Our Sussex

The countryside and the songs are as one to me; the safe-guarding of them equally important, both so vulnerable. Our beautiful landscape is seen by the avaricious as something to exploit, to concrete over and spoil, to drive unnecessary roads and railways through. It's often the same with our remarkable music, too, as people with very little understanding and knowledge of it seek to change its character. Contained in these songs are the lives and experiences of the people who sang them in the past, dismissed as peasants, often despised and neglected. Yet those same people were the carriers, knowing, by heart, hundreds of songs and ballads that have come down through generations, through centuries, bearing our musical, literary and social history; you might call it the archaeology of music.

In a way, a line was drawn when the collectors came along in Victorian and Edwardian times, and started noting down songs from ordinary people throughout the countryside. And of course, it didn't end there – collecting continued right through to the 1970s with the advantage of recording machines, giving a far more complete sound and understanding of the singer and the song. Thank heavens that they did, otherwise it all might have been lost.

There appears to be no subject that isn't sung about, and the songs themselves teem with incident of every sort. There are heroic deeds of bravery, acts of treachery, battles, sea-chases, true love so loyal it can survive incredible odds, lovers separated for seven long years (it's always seven) finding each other again, love that even returns from the grave; the dead can speak, although more often than not they plead with the living to stop mourning, to let them go, to let them rest. On the other hand there are careless false lovers, seductions, partings, adulteries; but the songs aren't solely about heartbreak and retribution, there are many erotic, saucy and frivolous sexual encounters too. There are the ballads that deal with the big taboo subjects: incest, infanticide, any number of murders, even cannibalism in the British Navy. Many are about wars, press-gangs sending men to 'fight abroad for strangers', transportation or execution. England's dark history imbues many such songs. They also tell of the everyday, drinking and gambling, 'night rambling and courting', poaching and hunting, working on the land or the sea. There are songs of witchcraft and magic, inexplicable but convincing happenings. And always that connection to the mystery of the seasons, those remarkable ancient turning-of-the-year carols, that can bring you to a standstill, taking you back in time while connecting you to the present.

One of the oldest songs that was still being sung in the field, albeit rarely, is 'Death and The Lady'. One version was collected from a Mr Baker of Maidstone, Kent by Francis M Collison in 1946, yet it harks back centuries, perhaps even from when the Black Death was stalking the country. It puts me in mind of the gripping scene in Ingmar Bergman's 1957 film, *The Seventh Seal*, where a knight, newly returned from the Crusades, plays a long game of chess with Death on a lonely Scandinavian seashore. So many songs open with the words 'As I walked out one morn in May' that it is like the device 'once upon a time' that prefaces many fairy tales. On this walk you might encounter a sweetheart or a seducer, a soldier returning from fighting abroad for seven long and weary years, or serving on board ship. You might encounter the Devil, who you could outwit, or you might meet Death, who you couldn't.

As I walked out one morn in May
The birds did sing and the lambs did play
The birds did sing and the lambs did play
I met an old man, I met an old man by the way

His hair was white, his beard was grey
His coat was of some myrtle shade
I asked him what strange country man
Or what strange place, or what strange place he did belong

My name is Death cannot you see
Lords, Dukes and Ladies bow down to me
And you are one of those branches three
And you fair maid, and you fair maid must come with me

I'll give you gold and jewels rare
I'll give you costly robes to wear
I'll give you all my wealth in store
If you let me live, if you let me live a few years more

Fair lady lay your robes aside
No longer glory in your pride
And now sweet maid make no delay
Your time is come, your time is come and you must away

And not long after this fair maid died
Write on my tomb the lady cried
Here lies a poor distress-ed maid
Whom death now lately, whom death now lately hath betrayed*

Bessie Jones, a remarkable woman and singer living in St Simons, one of the beautiful Georgia Sea Islands, also sang of a conversation with Death which has remnants of the English version. It was one of many songs that Alan Lomax recorded on our 1959 field collecting trip in the American South.

O Death, O death in the morning
Death, spare me over another year.

Hey, what is this I see?
Cold icy hands all over me
You say 'I am Death, no one can excel
I open the doors of Heaven and Hell'.
Well, I'm gonna fix your feet so you cannot walk
I'm gonna fix your tongue so you cannot talk
Close your eyes and you cannot see
You got to go and come with me

---

*I've recorded this song twice, with the tune I wrote for it, once for my album *Love, Death and The Lady* (1970), and then again for *Lodestar* (2016).

Well, Death, consider my age
And do not take me at this stage
Because all of my wealth is at your command
If you'll just move your cold icy hand

O Death, spare me over another year…

Vera Hall Ward of Tuscaloosa, Alabama, also sang her version to us.

O Death, have mercy
O Death, have mercy
O Death, just spare me over another year…

There are so many fragments of songs and ballads with perhaps just a glimpse of the original story; sometimes I'm tempted to restore them by linking the words to more complete versions, but often I accept them just as they've come down to us. Some of the early collectors, mostly middle and upper-middle-class men and women, with the leisure and wherewithal to go out 'in the field', tried to explain such elusive things when they printed their 'finds' in the first *Journals* of the Folk-Song Society, formed in 1899.

In 1908 Francis Jekyll and George Butterworth noted down the song 'Come All You Little Streamers' from the singing of Ned Spooner, an inmate of the Workhouse in Midhurst, West Sussex. Of this charmingly muddled song, Anne Gilchrist wrote in the *Journal of The Folk-Song Society* in 1913: 'I tried to give some faint idea of the strange and countless permutations of this kind of ballad… Clearing up some of the obscurities which have puzzled folk-song collectors.' She felt that the song was in a 'present woefully corrupt and incoherent state'.

O come all you little streamers wherever you may be
These are the finest flowers that ever my eyes did see
Fine flowery hills and fishing dells and hunting also
At the top all of the mountain where fine flowers grow

At the top all of the mountain where my love's castle stands
It's over-decked with ivory to the bottom of the strand
Fine arches and fine parches and a diamond stone so bright
It's a beacon for a sailor on a dark stormy night

At the bottom of the mountain there runs a river clear
A ship from the Indies did once anchor there
With her red-flags a-flying and the beating of a drum
Sweet instruments of music and the firing of her gun

So come all you little streamers that walks the meadows gay
And write unto my own true love wherever she may be
For her sweet lips entice me, and her tongue it tells me no
And an angel might direct us, and it's where shall we go

But for me, as a singer, it's delightful and perfect as it is with its utterly delicious last verse. That 'woefully corrupt and incoherent state' is its fascination and a good reason to sing it pretty much as it came from Ned Spooner. I'm sure he didn't puzzle over the obscurities, and neither do I, in fact I welcome them, trusting both the singer and the song.

It grieves and angers me that nowadays the term *folk music* has come to mean almost anything – a singer-songwriter, a pop star with a guitar or an accordion, as if that is its true definition. Anyone can claim to have written a 'folk song', completely ignorant of, or dismissing the fact that it's the long journey down through so many, many years that makes it the real thing, that essential handing-on by word of mouth by generations of singers.

I'm occasionally challenged by some people who maintain that folk song belongs to everyone (which indeed it does – if they want it) and therefore that anyone can write a folk song. I counter that argument by saying that a true folk song has undergone the 'handing-on' process. Of course, anyone *can* write a song, I'm perfectly happy with that (although not often happy with the outcome). What I object to is that they are denying the essential part played in it by those people who sang and handed those songs on to us, mostly people from the rural labouring classes who throughout their lives were exploited and despised, dismissed as worthless. I have always tried to redress that by naming the singer that I learned the song from, whether in person or from a book or a field recording. Then a second argument is flung up that somebody must have written that song in the first place, so why can't a song that was written last week be, or become a folk song, say in a hundred years. There's no proper answer to that since none of us will be around in a hundred years to prove it. In any case, music isn't handed down by word of mouth nowadays – it's sold to us by a worldwide music industry that all too often trivialises us, and the music, while influencing our tastes and preferences.

But having said that, there are songs that we do know were written at a certain time, many with the sole purpose of celebrating noteworthy events, such as 'The Murder of Maria Marten'. That ballad, in particular, was sold in its thousands as a printed broadside at the execution of the murderer William Corder at Bury St Edmunds in 1828. It passed into the oral tradition and was widely sung, and still is; it doesn't have an author's name. There is another song, 'The Poor Murdered Woman' or 'The Leatherhead Common Murder', written less than a decade later, that has also passed into the song tradition, and this time we know who wrote it. It is one of the finest, most moving ballads about an actual event.

> *The Times*, 14 January 1834
> Supposed Murder
> While the Surrey Union foxhounds were out hunting on Saturday last at Leatherhead Common, a most extraordinary and horrid circumstance occurred, which at present is involved in great mystery. About 12 o'clock as the huntsmen were beating about for a fox, the hounds suddenly made a dead set at a clump of bushes on the Common. As no fox made his appearance, the huntsmen whipped the dogs off,

but they still returned to the bushes, and smelling all around, would not leave.

Supposing there was a fox which would not break cover, the huntsmen beat the bushes, and in doing so, to their astonishment and horror, discovered the body of a woman in a state of decomposition.

Various rumours are afloat, some stating that the unfortunate woman was the wife of a travelling tinker.

Morning Post, 24 June 1834
Peter Bullock, alias Williams, a travelling tinker and knife-grinder, was charged with the murder. A young girl who was on the tramp with a couple, said that while sheltering in a barn with them, she heard Bullock talking about a woman who he called 'his dear Nancy'. He lamented her death, and upbraided himself with having been her murderer, and said he did the deed with a hammer after leaving a public house where they'd had a quarrel. He dragged her body to a wood, and left it there. (From Surrey Constabulary History.)

The woman's remains were buried on 15 January 1834 in an unmarked pauper's grave in Leatherhead churchyard. A local bricklayer, a Mr Fairs, was moved to write a song telling of her murder; all the details are so accurate it's almost reportage. It was sung locally, even some sixty years after the event, when Lucy Broadwood, our collector in Sussex and Surrey, was given it in 1897, by the Rev Charles Shebbeare, to whom it had been sung by Mr Forster, a young farm labourer, it being one of his favourite songs. Lucy printed it in her collection *English Traditional Songs and Carols* (1908) and in one of the early *Journals* of the Folk-Song Society where she noted 'its fine Dorian tune', but unfortunately made a reference to its 'doggerel words'.

In 1935 it was included again in a book called *English Folk Song and Dance*, but only 'as an example' in the words of the editor, Iolo A Williams, as 'a song of poor poetical quality'.

They were both wrong. The words have such a strength of feeling, compassion and tenderness for this 'poor murdered woman'. With its beautiful tune it is a noble song.

It was still being sung in the 1960s when I first heard it sung by Peter Wood at the Fighting Cocks in Kingston, Surrey, and it continues right up to the present day, taken up by several of the younger generation of singers. In 2013, Paul James and Simon Houlihan produced a programme for FolkRadio at the same time as an exhibition was mounted at the Leatherhead Museum by local historian Rev Alun Roberts, meticulously detailing the event, and using my recording of the song from *No Roses* (1971). Alun and I agreed that we would name the poor murdered woman, 'dear Nancy.'

It was Hankey the Squire as I've heard men say
Who rode out a-hunting on one Saturday
They hunted all day, but nothing they found
But a poor murdered woman laid on the cold ground

About eight o'clock boys, our dogs they throwed off
On Leatherhead Common, and that was the spot
They hunted all day, but nothing they found
But a poor murdered woman laid on the cold ground

They whipped their dogs off and they kept them away
For I do think it proper she should have fair play
They tried all the bushes but nothing they found
But a poor murdered woman laid on the cold ground

They mounted their horses and they rode off the ground
They rode to the village and alarmed it all around
It is late in the evening, I'm sorry to say
She cannot be removed until the next day

The next Sunday morning, about twelve o'clock
Some hundreds of people to the spot they did flock
For to see that poor creature, your hearts would have bled
Some cold and some violence came into their heads

She was took off the Common and down to some inn
And the man that has kept it his name is John Simms
The coroner was sent for, the jury they joined
And soon they concluded and settled their minds

Her coffin was brought; in it she was laid
And took to the churchyard that is called Leatherhead
No father, no mother, nor no friend I'm told
Came to see that poor creature laid under the mould

So now I'll conclude and I'll finish my song
And those that have done it shall find themselves wrong
For the last day of judgement the trumpet shall sound
And their souls not in heaven I'm afraid won't be found

NINE: *All Music Is Folk Music*

'All music is folk music. I ain't never heard a horse sing a song.'

So said Louis Armstrong. And would you be willing to try anything once except incest or Morris dancing? (This line is usually attributed to Sir Thomas Beecham.)

These are just a couple of the epithets used to deride folk music. On *Desert Island Discs* (18 January 2013), presenter Kirsty Young asked her guest Martin Carthy why 'we tend to have a very strong reaction for or against folk music?'

Such a lack of respect has always extended, as well, to the people the music actually came from, the poor of England: the farm labourers and their wives, the servants in the houses of the wealthy, the cottage lace and shirt-makers, the seamen and fishermen, the gypsies and, most heart-breaking of all, the inmates of Poor Houses and Workhouses such as Marylebone Workhouse, where there were 2000 inmates – husbands, wives and children, forcibly and cruelly separated. All of these people lived on the outskirts of society, but many of them, although often illiterate, knew old songs and tunes by heart, and kept, even if unknowingly, centuries of English song and dance alive. It seems to have been far easier to scoff than to listen, and to understand and appreciate how much of our social and artistic history is embedded in these songs, how beautiful are many of their words and melodies, and how intrinsically English.

Also remaining to a certain extent on the outskirts were the women collectors of folk song and dance in the late nineteenth and early twentieth centuries, women who did so much essential work that enriched our knowledge of our traditional music, but who are, by and large, unsung in comparison to their male counterparts. I've chosen just three to tell you about, three who are heroines of mine, and whose work I respect and celebrate.

It's not my intention or desire to undermine or devalue the work done by men whose work is rightly celebrated, such as Cecil Sharp, Percy Grainger, Ralph Vaughan Williams, or George Butterworth – that would be foolish. But it's worth pointing out that my first subject, Lucy Broadwood, was collecting songs and carols from local singers in Sussex and Surrey for at least a decade before Cecil Sharp got going.

Lucy was the niece of John Broadwood, of the Broadwood piano-making family, who was said to have been so captivated by the carols sung by the tipteerers and mummers at their traditional Christmas and New Year's appearances at Lyne in Surrey that he set about finding what other songs were still remembered by the local peasantry, and in 1843 published his first collection, *Old English Songs*. This fascination with traditional music, and the urge to save it, ran in the family, from Lucy's grandfather James to her father Henry, so it's little wonder that it ran in Lucy's blood, too. She started collecting songs in the late 1880s, and fifteen of these were included in an 1890 reprint of John's book but, while she also worked on the new edition, her name was not credited. However, she was invited to collaborate with her cousin, the music critic JS Fuller Maitland, on the book *English County Songs* (for which they both wrote arrangements) and this time Lucy was given full credit as co-editor. Vaughan Williams said of the book: 'This may well be the starting point of the modern folk song movement.' In 1908 she published *English Traditional Songs and Carols* – all of which had been collected by her.

Lucy was also a crucial figure in the founding of The Folk Song Society in 1898, acting as its Secretary for several years and editing its Journal for over twenty years before finally becoming President in 1928. And yet, as CJ Bearman wrote: 'she, and indeed the work of the Folk Song Society which she virtually personified for 25 years have been strangely neglected by modern scholarship.'* Even the English Folk Dance & Song Society itself which, after her death, had been given all her collection of notes, manuscripts and even phonographic cylinders, appeared to have placed little value on

Folk Music Journal, vol 3, no 5, 1997, pp 357-365.

her work, as I discovered when hunting for the missing 'Gilderoy' words. Truly, if Lucy had done nothing else but collect the 400 songs from Henry Burstow, 'The Poor Murdered Woman' and an exquisite carol 'The Moon Shines Bright' from the Goby gypsy family, she would have given a uniquely invaluable service to English folk song.

Fittingly, Lucy was buried at Rusper Parish Church, and an alabaster plaque designed by Thomas Clapperton, was hung in the church, and every year on May Day, the Broadwood Morris Men dance inside the church in her honour.

All the women collectors, including Lucy, were from wealthy and privileged backgrounds, gentlewomen with the leisure and wherewithal to undertake such work. Take Ella Mary Leather, who had the same passionate desire for finding and saving these precious songs, and with 'undaunted perseverance' chronicled as much as she could of her native Herefordshire life. She noted down not only songs and carols, harvest homes, Morris dances, broomstick dances and mummers plays, but also, as she lists in the preface to her book *The Folklore of Herefordshire*, old customs of birth and death and burial, witchcraft, sin-eating, ancient beliefs and superstitions that may still linger, and always fascinate; and all of the county's history from as far back in time as when rhinoceros, reindeer, elk, bison, cave lions and mammoths roamed there, and whose bones were found many layers down beneath the floor of King Arthur's Cave. Merlin himself is said to have been buried nearby at Longtown. From the making of the Saxon dyke to the Norman castles, to the Wars of the Roses and the English Civil War, the country people of Herefordshire were remembering and passing on their own songs and legends.

Once again, the workhouse, this time in Weobley, played a part in this history, Mrs Leather noting down thirty songs and carols from William Colcombe, an inmate there. One of the most remarkable carols she heard was the relic of a penitential song written by the novelist and ballad-writer Thomas Deloney after the great earthquake in the southeast of England in 1580, which caused part of London's old St Paul's cathedral to fall. The earthquake was taken as a sign that God was displeased, and this carol, published in the sixteenth century as a broadside ballad, persisted, almost incredibly, in Herefordshire until 1909, when 82-year-old Caroline Bridges sang it, with its sombre old tune reminiscent of 'God Rest You Merry Gentlemen', and with the scouring words:

> *Awake, awake sweet England sweet England now awake*
> *And to your prayers obediently, and to your souls partake*
> *For our Lord our God is calling all in the skies so clear*
> *So repent, repent sweet England for dreadful days draw near*
> *Let us pray, and to the living lord, let us pray*
>
> *It's woe unto the woman who big with child do go*
> *Likewise their silly nurses as they give suck also*
> *For there's never any man so stout, nor man nor woman looks gay*
> *But worms will eat your flesh, and your bones will waste away*
> *Let us pray*
>
> *Today you may be here dear man, with many a thousand pounds*
> *Tomorrow you'll be dead and gone and buried underground*
> *With one stone at your head, dear man, another at your feet*
> *Your good deeds and your bad deeds will all together meet*

Over time, a softer and more cheerful last verse came into being, ending

> *We'll shake off care and sorrow, put on our best array*
> *So I wish you all good morrow, God send us a joyful May**

In his foreword to Ella Mary Leather's 1912 book *The Folklore of Herefordshire*, E Sidney Hartland wrote of

> the steamroller of modern fashion crushing into one dead level all that had gone before. Our school

*I used this as the opening song on my 2016 album *Lodestar*, set to music arranged by Ian Kearey.

histories are little more than the story – often amazingly inaccurate – of the pomp, the pedigrees, the pretensions and downfalls of the ruling families. Of the people at large they hardly take account; and when they refer to local customs or traditions, it is with ill-concealed contempt.

Both Lucy Broadwood and Ella Mary Leather were occupied with saving and noting down the culture, but my third heroine, Mary Neal, had a social conscience as well as a desire to give back folk culture to ordinary people. In doing so, she was often faced with the petty and jealous male attitudes of the Victorian and Edwardian eras. Her mission was to improve the lot of working-class women in London, not only materially, but also by bringing into their lives some connection with music and dance as an antidote to the drudgery of their everyday lives.

Born Clara Sophia Neal in Birmingham in 1860 into a well-off family, she described her early life as 'a pageant of snobbery', typical of the Victorian age: 'everything must be correct on the surface, no matter what the reality.'

She was greatly affected by reading an 1883 pamphlet called *The Bitter Cry of Outcast London* which made her aware of the harsh social conditions of working class women's lives in the city. At the age of 28 she went to live in London where she joined The West London Mission that had been formed by Wesleyan Methodists. She dropped her name, Clara Sophia, and became Sister Mary. Throughout the seven years that she worked there, running an employment register and generally supporting poverty-stricken women, she also ran a girl's social club which met on two or three evenings a week. Her passionate longing, she said, was 'to bring some of the beautiful things of life within easy reach of the girls who earn their living by the sweat of their brow and lived lives of long, grey monotonous drudgery'.

With her friend Emmeline Pethick, who had joined the Sisterhood in 1891, the social club went from strength to strength. But in 1895, Mary and Emmeline broke away from what they felt were the restrictions of the West London Mission, and Mary's ambition started to crystallise and become more practical. Wanting to improve the working conditions and poverty caused by the lack of decent employment, Mary and Emmeline started up a tailoring business called Maison Espérance, promising an eight-hour working day, a living wage and good working conditions for young women. They also formed the Espérance Club, an after-work social club where their workers could enjoy getting together to drink tea, to talk, to join in with singing and dancing in the evenings; all this, Mary thought, being a way to bring a little light and joy into their lives. And they organised an annual summer holiday for the girls, setting up a hostel in Littlehampton.

Emmeline was the director of music for the club for about five years, until she left to get married in 1901, and at the wedding guests were entertained by the Espérance Club. It was reported thus:

> A dozen girls, dressed in the costume of Ancient Greece, performed a series of cymbal dances. The beautiful sight presented by the graceful attitudes and evolutions of the dancers caused great pleasure.

Emmeline's departure proved to be a bit of serendipity, leading to a new and beneficial direction for the Espérance Club. Her position was filled by the novelist Herbert MacIlwaine, an Irishman with a love of music. And it was he who, after reading in *The Morning Post* an article about Cecil Sharp and English folksong, was convinced that this would be an ideal choice of music to use for the club's Christmas party. He arranged for Mary and Cecil Sharp to meet and they got on well, finding in each other a mutual sympathetic interest.

At a later meeting, Mary asked Sharp if he knew of any dances that might be suitable for the Espérance Club girls to perform, and he told her how he had seen, in Oxfordshire on Boxing Day, 1899, the Headington Quarry Morris Men dance with William Kimber, a bricklayer, concertina player and gifted dancer; Sharp thought this might be just the thing for the Espérance girls. Without delay

Mary went up on the train, and persuaded Kimber to come down to London and teach her girls how to dance the Morris.

So successful was this passing on of the tradition, and so willingly was it embraced and so beautifully practised by the Espérance girls, that within surprisingly few months they formed Morris teams that were invited to many parts of the country, not only as performers, but also as teachers. There were many public performances, and so popular was it becoming that in 1907 Sharp published *The Morris Book*, which he dedicated to 'Our friends and pupils, the members of the Espérance Club', adding a tribute to Mary Neal. That the dances had come from a sound and fine traditional working-class source was all to the good.

Mary organised a conference to discuss the future of the Espérance Club and the possibility of forming a new association, The Association For the Revival and Practice of Folk Music, and Sharp was instrumental in its founding, his paramount wish being that the Board of Education would introduce genuine traditional songs into schools. For a while, the Society went from strength to strength with popular displays taking place throughout the country.

Sharp was unhappy with the aims of the Folk-Song Society, which had been in existence since 1899, so he initially supported this new society, over which he felt he could have more influence. But that didn't prove to be the case for long. Sharp worried that this burgeoning popularity of folk music might lead to a lowering of standards. Two different objectives were emerging: Mary's – the actual performing, enjoyment and teaching of the dances, and Sharp's – the collecting and notating of the existing traditional sources. A rift started to appear between them when Sharp felt that his position as the leading authority on folk song and dance was being undermined, or even usurped, by Mary. William Kimber, the Headington Quarry dancer, remembered Sharp saying, 'She isn't satisfied with having a ride in the conveyance, she wants to take the reins, too…'

Mary was inviting dancers from traditional Morris sides to come down to London to teach the Espérance girls, while Sharp was giving lectures on folk song and Morris dancing. He then formed his own rival side of female dancers drawn from the Chelsea College of Physical Education, and they gave a display of the Morris, along with William Kimber, at the Chelsea Hospital for King Edward VII – a bit of a coup for those times.

Mary, meanwhile, was becoming active in the Womens' Suffrage movement, involving the Espérance Group at several public gatherings. This was a step too far for McIlwaine, the Group's musical director, and protesting that he could no longer be associated with Mary because of her political associations, he resigned.

A year later, in 1909, things blew up again between Mary and Cecil. In his newly published *The Morris Book, Part II*, Sharp said: 'Here and there we have noticed in the would-be-Morris dancer a tendency to be over-strenuous, to adopt, upon occasion, even a hoydenish manner of execution'.

He accused Mary of having low standards – or in his words: 'no higher artistic standard of performance than that of which you and your club were capable' – and blamed her for sullying the reputation of the Morris: 'Already the opinion is getting about that the Morris dance is a graceless, undignified and uncouth dance, quite unfitted for educational uses'.

And there the two groups split – each seeking to be the official source for teaching Morris dancing in schools. Sharp was giving even more time now to collecting and studying the Morris while Mary began exploring other dance traditions across the country.

At this time, both Mary's and Sharp's sides were all female, although traditionally the Morris was a man's dance. In 1910, Mary took the rather radical step of adding young male dancers to her Espérance girls, albeit friends and relations of theirs, adding fuel to the flames by forming The Espérance Guild of Morris Dancing, and publishing her own *The Espérance Morris Book*. Sharp was stung and was scathing in retaliation, but then so was Mary, who wrote of, 'the blighting touch of the pedant and the expert.'

It was recognised that their tussle was becoming damaging to both movements. *The Times* newspaper, in a conciliatory piece, wrote:

> The spirit of joy which has been the chief characteristic
> of the one, and the spirit of accuracy which has

marked the other are now to be found in the classes of both teachers.

Both Mary and Sharp pressed ahead with publishing their own Morris dance books, but Sharp added to his reputation by publishing a sword dance book, a country dance book, and a book of *English Folk Carols*. Then in 1911, Sharp formed The English Folk Dance Society, which further polarised support.

People were taking sides. Sharp had some very strong supporters including Vaughan Williams, who went to a fancy-dress party dressed as Mary Neal wearing a placard that read 'Power Before Accuracy', the young composer George Butterworth, and Douglas Kennedy, who by now were dancing alongside women in Sharp's Morris dance demonstration sides.

Mary's response to this worthy list was to point out the class difference between Sharp's dancers and hers. She held that the average young lady or gentleman was unable to get near to the spirit of the dance, whereas her working lads and lasses from town or country could, and did. And to her great credit, for the May Day revels at The Globe Theatre in 1913, she brought the full traditional Bampton Village side from Oxfordshire to London.

Then came the Great War. Mary had lost ground to The English Folk Dance Society, which by now had a stable middle-class base. But as Mary admitted: 'In 1918 it was impossible to begin again; the world had changed'.

In 1937 she was awarded a CBE for services in connection with the revival of folksongs and dances. She died in 1947. In her obituary, her old friend Emmeline Pethick said: 'Sensitive to every injustice and to every tragedy she kept a gay and gallant front to life to the very end'.

Trailblazing collectors and historians, these women Lucy Broadwood, Ella Mary Leather and Mary Neal, have been constant inspirations to me in my own work, preserving, sharing and singing the folk music of England.

TEN: *Whenever You Look Up There I Shall Be*

> *There's many a dark and a cloudy morning*
> *Turns out to be a most sunshiny day*
> From The Copper Family, 'The Sweet Primroses'.

The South Downs, and their songs, had claimed me; I was to walk them for many years. And I was fortunate enough to find a companion who would walk them with me.

One evening in 1978 I was in the bar of the Cottesloe Theatre with my sister Dolly at an end-of-run party, when my eye was drawn to a tall, dark-haired man, with a rather wonderful profile. I pointed him out to my sister who smiled and suggested I go and say hello. I didn't have the nerve, but Dolly grabbed my hand, led me over, and introduced us. He told us his name, Philip Barnes, and he said he knew who we were, as he worked part-time in the evenings at The National Theatre to help him through his actor's training at Central School of Speech and Drama, and that as often as he could he came backstage towards the end of the *Lark Rise* performances, and had also been to Albion Dance Band gigs. So – my heart sank – a student? How young a student was he? I hoped he was at least in his thirties… As we talked, he mentioned that his parents lived in Brighton, and that he often went down to visit. 'Oh,' I said – the words came out without thinking – 'I live in Bexhill – just along the coast. Come and say hello if you're ever that way.' I wrote down my telephone number, Bexhill 411343, on a *Lark Rise* programme, and handed it over. He still has it.

A couple of weeks later, there was a phone call from him saying that he was in Brighton, and free – could he come across? The panic of being unprepared reared up – what should I do in the hour or so it might take him to get to Bexhill? Wash my hair? Tidy up the front room? What should I wear? In no time at all it seemed, he arrived on a moped, jacket flying. When I answered the door in my black corduroy trouser suit and a pink check shirt with a cluster of tiny pink fabric roses pinned on the lapel, he greeted me with the words 'You're smaller than I thought.' He explained later that he'd been used to looking up at me on stage...

I hadn't had a date for some eight years or more and I didn't quite know what to do with him, so thought it best to wander up the hill to the pub at Sidley, have a drink and talk. We dived into conversation easily, found a shared love of Shakespeare, books and music, and when it was time to go home, bought greasy spring rolls at the Chinese restaurant and wandered back down to Sea Road, with oil almost dripping off our elbows. It seemed taken for granted that he was going to stay the night, as indeed he did: it was the start of a relationship that has lasted nearly four decades, passionately as lovers for the first few years, then changing, as I knew it must, since I was eighteen years his senior, into a friendship that I value above all else. Philip soon became 'Pip' (after Philip Pirrip in *Great Expectations*).

We had such easy, good times in Bexhill in those early days, swimming from the peaceful beach, and on summer evenings sitting on the balcony of the De La Warr Pavilion drinking gin and tonics and smoking long, slim, elegant More Menthol cigarettes. We'd watch the sun go down, the domes of the bandstand growing luminous in the evening light. Pip got on very well with Polly and Rob, now teenagers, and we played endless and raucous games indoors of Mah Jong and cards. I still had a turntable then, and we played favourite albums: William Boyce symphonies, *The Transports*, Peter Bellamy's remarkable ballad opera with Dolly's arrangements, David Munrow's *Two Renaissance Dance Bands*, Ry Cooder's *Paradise and Lunch* and Irish singer Paul Brady's *Welcome Here Kind Stranger*. Curled up on the long sofa, we drowsily watched much-loved films, *It's A Wonderful Life*, *Casablanca*, *The Philadelphia Story*, *The Big Sleep* – which became a household joke, as I was never able to stay awake till the end!

I had also found someone who loved walking as much as I did...

Through woods and green meadows we oft times have walked
And of sweet conversations together have talked
Where the lark and the blackbird so sweetly did sing
And the lovely thrushes' voices made the valleys to ring…

From 'All Things Are Quite Silent', Ted Baines, collected by Ralph Vaughan Williams, 1904.

…and we must have walked thousands of miles together in that time, conversation never flagging except when a peaceable silence was right. We've sat with our backs against the sun-warmed flint wall of Jevington church, eating our sandwiches before setting off along the track that climbs up to Windover Hill, the path knotted with roots that almost form steps, except that they're uneven, and will trip you; where wild garlic grows on either side. We've traversed High and Over, and Windover Hill, walked from Lewes across to Mount Caburn and Glynde; sat gazing down at Alfriston, walked along the river Cuckmere from there to Exceat, where one time there was a swarm of bees in front of us, but just over the tops of our heads. At Pip's insistence, we braved it… I closed my eyes and he steered me through.

A favourite haunt of ours, set on the brow of a hill, is Friston Church, one of the most beautiful of the Sussex Downland churches. It's one of my delights to swing open the rare tapsel gate (one of only six in Sussex and found only in this county), and head into the churchyard. On a spring day it is bright with daffodils and shining celandines, the grass fresh and green. At the eastern end is a traditional handmade split-rail fence, bleached by sun and wind, and with a tracery of silvered myrtle-green lichen, and a wicket gate that opens onto a long sloping meadow bordered all down one side by a thick-set hedge of blackthorn, white with blossom, known here as a blackthorn winter. It leads down to the village of East Dean.

Here you can sit outside The Tiger Inn, overlooking the village green that is surrounded by flint cottages, sipping a glass of Harvey's best bitter, and contemplating your walk down across to Crowlink and the great chalk cliffs, the Seven Sisters, and to the sea, the English Channel.

But back to the churchyard, which holds the most touching of simple graves; a plain wooden cross, topped by a little arch, with the words WASHED ASHORE carved there. I am moved by the compassion shown by the villagers who brought that unknown body to this peaceful churchyard and buried it here.

As a lady was walking down by the seaside
A poor drowned sailor she chanced there to spy
When first she saw the sailor, it put her to a stand
For she knew 'twas her true-love by the mark on his hand

She put her arms round him, she called him her dear
She wept and she kissed him ten thousand times o'er
Saying Now I am contented to lie by your side
As she kissed his cold lips and heart-broken she died

In yonder green churchyard this couple was laid
And a stone for remembrance placed over their grave
Saying Our joys they are all over, all pleasures are fled
We shall lie here for ever, the grave is our bed

'The Poor Drowned Sailor', collected in Oxfordshire by Cecil Sharp circa 1911. Singer not named.

For the most part Pip and I have walked in benign weather; just once though, we stood sheltering under a stand of hawthorns at the top of Black Cap in a frightening, elemental howling gale. We've walked through fields of almost impenetrable head-high rape from Lewes to Rodmell and back along the Ouse, keeping a sharp lookout for herons lifting themselves away from the river; then resting by the reed beds on the Old Railway Nature Reserve at the edge of Lewes, listening for the hidden warblers there. In the other direction, heading inland along the river, is Hamsey, where a Saxon church sits in isolation. It's a favourite place, and one that we liked to visit in the springtime. There's a hawthorn tree that grows aslant

Shirley and Pip Barnes.

behind a gravestone, and when the May is in blossom, it froths and tumbles over the headstone.

Three years back, Julian Bell the artist, who lives in Lewes, said he'd like to paint my portrait. He asked me what parts of the Sussex landscape I loved best so that he could set me in the right background, and Hamsey was one of several that I mentioned. Julian cycled out, made a quick oil of the little tombstone, with great trees behind it, painted so incredibly that you could not only see the movement of wind in their branches, you could almost hear it as well. When I saw this painting in Julian's studio, I begged him not to sell it to anyone but me. A short while later, when the large portrait was finished, he made me a gift of the Hamsey oil. Two years after that, his studio caught fire and everything was lost – everything – hundreds of paintings including this portrait. 'That must feel like a bereavement,' I said to Julian. 'No' he replied, 'Nobody died, nobody was hurt. I can always paint again.' I doubt if I could have been that philosophical, but I am so grateful that I was given the Hamsey painting in time.

Pip and I have walked every one of the Seven Sisters, the name given to that serene and majestic range of chalk cliffs that fall and rise between Eastbourne and Seaford where they end in a thrift-covered cliff edge. There were two constants on our walks – larks singing, and a twin-engine plane slowly droning in the sky; it had a 1930s feel to it, almost as if we were characters in a pre-war railway poster. We have never tired of their beauty and always valued their power to restore. Pip was occasionally anxious and a little depressed at the precarious career he'd chosen; it offered no security, no guarantee of work. Occasionally these moods would lower over our walks on the Seven Sisters, until one day I made up a mnemonic for them: *How Shirley Rebuked Barnsey For Being Woeful*: And once recited, Pip would ruefully smile his way out of his mood.

> *H*aven Brow
> *S*hort Brow
> *R*ough Brow
> *B*rass Point
> *F*lagstaff Point
> *B*ailey's Hill
> *W*ent Hill Brow

Crowlink is still a favourite spot even though my ability to walk is somewhat curtailed nowadays. The steps down to the beach that were there a couple of hundred or so years back have been taken by the sea, but it once was a place much frequented by smugglers who landed gin from Holland. It was known as Crowlink gin, and was of such a good quality that it was mostly sold in London for a better price.

We were there, sitting on a tussock close to the cliff edge one summer's day, when the Naked Rambler came swinging by, deep in conversation with a clothed companion. They were about to start up an incline as a group of young women were coming down it; we could hear the giggles from quite a distance. We watched both parties negotiate the meeting... And then, a rhinoceros appeared behind us – well, a walker in a bulky sea-green rhino costume bearing a sign that said he was walking for the Save the Rhino charity. So we gave him a fiver and a bottle of water to help save *him*, and off he went, pleased.

Four months after Dolly died in 1995, Pip and I took ourselves to Venice for a week. I had found it so hard to come to terms with her too-early death, and needed something to lift my spirits. It was winter and the days were bitterly cold but sunny, the city suffused with a beautiful light, the skies apricot and lavender at sunset. Without intending to, we were there at Carnevale, and we bought masks; it was an extraordinary, transforming experience. Mine was a harlequin mask that just covered my forehead and eyes, and I felt safe behind it, gazing out at the world, but invisible to other people. Pip, on the other hand, chose a bird mask with a long curved beak, and he said that he felt predatory behind it. Not that he behaved in any way that was unseemly, but he rather enjoyed feeling that he *could* have if he chose.

We caught the vaporetto out to the peaceful island of Torcello to visit the beautiful Byzantine church there. (Although I am not religious, I love churches.) We lit candles – mine for Dolly, Pip's for his father who had died two years back, and for his mother who was ill. And we both felt better.

When my 'renaissance' started, a decade or so back, Pip became a colleague, as well as a friend. He helped and encouraged me, worked alongside me on my 'talk' shows as an actor, and most recently playing on my *Lodestar* album, and at the *Lodestar* concerts as musician, singer and compere. Ours has been an enduring friendship. And that makes us smile, as back in the days when I first started seeing Pip, certain members of the Albion Band warned me that I was making a mistake! It's good to have proved them wrong.

Pip was, and is, in every show, and to stand on one side of the stage, with him on the other, is always reassuring as we share an evening.

> Whenever you look up there I shall be, and whenever
> I look up there will be you.
> *Far from the Madding Crowd*, Thomas Hardy.

I consider myself fairly sceptical when it comes to ghosts and inexplicable happenings, and yet – I have seen ghosts, of sorts…

On one occasion when Pip and I were walking across the Downs on our way to Jevington, as we came down a slope towards the Bottom (the name given to the valleys in the Downs), a small flock of little dark-woolled sheep appeared out of a hawthorn thicket to our right and stood directly in front of us, facing us in what seemed like a rather challenging stance. We stopped and stood still, not wishing to disturb or alarm them. Then as suddenly as they had appeared, they vanished. There was no sound of hooves trampling through the thicket. We looked at each other astounded, and walked into the trees to see if they were there. There was no sign of them, no droppings, not even the tufts of wool you would have expected to find, tugged from their fleeces by the sharp thorns of the may trees. One minute there, next minute vanished without a trace. Perhaps it was a mirage – after all the words downs and dunes have the same derivation…

Two other memorably strange experiences occurred on the Downs as well, this first back in the 1970s. Ashley (my then husband) and I were out with Mardi Gras, a very tall woman I had met while queuing in the Post Office in Etchingham. (The service at the counter was always rather desultory). 'I say, what's your name?' she asked me in very upper-class tones. 'I rather like the look of you. I'm Barbara Huelin. My friends call me Mardi Gras.' And friends we became for many years. She had red hair and a heart of gold. We'd driven over westward from Etchingham to walk at Chanctonbury Ring, high up on the South Downs, the site of an Iron Age hill fort, where later, two Roman temples were built within its defences. Old legends have it that you might meet the Devil there; more recent ones that it was a good place to see UFOs.

It was a weekday, and we had the place to ourselves. As we stood gazing down across the Weald from the beautiful stand of beech trees that had been planted in 1760 (and would later be destroyed in the Great Storm of 1987) I could hear the sound of Morris bells on the air. I asked Ashley if he could hear anything. 'Yes, Morris bells,' he replied. I asked him to sing the note he could hear, and it was the same as mine. Mardi Gras couldn't hear them. We looked and looked to see if there were any errant Morris dancers up there or in the fields far below, but nary a one, as Grandad would say. Mind you, Ashley was recording the album *Morris On* at the time!

The third encounter was a somewhat more unsettling experience. The name of the place is Balsdean, between Brighton and Lewes. Pip and I have walked through it twice, and vowed never to go there again. It's a deep valley with steep slopes on either side, so that the daylight scarcely reaches the floor, especially in winter when the sun is low in the sky. And it is always cold, whatever time of year. Both times I've walked it I've had the distinct feeling that I am being watched, and as I looked up to the top of the slopes, there at the corners of my eyes I thought I glimpsed Roman soldiers in ranks lining the ridge of the hillside, and they weren't pleased that we were there. And beyond them I had the impression of Stone Age people watching – or might they have been the Celts that once inhabited the Downs?

Pip doesn't see the figures, but he, too, feels uneasy in the place. Fanciful? Maybe. But the memory of it is a powerful one.

Although I am fascinated by signs and tokens as they appear in songs, I am, generally speaking, a down-to-earth person, but strange things can happen to us whether or not we choose to believe in them.

On rare occasions in my life I've felt that I could pluck thoughts out of peoples' minds. When I lived in Blackheath with my first husband Austin John Marshall, a small garden fete was held on the green lawn opposite our house, and I entered the 'guess the weight of the cake' competition. I picked up the two-tier chocolate cake, looked at the stall-holder, and said 'Three pounds, thirteen and a half ounces.' I could see by her startled look that I had guessed it right. Polly and Rob were so thrilled when at the end of the day we carried it home for tea. And at the same fete Rob entered a charity balloon competition. You wrote your name and address on a printed slip attached to the balloon with the request that whoever found the balloon would post the card back to the charity, and whichever balloon had travelled furthest would win. About three weeks later, there was a knock at the door, and a gentleman had come to give Robert his £10 prize (a lot of money then). His balloon had been picked up by an English couple on the beach at Rimini!

Once when Uncle Fred was presiding over an evening of literary quizzing at his home with family and friends, he read a quote and asked who wrote it. Everything went silent until I yelled out 'William Hazlitt'. The silence then was a stunned one – even Fred looked amazed. I'd never read anything by Hazlitt, but it was the right answer. Fred congratulated me which made me feel very proud, but I knew it was right because I'd taken it from Fred's head! I wish it would happen more often!

Once in around 1970, when I was singing solo at a folk club in Sudbury, I was given accommodation for the night with the people who ran the club. They lived in a beautiful period terrace, and had just bought the house next door which they were in the throes of redecorating – and they put me up all alone there, in a bedroom on the top floor. It was midsummer, and very warm, but the minute I went into that room, I felt icy cold. I sat on the bed for a while and decided not to undress. But being tired after the travel and the performance, I got under the covers and tried to sleep. I still couldn't get warm, and I felt very afraid; there seemed to be some dread presence in the room. I lay there until daylight – happily early as it was high summer, then got up, picked up my bag and my banjo and walked to the station and waited for the first train to take me back to London. I mentioned this one day to Dave and Toni Arthur. Toni's immediate response was to say that she'd experienced the same thing in that room – but she had actually seen what it was – an old woman sitting in a chair at the end of the bed, staring malevolently at her…

My mother saw a few ghosts, and she told of the family stories – ones that I think must have occurred in many families during the First World War. My Grandfather had been conscripted into the Army – all in secret of course, no one knew where he was. But Granny dreamt one night that he walked up the garden path to the cottage, waved, then turned aside and vanished before he got to the door. She learned later that was the day his regiment was sent to South Africa, India and Burma, and it would be five years before she saw him again. He kept a diary of that time which I have; here's a part of it. It starts in Lewes, outside the Town Hall, in the days before there was a War Memorial opposite.

> We left Lewes on Feb 8th 1917. At 9a.m. we had orders to have everything ready to take to the Town Hall at 10.30p.m. we paraded there with kit bags and packs, etc. and marched to the station and by the time we were all in the train it was 12.o.c. midnight. We arrived at Exeter 7.45a.m. Friday where the Mayoress supplied us with tea and buns and cigs.

> After another 12 hours in the train we arrived at Devonport, looking worse for a shave & wash. After standing on the Quay for 2 hours we boarded the Royal Mail Boat - the Balmoral Castle - a liner of 13.361 tons, seven years old.

> Then we had a good look round and wondered what sort of time we were in for. It was fun to see us trying to get in our hammocks; in fact the first night most of us fell out, for it's very funny the way they have of tipping you out.

> *Feb 12th Monday:* We left Plymouth for Cape Town, South Africa. The convoy consisted of six destroyers, five troop carriers and one armed cruiser. The night we left, the German submarines were waiting for us. The leading boat of our three had a torpedo fired at her and we all scattered. Some went miles out of the way, but I'm glad to state that none got hit and two of our destroyers rammed the submarine and she went to the bottom. For a few days we were all separated,

one boat for instance went up the Irish Channel, but eventually we found each other in mid-Atlantic, a destroyer to each boat. On Feb 20th these left us, as we were supposed to be out of danger – to a certain extent.

Feb 26th: We first sighted land at 11.15a.m. and 12.30 we anchored at Free Town, Sierra Leone and stayed there three days. Officers and passengers went ashore and brought back fruit and things. Every day natives came alongside the boat in canoes, dozens at a time. Some were quite naked, others wore loin cloths; they brought fruit, beads and curios to sell.

A mail boat called and departed on the 28th; she took some of our letters. This boat had General Smuts* on board, so we knew that our letters would get home safely. We took on a fresh supply of water and started for Cape Town at 11.a.m. We were inoculated for cholera. After two days sailing we crossed the Equator. We had a most terrific thunderstorm. I have never seen anything to equal it and being on the ocean made it so much worse. We all got soaked. What a night!

Tuesday March 13th: At Cape Town the passengers left us and the Colonel went ashore and got permission to take us for a March. I were in the drums then. We disembarked at 1.30 and our Bugle Band played the troops through the town. What a lovely place it is. As soon as we broke off I went to the Town Gardens and had a good look at the lovely flowers there.

We left Cape Town the next day for Durban, 860 miles up the coast; it took three days to arrive there.

*General Smuts was a Boer who fought against the British in South Africa during the Booer War.

Saturday March 17th: Soon after breakfast we disembarked and put our kits on waggons, then marched thee miles to the Camp which is called The Imperial Rest Camp where we were put under canvas. After a good night's rest we were up at 5 o'clock and taken for a good bathe in the sea, and I can say we wanted one jolly bad! We were never allowed to go there again as sharks were frequently there. A horse had his legs bitten off and several natives lost their lives.

Sunday March 18th: We were allowed in the town in the afternoons. My pal and I had some fine trips out. First we went to Umbilo all over the banana plantations and pineapples. Every day my pal and I used to go for these trips through the native villages. We saw some lovely sights – but don't the natives just keep their eyes on you! I had plenty of rickshaw rides and such fine chaps to pull you about! They dress in such queer fashions – some have horns and feathers, some paint their legs and body.

We left Durban Friday April 13th on The Empress of Britain and anchored in the bay for seven days. This boat is 18,000 tons, a fine one, but so dirty, full of lice, bugs and beetles. My Company – A – were put down the very lowest – you couldn't open the port holes on account of them being below the water. We had to take our meals, and sleep there. We used to strip, for it was just red hot. One of the Somersets died, and another taken ashore in a serious condition.

On April 20th we steamed out of Durban en route for Bombay, and when we were three days out we passed some islands which was supposed to be inhabited by cannibals. On the fourth day, a chap in the Black Watch died, and was buried the same day, then another died.

Some of the Bedfords were inoculated but their arms began to give them trouble. The first to die through this was Sgt Evans and Private Harris. Some more and I were picked out for the Burial Party, and I think anyone who has done this sort of thing, think it most sad. They just put a sacking around and sew it and put weights on their feet, lay them on a plank and let them slide off into the sea. Such a hard way of doing things.

Grandad lived into his eighties and died before Granny did, but when she was an old lady, a widow, I heard her say on two occasions as she sat on her bed sorting through her belongings: 'I'm not ready to come yet, Fred.'

My mother had several ghostly experiences, some frightening, some amusing. In 1957 she, Dolly and Jonathan had moved from Athelstan Road to an isolated and dilapidated Tudor farmhouse, Bridge Farm, where they hoped to be self-sufficient. It was nicely isolated down at the far end of Rocks Lane near Coghurst, with an orchard and fields at the back sloping down to the railway line that ran between Ore and Rye, the noisy steam trains belching their way through the countryside. As children we'd loved being on the bridge at Coghurst (see photo on page 62), waving hello to the driver, then dashing through a cloud of smoke to the other side to wave goodbye; it was always a thrill when the driver waved back. The bridge was made of cast-iron, its floor of heavy, thick, bleached wooden planks, sun-warmed on a summer's day to our bare feet, but full of large and spiteful splinters.

Soon after the three of them had settled in, Uncle Fred and his wife Jacquie joined them, and became part of the self-sufficient smallholding. They kept chickens, geese and goats, and grew all their vegetables, with an abundance of apples from the orchard. Uncle Fred and Jacquie weren't perhaps the best suited to country life; they both disliked the goat and were scared of the geese, and while Jacquie gardened with enthusiasm, she found it impossible to tell the difference between young vegetable seedling and weeds. They returned to life back in town after a couple of months.

It was here at Bridge Farm that Mum saw, more than once, in the large kitchen, a very cheerful man naked in a bath, apparently singing and scrubbing his back. Of course, everyone dismissed this as foolishness, until the day the floorboards had to be taken up for some reason. There, in the space beneath the floor was an old-fashioned iron bath tub… but unoccupied!

One night at Bridge Farm, when Mum was there alone, Dolly and Jonathan having gone up to London for a couple of days, Mum had this experience that she wrote down:

> *June 23rd 1957 Monday:* 'I had gone to bed at 10.30 – night was dark – went to sleep – woke with a start at 11pm to see white and green flashes on the ceiling. Watched for a while wondering what caused them, then thought perhaps the caravan was alight – 300 yards away – jumped out of bed and looked across the field – caravan OK, but thought I saw more rays, green and white, coming down through trees – thought it was an illusion or eyes playing tricks. So concentrated on one space between trees to prove that I did see rays – presently ray appeared in chosen spot. Began to get apprehensive as I was in cottage alone. Looked at caravan once more – about half an hour had elapsed – tested my pulse – normal – or at least not racing, pinched myself to see if I was definitely awake – turned cold tap on in wash-basin and bathed my face and eyes to ensure that I was definitely awake – walked around room quietly. Had another look out of the window – time 12.15. As I looked through trees saw outline of space ship – stared horrified at it. Tested myself again – and mentally – was I mad? Tried to think rationally – seemed quite normal, definitely awake. Space ship made, as far as I could see of some very light material – or metal rather (in weight) seemed very pale khaki in colour – but it was a very dark night. Also could not judge distance away – seemed close and not much larger

than our cottage – but might have been more distant and larger. While wondering about it and beginning to feel –though frightened as I was in cottage alone – interested. I hear strange humming – like from a huge army of bees – but not so high pitched – a beautiful, deep, melodious sort of humming – wavering – began to get frightened – felt cut off from the rest of the world – tested myself again – moved as little as possible because I didn't want to be seen as I was standing at the open window. As I listened and watched, waves of gentle light, well, only a glow of light, came from the space ship, wider and wider like waves made when stone thrown in pond – really frightened now – shut window noiselessly and crept back to bed. Time 2.17 – lay trembling in bed watching white and green light on ceiling still – wishing it was morning – feeling terrified – felt that waves of sound and gentle glow were trying to draw me into their folds – resisted with all my might the wish to go to the space ship – felt pulse, a bit erratic, heart rather loud – thought I was mad or going to be ill, lay as quietly as possible and tried to keep calm and think rationally. Now a sound like some soft material nibbling the window – peeped over bed clothes – time 3.01am. Saw little silver being beckoning me through the glass – silver skin or clothes – beautifully soft and as flexible as my own skin – seemed to be non-porous, curious shaped hands. I'm afraid to draw them as I feel I shall be committed to their influence or make them earth-bound.

I longed for day – felt terribly cut off from the rest of the world – felt that everything had changed for me and I could never be the same again. Presently an owl flew across the orchard and I felt at least another earth mortal was alive on this awful night – felt comforted – did not feel frightened – that space ship and occupants meant me no harm physically – it was all too gentle. I felt that the power in it, or controlling it was benign. BUT I did not want to be controlled by any other mind than my own, and resented tiny beings coming from anywhere and trying to make me do things – also was not sure that I was not suffering an hallucination and felt that to step out of window and follow my strange madness – if it was madness – was harmful to me and I might not regain my sanity. I lay in bed, fists clenched, fighting. Last time looked at clock 4.27 am. Afraid to look over bed clothes any more – very frightened – dawn appearing, suddenly without at first being aware of it, all noise, all fear, all light had gone. I felt safe, fell asleep, woke at 8 am or thereabouts.

After effects: warned my household not to get too near me as I felt in some way I was dangerous to other people – or felt different, a feeling that persisted for a month very strongly – laughed at of course, they didn't know what to think of it all, but that night is all still vivid to me. Regarding the glass in the windows and why the little beings didn't come through it, had some strange knowledge – though how I came by it – that sand in glass was not passable by silver people. The silver beings seemed to be in control – happy control – of larger beings – not seen but felt, and benign. My daughter had a strange dream on the same night – dreamt that space ships had landed by the cottage and that I was terribly frightened.

Dolly went back to the cottage the next morning, so anxious was she; and there was another strange coincidence – a farmer wrote to the local paper looking for an explanation of the green and white flashes he had seen that same night…

Amusingly enough, three years earlier I'd sung a song written by Ewan MacColl called 'Space Girl':

My Mother told me I should never venture into Space,
But I did, I did, I did
She said no girl on Earth should trust the Martian race,
But I did I did I did
A rocket pilot asked me on a voyage to go,
And I was so romantic, I couldn't say no,
That he was just a server robot, how was I to know?
So I did, I did, I did

I doubt if Mum's account of her visitation will endure, but there are strange and unlikely events, held to be true, that have lasted in songs and ballads for centuries, notably for me, the ballad of Lord Allenwater, a story over three hundred years old. It's the true story of the arrest and execution in London in 1716 of James Radcliffe, third Earl of Derwentwater for his part in the first Jacobite Uprising a year earlier. He was just twenty-seven when he was beheaded for treason, and he left a wife, a son and newly born daughter. He was said to be much loved by the tenants on his great estates in the Lake District; and the legend sprang up that on the night he was executed in London, the rivers on his land ran blood, and that the Northern Lights shone more brightly than they ever had before, and were known ever after as Lord Derwentwater's Lights. The ballad was found only rarely in England, but in 1904 a Mrs Emily Stears of Horsham in West Sussex (and great-aunt to Ian Anderson, musician and proprietor of the world music magazine *fROOTS*), sang it to Ralph Vaughan Williams, although by the time it had reached Sussex, the name Lord Derwentwater had vanished, becoming Lord Allenwater. The song is full of signs and portents, and James Radcliffe is quite clearly a hero, maintaining that he was not a traitor, defiant to the end.

The King has wrote a long letter and sealed it up with gold
And sent it unto Lord Allenwater to read it if he could

The first two lines Lord Allenwater read they struck him with
surprise

The next two lines Lord Allenwater read made tears fall from his eyes
He goes up to his gay lady as she in childbed lay
Saying 'Up to London I must go for I'm sure there is great need'

'Well it's if to London you must go, before you go away
Make your will my dear' she said, 'lest you should go astray'

'Well I will leave my only son my houses and my lands
And I will leave my dear wedded wife ten thousand pounds in hand'

He goes out to his stable groom to saddle his milk white steed
And says 'To London I must go, for I'm sure there is great need'

And he put his foot upon the stirrup, the other across his steed
And the gay gold rings from his fingers burst and his nose began to bleed

And as he was a-riding along the road his horse fell against a stone
'O there's signs and tokens enough I've seen, I'm sure I'll never return'

And as he was a-riding up a merry London street, so close by to the Whitehall
O the lords and ladies stood looking hard, and a traitor he was called

'No traitor at all,' Lord Allenwater cried 'No traitor at all,' cried he
'Why I vow I could find you three score men to fight for King Georgie'

Then up and spoke a grey-headed man, a broad axe in his hand
'Deliver yourself, Lord Allenwater, your life's at my command'

'My life I do not value at all, my life I do give unto thee
And the black velvet coat I have on my back, you take that
for your fee

There is forty pounds in one pocket, pray give it unto the poor
And there's forty-five in the other one, pray give it from door
to door'

And he laid his head upon the block, the man gave a mighty
blow
'Now there lies the head of a traitor,' he said. But it answered
and it said 'No!'

In spite of the stark cover of our 1970 album *Love, Death &*
the Lady, with Dolly and me dressed heavily in black and gazing
moodily out, and which caused some people to believe that we
might be witches, it wasn't, and isn't true. But it was at a time when
there was a great interest in songs about magic, fairy and elfin
visitations, the most popular of which was 'Tam Lin', recorded by
Fairport Convention on their 1969 album, *Liege & Lief.* Once heard,
almost everyone wanted to perform it, and as time went by, the
new cover versions grew more and more frenzied. People started to
hunt through Child's *Popular Ballads** searching for similar magical
ballads, or wrote their own. Even though the Fairport version was
thrilling, I was never quite convinced of its authenticity, and indeed,
A L Lloyd confessed that he had 'cobbled it together' partly from
Child's *Ballads* book and partly from fragments that had turned up,
he claimed, from 'mostly Scots travelling people.'

Fairies and transformations weren't of interest to me; I cared far
more for those more subtle mysteries that were in the songs, relics

**English and Scottish Ballads* by Francis James Child, originally
published in eight volumes in 1860 and reprinted in multiple
editions since, the most popular being *English and Scottish Popular*
Ballads Edited from the Collection of Francis James Child (1904),
edited by Helen Child Sargent and George Lyman.

of past beliefs now accepted as a part of the story that didn't require explanation or even understanding by the singer. This is where field recordings come into their own; the song is intact in that version the singer has given.

Take 'George Collins', for example, a ballad sung by 80-year-old Enos White of Axford, Hampshire, to Bob Copper in 1956. Rarely found, it tells how young George, while out riding one day, encounters 'a pretty fair maid a-washing her white marble stone' by a stream.

Although he is betrothed to Fair Ellender, he kisses the girl (and here is an element of magic) who turns out to be a water-sprite. George divines this and, realising that the kiss is fatal, returns home to die.

> *For if I should die this night*
> *As I suppose I shall*
> *Bury me by the marble stone*
> *That's against Fair Ellender's hall*

Not only does he die, but his Fair Ellender too, and in the final verse:

> *The news being carried to London town*
> *And hung upon London's gates*
> *There's six pretty maids died all in one night*
> *And all for George Collins' sake*

There are several theories, the water sprite being the most common, but more recently it has been suggested that George had a venereal disease, which might account for the multiple deaths… but I think I'll pass on that one. In any case, not everything has to be explained. I doubt that Enos knew the full implications of the story – he certainly didn't mention them – and I wouldn't expect that the word 'water-sprite' ever passed his lips. He was a farm worker, a carter, a man who could neither read nor write, but accepted the ballad as he had heard it sung by the singer before him from whom he learned it. So the mysteries remain there buried in the song.

There are, of course, many songs that contain a frisson of the supernatural; for instance, is Reynardine a man or a fox?

Sun and dark she followed him
His eyes did brightly shine
And he led her over the mountains
Did this sly, bold Reynardine

There are many songs that tell of ghostly visitations from dead lovers whose souls are prevented from finding rest because of the over-weening grief of the loved-ones left behind. After a year-and-a-day of mourning, the dead return to beg to be let go.

It's I, my love, sits by your grave
And will not let you sleep
For I crave one kiss of your clay cold lips
And that is all I seek

But lily, lily are my lips
My breath comes earthy strong
If you have one kiss from my clay cold lips
Your time will not be long…

We sing these words although we know that in our world, this isn't real or true, but in the song that age-old belief holds us and convinces us still. So for me, the fascination is that the songs still contain these golden shards of long, long memory, and are enhanced by them.

ELEVEN: *The Sea Glass Years*

In 1980 Dolly and I were offered a two-week tour of Australia, including a concert at the Sydney Opera House as part of the Sydney Folk Festival. Dolly turned it down as she didn't want to leave her young son, and I told the organisers in that case I was sorry that I wouldn't be able to accept. They came back with an offer to provide me with a harpsichord player for the main concert; I would just have to take Dolly's scores with me. They offered an all-expenses-paid tour, and a fee of £600 – a small fortune then – and I'd be sharing the tour with Peter Bellamy of The Young Tradition. I decided I couldn't pass this money by, so I accepted, even though I realised I would have to sing unaccompanied for the rest of the gigs as I had sold all my instruments, my five-string banjo, the dulcimer and even This Instrument (to Ian Kearey). The money from this had kept us going while Polly was at Oxford (the first in our family to go to university), and Rob still at sixth form college.

So on a bitterly cold snowy January day I hugged Polly and Rob, looking so pale in that wintry light, and left for Heathrow Airport. It was so cold that our plane's wings had to be de-iced before we could take-off, not the most reassuring start. However, the flight was incredible. We touched down at Dubai, then to Australia, landing at Perth, before setting off to Sydney – another thousand miles across the almost unimaginable vastness of the continent. Then at Sydney Airport, Peter and I walked out into the reception hall, to be greeted by the Sydney Morris Men, dancing to welcome us, policemen dressed in shorts looking on, smiling. It was the Australian summer, the heat was intense, and I felt such a sense of well-being and freedom. It was so relaxed and friendly that all my worries fell away – just for a short while. I had to face the prospect of singing at the Opera House, in two days' time.

I had an afternoon's rehearsal with the harpsichord player, a lovely woman, Winsome Evans, and she played Dolly's arrangements with understanding and many extra flourishes. One of the songs I sang was Uncle Fred's 'Come My Love', and the recording from that concert is on my box set *Within Sound.* Can you imagine what it was like walking onto the stage at The Sydney Opera House, the responsibility of it, not knowing what might happen? I didn't do too badly though, and the audience was receptive and warm... I was staying in Sydney with Diana, Austin John Marshall's sister, her children and her new husband, John. At home after the concert, everyone lavished generous (though not fully deserved) praise on me, with the exception of the husband. 'Call that folk-singing?' he said. Taken aback, I asked him what was. 'June Tabor,' he replied.

That concert was safely over, but I had several more gigs to do all over the continent, without Winsome. The next one was in the open in a market place in Sydney and I had to sing unaccompanied. It was humiliating. I think it was in Melbourne that I borrowed a banjo for the concert, but I didn't have a thumb-pick, more or less essential for a 5-string, and the capo wasn't very secure... so I struggled with the accompaniments. My confidence level was so low that I felt that it had all ebbed away. Somehow I got through that evening, but even nearly forty years later, I still have nightmares about being on stage totally unprepared, although sometimes they take the shape of me being on stage in a play, and I haven't learnt my words.

Peter Bellamy and I were sharing all the gigs; he was as supportive as he could be, and we did sing some songs together. We flew to Tasmania to the Folk Festival there, so I was certainly getting around, and being in Australia and spending time with Australians was a wonderful experience. It would have been perfect if it had just been a holiday! Even so, I was relieved when it was over; I had just about got away with it, I thought, but really I felt humiliated at not doing better. On the plane, Peter and I were upgraded to seats in the upper cabin. We sat side by side for the long journey home, Peter chain-smoking. And he did that classic thing of looking at his watch to tell the time while holding a glass of beer – and it spilled all over me! By time we reached London, I was kippered with all the smoke.

I made it home to Bexhill, laden with two sheepskin rugs that Diana had bought for Polly and Rob, relieved to have made it safely back.

Although my Australian earnings seemed like a lot of money, they didn't last long, and I realised I'd have to accept that, after the emotional distress of *Lark Rise*, I was no longer a reliable singer, and that I'd have to find proper full-time work. I was cleaning one day a week out at Jonathan Clowes' weekend home at Penhurst – a tiny village near Battle. Jonathan's gardener drove me out and back every week and handed over £20 cash at the end of the day's work. I could have got a full-time job in the local Sainsbury's in Bexhill, but thought that would feel like too much of a defeat.

Rescue came in the form of an offer from Jonathan – would I like to work at his literary agency in London for two weeks, at £75 a week and a lift home on Friday afternoon? Yes, I would, and off I set in my best black dress, ready to polish my typing skills. Jonathan and his partner Ann Evans were very successful, with prestigious clients, including Kingsley Amis, Elizabeth Jane Howard, Doris Lessing and David Nobbs, the creator of *Reggie Perrin*. I heard that CJ – Reggie Perrin's boss in the TV comedy – was JC, based on Jonathan, but with the initials reversed! To my amusement I discovered that one of Jonathan's clients was Len Deighton, whose original manuscript of *The Ipcress File* I had typed some twenty years earlier, although by now Len was sending his manuscripts on a disc, one of the first people to do so. There was one other person working there who showed me the ropes, Anne-Marie Nation-Tellery. We hit it off straightaway, becoming firm friends, and I'm happy to say we still are. She told me later that she was dreading the arrival of 'a friend of Jonathan's' to work there, but was mightily relieved when I turned up. She was always cheerful and funny, unfazed by the status and fame of the clients, and sometimes quite dismissive in her breezy manner.

My first task was to learn how to man the switchboard. Oh God! Panic set in straightaway. I had to push switches up or down in order to speak to Jonathan or Ann, and down or up to speak to the caller, and then another manoeuvre to put the call through. I simply couldn't get the hang of it at first. It reminded me of the day when

I was ten or so when Mum took Dolly and me down to the public phone box in Ore village to show us how to make a call if ever there was an emergency. Such things scramble my brain. I never did sort out when to press Button A or when to put the money in (two coppers) or press Button B – except I think that was to get your money back if the first operation didn't work. How confusing was that – too many 'ifs'. Luckily, I didn't ever need to make an emergency call, so that was OK.

Jonathan ran his office from his home in Camden Town, and he percolated wonderful fresh coffee every morning – I think it was a special blend of Blue Mountain and Java coffee beans that were delivered regularly. We were allowed a cup at the start of the day's work, served with double cream. If a client had a morning appointment, we could give them coffee, but Jonathan insisted that we didn't use a fresh grind but just added more boiling water to what was left in the percolator. The day came when Kingsley Amis refused to drink his coffee, saying it tasted of nothing but water. As it was I who had given this diluted brew to him, I got the blame, but ever after that I ignored Jonathan's rules and made fresh coffee each time, shaking my head over such a petty economy in such a classy office. Jonathan's business partner (and later his wife), Ann Evans, wasn't as helpful as she might have been. The first week there, while I was still finding out what was what, she'd come into my little office/reception area, toss a manuscript or book into my in-tray and tell me in an unintelligible gabble to post it to some foreign publisher in Sweden, Italy or Japan, not waiting to see if I'd got the name right before flouncing away. That seemed to me a rather careless way to do business, but Anne-Marie helped me out. I must have done alright because the two weeks turned into two years. I rented a bedsit from old friends of Alan Lomax's in Hampstead, Frances and Nat Brown, and still managed to keep us going, even with paying a mortgage in Bexhill and rent in London. But how wonderful it was to get home at the weekends, and how I hated going back up to London on Sunday nights. Sometimes I was so broke I just had enough money for my fare on the 24 bus from Victoria to Hampstead Heath; I'd walk down to work at Camden

Town in the mornings. As I came out of Victoria Station one very rainy night, I spotted a soggy pound note on the pavement; I was delighted at such an unexpected gift. You may find it hard to believe that I could have been so broke, but I just was!

I was still keeping up with a few folk friends, and Jane Winder, who had once acted as an agent but was now working in the bookshop in The British Museum, told me what a great place it was, and that she was paid £100 a week (I was getting £75 at Jonathan Clowes). She suggested that I get a job there, so I handed in my notice with Jonathan, and had a wonderful surprise with my final pay cheque. The accountant had added two years' holiday pay which, naïvely, having been always self-employed as a singer, I hadn't realised I was entitled to. Going to the Museum was a good move – and I had two wonderful years there, meeting people from all over the world, occasionally being recognised by visitors, one girl admiring the dress I was wearing, saying she remembered me wearing it at a concert in Regent's Park (what a memory she had – as that was some years earlier) adding that it was an antique, wasn't it? I didn't like to tell her that I'd bought it brand new from a dress shop in Heathfield when I was living in Etchingham!

In most lunch hours I'd wander around the museum, and the exhibit I loved most was the Anglo-Saxon Alfred Jewel, which was then on loan from the Ashmolean Museum; it's a thing of such beauty – a tear-drop-shaped gold-framed miniature in exquisite greens and blues, that held a portrait of King Alfred, gazing away to the side with a distant look in his eyes. It moved me profoundly. And still does. If there was ever anything I really coveted, it was that Alfred Jewel.

One Friday quite out of the blue, Jim Lloyd, presenter of the Radio 2 folk programme, phoned me at the Museum. He'd recently been appointed Director of the English Folk Dance and Song Society, and said they were looking for a public relations officer to work at Cecil Sharp House and that the position could be mine. It was urgent – I could have the weekend to make up my mind. Jim's wife Frances Line, who would be made Controller of Radio 2 in 1990, had commissioned a broadcast of *Anthems in Eden* back in

1968. I knew them both, and agonised over this decision. Was this my chance to get back into the world of folk music, where part of me felt I rightfully belonged? Was I still clinging onto the rather forlorn hope that I was really Shirley Collins, the folk-singer, and not a shop assistant, however elevated a one?

And yet... and yet... I was so established and happy at the British Museum. But a false sense of hubris kicked in, or perhaps it was vanity at having been sought out, and I phoned Jim on the Monday morning and accepted the post. It turned out to be a huge mistake; I had been misled. I wasn't a public relations officer, I was secretary to the accountant there, a bad-tempered, secretive, rather paranoid man. He scarcely spoke except when he wanted me to type a letter, never smiled, and hardly acknowledged my presence. I was so frustrated at having put myself in this position. At the end of the first week I asked my manager at the Museum if I could have my job back, but she said no – it was not her policy. I was so unhappy there, and so angry with myself.

My only friend and ally there was Malcolm Taylor, the librarian of the Vaughan Williams Memorial Library. Malcolm was arguably the best thing that ever happened to the English Folk Dance & Song Society, and Cecil Sharp House. He started there in 1979 as Assistant Librarian, and within two years he had been promoted to Head Librarian. He too felt, as I had, that the Library was a forbidding, forbidden place, and the first thing he did was to put a window in the Library door – letting light in, making it open and welcoming. Over his years there, he was awarded several honours, notably an OBE in 2002 'For services to music, librarianship and heritage', and he was the first non-musician to be given the Good Tradition Award at the BBC Radio 2 Folk Awards. And this was before he'd set up and launched *The Full English* – the world's largest free digital resource for English traditional song, music, dance and culture, comprising some 54,000 items. It was an extraordinary achievement, and all done with grace, modesty and good humour. He still is an eloquent communicator, speaking with passion and knowledge. He loves cricket and walking the South Downs – and there you have it – he's an ideal Englishman, a national treasure. Malcolm had this to say of my time there:

> EFDSS Director, Jim Lloyd, managed to persuade
> Shirley back into the fold with a promise that
> she would become the face of folk music for the
> EFDSS. Sadly, this role never came to fruition,
> and some of her frustration with her 'temporary'
> secretarial post was vented by her marvellous temper,
> often followed by a cooling-down period when
> she sat on the banks of the local Regent's Canal.
> *English Dance & Song,* Vol 77, No 3, 2015.

But I had made an enemy at Cecil Sharp House which made things even frostier – Jim Lloyd's secretary. A problem arose about the 'top of the milk.' I always arrived first at work, made myself coffee, and poured in the top of the milk.* This didn't go down well with her and complaints were made. I had to either shake the milk up, or wait until everyone else came in. To be honest, though, if someone else had taken the cream, I'd have been annoyed! But I'd had enough of that pettiness – I wasn't happy there or doing anything useful or even remotely connected to folk music. I left after six months, and went home. Home by now was a flat in Brighton that Pip and I had bought together – I'd sold the Bexhill flat while I was at The Museum. Polly had finished her three years at Oxford and moved to Brighton, Robert to Hastings where he was making a name for himself as a cricketer.

I saw an advertisement in the *Argus* – 'Manager wanted for Oxfam shop'. That might be a lark, I thought, so I applied, and went for the interview which was held in the North Street Brighton shop. The area manager was a young, very attractive woman, and she introduced me to the volunteer staff. I eyed the middle-aged, middle-class ladies warily; they eyed me stonily back. Resentment filled the air – they'd been used to managing perfectly well without a paid manager. I tried to say all the right things, but I wasn't winning

---

*You may remember that this had also got me into trouble with Alan Lomax's ex-wife Elizabeth when we lived together in Highgate!

them over, and didn't get the job. It went to a rather fussy, portly, snappily dressed man who I supposed the ladies thought wouldn't interfere too much with the way things were being run. A month or so later, a call came from Oxfam, saying they'd like to consider me to manage a new 'flagship' shop/café they were opening on the Western Road in Brighton – and this time, the job was mine. It was a taxing time getting the shop fitted and collecting the donations of clothes, bric-a-brac, books, anything that would sell – during which time my District Manager vanished to India for a week. On her return she insisted that we also get the café up and running, but without any money set aside for it. For tables, we begged for old sewing machine trestles, we scrounged around for chairs, many of which, when they were donated, proved to be unsafe and in need of repairing and varnishing. This last task was done the evening before we opened.

I had asked Brighton Morris if they would come and dance at the 'Grand Opening', which they kindly did, dancing on the pavement outside and throughout the shop. But when they sat down to rest on the chairs, every one of them got stuck. The varnish hadn't dried and their jeans were ruined. I was mortified, but they forgave me, and since that day I have only asked them to dance at my proper gigs – years later, when I was Shirley Collins again – at the South Bank and later on the *Lodestar* shows. I hope that made up for it! I think all was forgiven – they did, after all, make me their patron in 2014.

The café proved to be a burden. It was on the first floor above the shop, and many people couldn't or wouldn't make their way up to it. We had recruited a variety of volunteers, many of them post-grads filling in time until they'd decided what to do with their lives, others were retired people, the salt of the earth, willing and sensible. The young volunteers didn't have much of an idea about catering – even though it was simple fare that we offered – sandwiches, jacket potatoes with a choice of toppings, the best-seller being sour cream with chopped spring onions. I gave that task to one young volunteer who, when she'd finished, handed me a bowl containing the little white bulbs – she'd thrown all the rest, the green bits, away! She said she hadn't ever seen a spring onion before, let alone eaten one.

An officer from the fire brigade came to inspect the café before we opened, and said that we'd have to put fire doors in at the top of the stairs, and that they would always have to be kept closed. My manager thought that would be even more of a deterrent for customers, and instructed me to keep them open. I wouldn't do that, and it was the first of several major fallings-out that we had. She also wanted me to be smartly dressed and to oversee the shop, but I was more of a hands-on manager – I wouldn't expect any of the volunteers to do jobs that I wasn't prepared to do myself. I lasted there for over two years, until I decided I'd had enough of carting heavy black sacks around, and clearing the toilet of clothes that some customers stuffed down it – why would anyone do that?

During my Oxfam years Pip and I sold the flat, driven out by hellish noisy neighbours overhead, and I rented a house in pretty North Gardens. Pip shared this with me, although he was away quite a bit – he'd landed a contract with the Royal Shakespeare Company, a tour of Australia.

We entertained a good deal, sitting with drinks in the upstairs front room where the evening sun shone through, before moving downstairs to the basement for dinner. I'd made two good friends, Mirella and Chris Marlow, well-dressed and witty, their friendship was to prove essential and supportive, and lasts to the present day. I'd met Mirella at Oxfam – she came as a volunteer, and we hit it off straightaway. She was tall, intelligent, well-read and blonde, with natural cupid's bow lips. Chris, her husband was a music teacher, elegant, well-dressed and witty. Old friend and musician Ian Kearey and his wife Rivka were regulars too, and the laughter and conversation never flagged.

I needed a bit of a break after the Oxfam slog, and stayed unemployed for a couple of months, until one day in 1989 I heard from Jim Lloyd again who by then was on the board of South East Arts. He told me that they were creating a post of a Folk Animateur (no, I didn't know what that was, either) and would I like to apply? It was an eighteen-month trial, and the brief was to create awareness of traditional music and arts in the Sussex area. I got the job! One of the first things I did was to talk to the Schools Music Officer for Sussex, saying I'd like to take traditional song and dance into schools, like a modern Mary Neal. He dismissed the idea breezily, saying it was already in place. That's good, I thought, then asked him what it was. He replied, 'Oh we've got a gamelan orchestra and a steel drum band.'

My lack of administrative skills were something of a stumbling block at first, but I soon picked things up. I gave some financial support to local projects and paid Chris Wood's air fare to Canada so that he could study Quebecois fiddle-playing (Chris thinks it was an Art Council grant, but in fact I paid it out of my salary). I put Roadshows into six village halls where Bob Copper talked about Sussex rural life and folk song and people could learn quilting and corn-dolly making, bring infants to listen to nursery rhymes and play dance-games, rounding off the day with a Barn Dance with The Sussex Pistols, a band formed of local musicians Vic and Tina Smith, Ian Kearey, Bing Lyle, and Naomi Russell (whose early death remains a cause for grief). They still flourish today as a working band. And it was at this point I was given a bit of excellent advice by Jim Lloyd. I showed him the leaflet I'd written about the Roadshows to put through the letterboxes of the chosen villages in which I begged people to attend. He told me to never use the word 'beg' – that smacked of desperation – but to substitute it with 'urge'. Right at the beginning I decided to have a big banner made that we could stick up wherever we went. It was rather costly, and when it came back from the banner-makers they had spelt Wealden wrong, they'd got it as Wealdon, so back it had to go. That wasn't the only frustration.

Because I didn't drive, one of the stipulations of being given the job was that I learn to, with the promise that when I'd got my driving licence, South-East Arts would provide me with a car. This wasn't something I'd ever aspired to, or even wanted – but in order to keep the position, I spent six months and far too much money on driving lessons, and managed to pass first time. But then the promised car wasn't forthcoming. Another four months passed before it was available, during which time I had completely lost my nerve about driving, and paid other people to get me around. I only had another few months to go in any case. After the final meeting at the Arts Council in Tunbridge Wells, I sat in the front seat of the upper deck of the 28 bus back to Brighton feeling a huge sense of relief. A little way along the bus route I spotted Chris Marlow waiting at a bus stop – I told him my news, and by coincidence he said he'd just that very afternoon resigned from his job and was feeling great. When we got to Brighton, we got off together to celebrate with a gin and tonic.

I gave myself a couple of weeks of freedom, then went down to the Job Centre to sign on. The advisor who interviewed me offered me a job there – and told me that if I didn't take it I wouldn't be able to claim benefits – so I took it, and was there for nearly five years until I reached retirement age, which was sixty for women then.

I had to sign the Official Secrets Act, so I can't mention the nefarious things that went on there, although I can talk about the ludicrous ones. I worked alongside Paul, an eighteen-year-old who I kind of took under my wing. Our desks were next to each other; we shared the same dim view of the management and the system, and we exchanged scurrilous remarks and raised eyebrows all day long. One time we were put on the same training course; my heart sank when the woman who was running it divided us all into 'syndicates' of two or three people. Why not 'groups'? I whispered to Paul. He gave a disdainful snort. Why is it considered necessary to dress things up or make them sound more important by using pretentious and inappropriate long words? I think the worst, yet most amusing I ever heard was the word 'dilemmarising'. 'And what have you achieved at this meeting?' 'We spent the time dilemmarising.'

O England, what have you come to?

I endeared myself to Paul one Christmas by giving him a present of a box of Sobranie Cocktail cigarettes, each in a beautiful pastel-shade, and he said he felt instantly sophisticated smoking them. Our friendship was further cemented by our desire, or rather need, to have windows open; we were on our own there. Some days seemed to be spent opening the windows that had been closed by other people – 'it's so cold – it's so draughty,' they complained. Lord, how I despised them – especially as the only staff-room in the building was a smokers' haven, and consequently so stinking and fuggy that you needed a bit of fresh air when you went back to your desk after a break.

One day Paul and I were threatened with a Stanley knife by a drunken claimant. The manager reluctantly sent for the police at my insistence; the copper who turned up quite a while later merely told me to watch out for our attacker in future, in spite of the fact that I'd told him I knew who he was. It was all so casual, no action then nor subsequently on the several times claimants bashed their chairs against my desk – that's threatening behaviour in my book, but there was no security, no screens, we just had to take it. Paul and I are still in touch – he left The Job Centre after a couple of years to go to University, and is now Professor and Head of the Department of Sociology at the University of York, living very happily with his partner, Rob, and he has recently been awarded a Leverhulme Trust Research Fellowship.

I often wondered what on earth I was doing there, especially the day one of the young men who'd got a temporary job said how much he hated coming into the place and being advised by old ladies who told *him* what to do while knowing nothing of the world. The embers of my 'other' life flared up. I hissed at him that I hadn't always been there, that I'd been a singer, made albums, sung at the Royal Albert Hall, the Royal Festival Hall and the Sydney Opera House. He was taken aback by my rage, and apologised – but I'm not sure he believed me.

I held on. I knew the end – my sixtieth birthday on 5 July 1995 – was in sight.

Then my Brighton landlord wanted his house back – he was coming home from working in Bahrain. By now Pip had formed a new relationship and had moved out – not entirely unexpected as I'd always known that while our romance couldn't last, I had always hoped that our *friendship* would. I moved up to the Seven Dials in

Brighton for a couple of years – again in a rented flat with noisy neighbours above and below, although there was the consolation of a garden with a beautiful pear tree and an Italian deli two minutes away.

Then when the noise got too much to bear any longer, a friend, Rebe Cleveland, who I'd known for many years through the folk music world (she'd been married to Eddie Upton, our caller in The Albion Dance Band and was now married to Dan Quinn, film buff, master melodeon player and fine singer), offered to rent me her late parents' ground floor flat two minutes from the sea in Hove – reassuring me that the man who owned the overhead flat was a policeman. Great, I thought, he's bound to be well-behaved. The very first night after I'd moved in, I was woken at three in the morning by the sound of loud music and heavy feet pounding up and down the stairs and overhead. I got out of bed, went to the bathroom extension at the back of the house where it was a bit quieter, sat on the lavatory, put my head in my hands and wept; and this was to be the pattern for some months.

The young policeman went out clubbing when he'd finished work, and then brought people back to the flat to continue partying. I was in despair. I tackled him about it one day and he said 'I'm going to lead my life.' 'Yeah,' I replied, 'I'd like to lead mine, too.' He was a violent man, he and his girlfriend often fought; you could hear things flying, and once he kicked the front door in. It was a huge relief when he announced he was going to move to the States. Rebe bought his flat – and now owned this pleasant semi-detached house just minutes from the sea. She looked for new tenants for the top flat, and rented it to a young couple. 'They're very nice,' she assured me. 'What do they do?' I asked. 'Oh he's a drummer in a rock band,' then seeing my horrified look said, 'But he assured me that he keeps his drums in a studio, not at home.' He kept neither his word, nor his drums in a studio. I was in despair again.

Many days I'd wander along the beach, collecting sea-glass, and I still have thousands of pieces. By now my son Robert had two little children, and I spent a good deal of time with my grandsons Joe and Louis. Joe, the older of the two, especially loved being on the beach, helping me find sea-glass, paddling and playing all sorts of games; his favourite was finding driftwood to act as blunderbusses, and we'd fire shots out to sea to scupper the pirates' ships. 'Shoot through the tadpoles!' Joe yelled one day; I gently corrected it to 'portholes', but cherished the mistake.

Eventually Rebe decided she'd had enough of difficult tenants, and my complaints, and put the house up for sale. But she said she was planning to buy again, and I could still be her tenant if I wished – and suggested I start looking for somewhere suitable – a small house, perhaps, not a flat. I told her it had always been a hope of mine that one day I'd live in Lewes, and she suggested I go and look there. Pip volunteered to spend the day with me, and after traipsing through most areas of the town, we found ourselves in the late afternoon at the back of the castle, walking down narrow New Road, with its small Victorian terraced houses on one side of the street and a view across to a tree-lined meadow on the other. 'What a pretty street,' we both said, and then noticed a 'For Sale' sign and a blue ceramic plaque bearing the words 'The Cottage'. It was empty; we peered through the letter-box and I fell in love with it. I phoned Rebe that evening and told her; we came out together the next day to the Estate Agents, and were shown round 'The Cottage' – one sitting room and kitchen downstairs, a bathroom and two bedrooms above, and a courtyard garden at the back that gave on to a great bank of tall trees, ashes and sycamores. She liked it and thought it would be suitable and a good investment. 'So buy it now, please, Rebe,' I urged – or begged. She needed a couple of days to mull it over she said, and then she'd make an offer on it. I was on tenterhooks for days until the offer was accepted, then more weeks of anxiety until the contracts were exchanged. Pip helped me to move on 30 January 2003, a snowy day. Late that night, when I was settled in, we walked to the end of the road and looked back along the red brick terrace, the snow gleaming in the lamplight. It started snowing again… and I felt contented and safe home at last.

So the world turns. The wilderness years, the sea-glass years were behind me.

There are four key people in the world of music who have especially supported and encouraged me over the years, particularly during my time in the wilderness.

There is David Tibet, an artist, poet and founder of the long-running cult band Current 93, who tracked me down in the late 1980s and would become a loyal and important friend, eventually helping me to start singing again in 2014. In 1992 David put out, on his Durtro label, a compilation CD *A Fountain of Snow* and in 1998, *Harking Back*, a CD of live performances by Dolly and me, from Dublin in 1978, and from London in 1979. He also persuaded me, in 1996, to sing a track, 'All the Pretty Little Horses', on his Current 93 EP *The Starres Are Marching Sadly Home* and then, in 2006, 'Idumea' on *Black Ships Ate the Sky.*

After 'All the Pretty Little Horses' it would be another six years before I'd attempt a further recording, this time for Martyn Wyndham-Read who possesses one of the most beautiful voices I've ever heard. In 2002 he was compiling a double album for Fellside Records, *Song Links – a Celebration of English Traditional Songs and their Australian Variants*; he asked me if I'd contribute a song, and as he and his wife Danni are such good friends of mine, I agreed. As it happened, I'd just found, in an old book of nursery rhymes, a set of words for 'Babes in the Wood', a favourite song from The Copper Family repertoire. These words were slightly different though, and I became obsessed with the song. I re-worked the tune, and longed to sing it. So when Martyn asked, I thought I'd take that leap into the untried and recorded it, greatly helped by an utterly lovely arrangement for concertina by Iris Bishop. Although I hadn't really the voice to do it justice, there was something about the whole thing that worked. One person said it reminded him of his grandmother singing, and a BBC announcer said I sounded like Tom Waits! But, as I listened to it, at least I thought, I still knew how to 'tell' a song properly.

How would I have made it through to my present position without David Suff, who is Fledg'ling Records and also a close and dear friend? He frequently visited me in Brighton and Lewes over the

Shirley with David Tibet, 1992.

years, in the early days bringing with him his toddler son, Matthew, and we'd sit on the beach eating fish and chips and skimming stones in the sea. First and foremost David is a world-renowned artist, he's a master at painting topiary, his work exquisitely detailed and beautiful. I'm so fortunate; he gave me his original portrait of two legendary Morris musicians: Jinky Wells, fiddler with Bampton Morris, and William Kimber, concertina player with Headington, most likely taken from the 1931 photograph of the two of them together; and another Morris-inspired work, an original of a Hobby Horse titled *Oss Oss for Shirley 1995*, which was a sixtieth birthday present. They are prized possessions.

Not only has he owned Fledg'ling Records since the early 1990s, he also jointly heads Topic Records. As early as 1963 I had recorded an EP *Heroes in Love* for Topic, and Dolly and I had made our first album together, *The Sweet Primeroses* in 1967, my *Adieu to Old England* in 1974, and what was to be the final album with Dolly, *For As Many As Will* in 1978.

On the Fledg'ling label, 1995 was a bumper year for me. David put out the *Etchingham Steam Band* CD, *The Holly Bears the Crown*, the Christmas album that Dolly and I had made with the Young Tradition back in 1969 for Decca Records, but which hadn't been released because the YT broke up soon after. It didn't see the light of day for sixteen years, until David released it. He also re-issued my 1958 album *False True Lovers*: half of those songs that had been recorded by Peter Kennedy and Alan Lomax that year. It had come out on Folkways USA, and the other half of the songs on *Sweet England*, for Argo in England. In 1999, Fledg'ling re-issued *For As Many As Will*, *Adieu to Old England*, and *The Power of the True Love Knot*, while among the re-issued EPs were *Alan Lomax and the Ramblers*, *Shirley sings Irish*, *English Songs Vols. 1 & 2*, *The Foggy Dew*, and *The Bonny Cuckoo*, which has one of the most exquisite sleeves painted by David. Then in 2002, the thing I appreciated most of all, he produced a four-CD box set, *Within Sound*, an overview of my recording career from 1955 to 2002, with, as always, the most beautiful artwork (and which also contained 'Babes in the Wood').

On 5 July, 2015, for my eightieth birthday, he organised a day's entertainment at the South Bank. In the afternoon, the comedian Stewart Lee and I were in conversation in the Purcell Room; there were performances by Brighton Morris, The Belles of London City, Pete Cooper, Dave Arthur and Dan Stewart, and a folk play, *The Little Gipsy Girl*, specially written and produced by Polly Marshall, my daughter. The evening culminated with a performance of *No Roses*, with Stewart Lee, Stewart Estell, John Kirkpatrick, Olivia Chaney, Lisa Knapp, Sam Lee, Graham Coxon, Alasdair Roberts and Trembling Bells. A short time before the day I still hadn't decided what to call the whole thing; then on the eve of a visit from David to show me his artwork for the publicity and programme, 'All in the Downs' came into my head. Next day when he arrived and I told him this, he smiled, then chuckled, opened his artwork, and there was a beautiful drawing of – The South Downs!! He had put together a special souvenir programme for the entire event, and included a bonus – *The Bonny Cuckoo* EP. And I also love David for the clothes he wears, especially his purple suit lined with scarlet silk, worn with red shoes.

The fourth person who has kept me afloat is my music publisher, Pete Lawton, who painstakingly over the 'wilderness' years made sure that I was receiving all the royalties I was due, as these had petered out or even vanished. He chased up money that I didn't even know I was owed, a fairly thankless task for him, as he couldn't have made much out of it. He's a lovely man and we share a liking for the books of Daniel Defoe.

So I wasn't ever really alone.

TWELVE : *By The Mark On Her Hand*

One May morning I chanced for to rove
And strolled through the fields by the side of the grove
It was there I did hear the harmless birds sing
And you never heard so sweet as the birds in the spring
From The Copper Family

Around 1993, my sister Dolly was back living again in Sussex. For some years, while she was married to her second husband, Stuart Hollyer, a geologist, her home had been in Lincolnshire. She had left that marriage and rented a cottage just outside the village of Balcombe, and was settled there with Fusty, her tabby cat, and her piano. Its wood had a deep honey tone that glowed in her living room, and had a wonderful, warm presence.

I was still working at the Job Centre in Brighton, and escaped every weekend to go walking or cycling with Dolly. Friday summer evenings we'd sit out in the garden, or in winter, by the fire, doing the Ladygram – a rather fiendish literary crossword in *The Lady* magazine. By filling in the clues onto a grid, you could work out the title of a book, its author and an excerpt. It took me a while to get the hang of it, but I still do it every week.

We had such good walks or long bike rides in the glorious countryside around Balcombe, whatever the season. Dolly once took me to see a wood ants' nest; it was at the edge of a wood that bordered a lane. The large ants were on the move, and the entire swarm was flowing over the fence in their many thousands like a dark waterfall. We stood spellbound – and not a little queasy. One afternoon as we were walking along a lane by tall clumps of rosebay willow herb, the plants released their seeds in a cloud of white that floated above and around our heads before drifting on the breeze to find new places to settle. I've never experienced such a magic

moment again. Then there was the morning in autumn when we had got up early to go mushrooming; the whole field was glistening silver in the pale sunlight, the grass hung with spider gossamer.

In the evenings at Balcombe Dolly would play her latest compositions to me, sitting so upright and straight-backed at the piano, as she always had, looking almost regal. While she was in Lincolnshire she had completed a secular mass, *Missa Humana*, her setting of the words written by the poet and novelist Maureen Duffy. In Sussex she was composing her settings of several First World War poems, and a new, full orchestral arrangement of John Gay's *The Beggar's Opera*. The text she was working from was a presentation copy, published in 1921 by Heinemann, with facsimiles of the eighteenth century tunes, and with colour plates of the costumes. It's printed on thick paper, now heavily foxed, which looks so appropriate, and has a name-plate: 'This book belongs to Dolly Collins'. Now it is on my bookshelves, but is always called 'Dolly's Beggar's Opera'.

She also wrote one folk-song arrangement that proved to be her last, the exquisitely tender 'The Poor Drowned Sailor', which she'd found in a book of folk songs collected by Cecil Sharp. I tried to sing it, but even in front of Dolly I didn't dare, and in any case it was too high for me. I kept the arrangement separately for years, hoping that one day I might attempt it; and eventually I did, on *Lodestar*, but called it 'Washed Ashore'. Ian Kearey re-worked Dolly's arrangement for guitar.

I had always thought of Dolly as a strong woman, but I was aware that her health wasn't good. She had worked too hard all her life, and was always on the go, working extra hours in garden nurseries, even when she moved down to Balcombe. Evenings she spent knitting or crocheting or making preserves when she wasn't at her piano. She was wearing herself out, too, being deeply troubled by the plight of her dear friend Mike Clifton, the sculptor, cook, designer, singer and Morris dancer, who had worked often with us in the past and was now dying of AIDS. After his death, she felt that she hadn't done enough to prevent it. Of course, this cruel outcome was beyond her control, and she had spent many hours travelling up to his London hospice to sit by his bedside; but she couldn't forgive herself. It took its toll.

My mother and stepfather Harold Williams lived close by in Haywards Heath, and every Friday Dolly drove Mum to the shops. On the morning of 22 September, 1995, around 9.30am, I had a phone call from Mum, worried that Dolly hadn't arrived, and that when she telephoned her, the number was engaged. She asked me to phone Dolly's landlady, who lived in the house next door. I got through to her, and she said she'd go round to see what was up. A few minutes later she rang back to say that I should come up straight away, that Dolly had collapsed. 'Is she alright?' I asked. 'I think you should come up,' was her reply.

I didn't know whether my sister was alive or dead. In a daze, I rang for a taxi; when it arrived, it wasn't an official Brighton cab – it wasn't smart, and neither was the driver. He also wasn't sure where Balcombe was, he said, having never been there before. I gave him directions and off we set up through the Sussex countryside.

It was one of those golden September days, the air hot, but light, the sun gilding the fields, burnishing the stubble; a golden light shone through the trees, dappling the road. It was a day of such perfection that you'd have thought nothing bad could happen. The driver persisted in chatting; it was exhausting and I explained to him that I was on my way to see my sister who had collapsed, and that I needed to sit quietly.

When we reached Haywards Heath, instead of heading onto the Balcombe Road, the driver somehow managed to turn into Sainsbury's car park, then had difficulties finding his way out of it. We were just going round in circles. This was a nightmare. I didn't know what was waiting at the other end, although I think I knew in my heart that Dolly was dead. The gold of the day mocked, rather than comforted me. How could she die on such a beautiful day?

It brought back memories of those walks we'd had as children, particularly on early autumn days when, with baskets full of field mushrooms and blackberries, our fingers and mouths stained with their juice, our skins sweet and salty from the heat, we'd walk back over harvested fields, the spiteful sharp stubble scratching our bare legs. We just had to make it to the Guestling bus stop, and sit on the bench in the black wooden hut waiting for the East Kenter with its maroon livery to carry us and our bounty back to Ore Village…

When we eventually arrived at Dolly's cottage, there was a police car parked outside, and standing at the gate, a small group of people: Dolly's landlady, a neighbour, a nurse who lived just up the lane, a doctor and a policeman. 'Is she dead?' I almost shouted, the words springing from my mouth. They nodded. For a long moment I was numb, then started weeping, the young policeman holding me gently against his shoulder. The doctor told me that Dolly had suffered a massive heart attack. She had been found by her phone, which was dangling from its cord. Oh God! Had she tried to phone for help? The thought that she had failed was unbearable.

I asked if I could see her, but the doctor said it would be better if I didn't, explaining that Dolly's face was suffused with blood; better that I wait until later. Then came the dread realisation that I would have to break the news to Mum and to Dolly's son Tom, or Buz as he had chosen to call himself. The policeman offered to do this for me, but I knew I would have to do it myself and in person to my mother. I said I must go straightaway to see her, and the policeman drove me there. I was so grateful for his kindness and sensitivity and his willingness to try to make things easier. I knocked at Mum's door, and when she answered it, instead of breaking the news gently, I found myself blurting out, 'Mum, Dolly's dead!'

And her response, 'I'd better put the kettle on', was not uncaring, it was stoic in the extreme.

Later, once home that evening I phoned Buz on his narrowboat in Leicestershire. 'I'm afraid I've got very bad news, Buz.' 'Has Granny died?' he asked. 'No, darling, it's your Mum.' What can you say to news like that? He said he'd have to call back later, and when he did, asked if he could come down with his wife straight away and stay until the funeral. Of course, that was alright. I then phoned

Stuart, Dolly's estranged husband, who asked if he could come straight down. It was going to be a houseful.

Stuart was a tower of strength, even while he was suffering the loss of his wife. He told me that he'd fallen in love with Dolly many years back on her wedding day to her first husband, Dave Busby, in November 1968 when he, as one of the Chingford Morris, danced down through Battle High Street, and that he'd loved her ever since. I don't know how he stayed so focused throughout everything there was to do, driving us to the Registry Office in Haywards Heath to get all the necessary paperwork done, to the funeral directors, preparing for the funeral; I see it as his final act of love for her. Really, though, for all of us it was a stunned calm, we were sleepwalking through it all.

On the day Stuart, Pip and I went to the undertakers to see Dolly in the chapel of rest, we gripped each other's hands as we were shown in. Dolly was lying there; a coverlet over her and her hands neatly folded across her chest. 'That's not Dolly!' I cried. 'We haven't lost her!' But, of course, it was her. The pathetic sight of her hands, scratched from the gardening she loved to do, her fingernails still with earth under them, stays with me. Yet there was a feeling of elation that somehow she *was* still with us.

Well, of course she is with us in the sense that her music can still be heard. She had a rare ability to support a song and enhance it with her beautiful harmonies. If I was praised as a singer, it was in great part due to Dolly's accompaniments. She died too young at the age of sixty-two. Alan Bush, the composer under whom Dolly had studied, died that same year, a month and a few days later than her, but he had lived to the age of ninety-five.

I had lost a sister and a great companion, but had all my memories. I remember our happy Christmases out at Bodiam, where she lived for many years; the family crowded into Dolly's small front room that held the Christmas tree and was hung with foliage and the old-fashioned paper chains she insisted on making each year, the sort, that as children, we had made at the kitchen table, gluing strips of coloured paper together with a paste made of flour and water. No wonder they kept falling apart and floating down! The walls were pinned with quizzes that Dolly had been saving from *The Guardian* and *The Observer*.

One very merry time when the rum punch was flowing, we were sitting in a circle playing the alphabet game – on this occasion it was 'name a ship in alphabetical order'. We had reached F – and it was my daughter Polly's turn. There was a long thoughtful silence, then suddenly she leapt off her chair and shouted 'Oh Frigate!' 'Polly!' her grandmother admonished her, begging her not to swear, which set off a chain of laughter, and it was some time before the room was brought to order again.

Dolly's Christmas dinners were feasts, with so many dishes being brought out from both the Aga and the gas oven, along with a huge roast goose, that there was scarcely room on the table for the dinner plates. Throughout the year though, Dolly was more frugal. Being a keen gardener, she grew most of her vegetables and fruit. She also still cooked dishes that had been typical of our childhood diet: steak and kidney suet puddings, bacon and leek roly-poly, stews with dumplings, bread and butter pudding, apple charlotte, steamed jam puddings, baked apples stuffed with raisins, drenched in golden syrup (although there hadn't been much of that during the years of rationing) then wrapped in a suet crust. Sometimes you could not get up from the table.

Going for walks with Dolly was a constant delight. In the evening, she knew where the badgers' sett was, where the bats and the barn owl flew. She knew the names of so many wild flowers, names that have enriched the English language: enchanter's nightshade, goldilocks, hairy bittercress, shepherd's purse and speedwell, woodruff, lady's bedstraw, saxifrage, milkmaids, creeping cinquefoil and creeping jenny, water avens, viper's bugloss, yellow archangel, bird's foot trefoil, touch-me-not, and devil's bit scabious… and that scarcely skims the surface.

She noticed things that other people might miss – perhaps a bird's nest deep in a hedge – and she knew which trees made a proper hedgerow – hawthorn and blackthorn, dog rose, field maple, hazel, hornbeam and holly. Once, as we were walking through the woods towards Ardingly Reservoir to watch the crested grebes fishing, diving under water and surfacing a fair distance away, Dolly stood still and shushed me. We watched spellbound as a purple emperor butterfly fluttered around the tall foxgloves growing there. It was the only time I had ever seen one. I have Dolly's collection of books of wild flowers, fungi, apples, birds, moths and butterflies, all with their unique names. Who could resist the skippers, dingy or grizzled, chequered or silver-spotted, the clouded yellow, the brown hairstreak, or the painted lady and the gatekeeper (there's an alternative title for *Lady Chatterley's Lover* if you like!). The name of a moth, the lappet, is one of my favourite words, along with lynchets, those long, ancient terraces that can still be seen on Dorset hills, and on the South Downs.

Dolly's ashes were scattered on open country in Balcombe where deer roam, and rabbits abound – a favourite walk of hers. It still feels too lonely a place to me, and there is no marker there, except for the daffodils that we planted. Far better as a way to celebrate her life is the Woodland Trust's Springfield Wood, at Salehurst, near to

Opposite: Excerpt from a score for 'The Poor Drowned Sailor' by Dolly Collins.

Poor Drowned Sailor

3 Verses

Bodiam, where I think she was at her happiest. Twenty years ago, not long after her death, Stuart, Pip and I planted many saplings there in a field that the Trust had acquired; it's now a healthy young wood.* Later Pip and I had a bench in Dolly's name placed in Butcher's Wood, the Woodland Trust's ancient wood at Hassocks, and we visit there each spring at bluebell time.

Seven years after Dolly's death, her son Buz committed suicide, in August 2002. He had been living on his narrowboat 'The Maid in England' in Loughborough, and had been suffering from depression, although I hadn't been aware of this. When I took the phone call from his estranged wife, I felt that my blood had turned to lead. I had never experienced such a sensation of unbearable heaviness before, even when Dolly died. I felt grateful at this point that she had gone and wouldn't have to bear this, but I also thought that if she was still with us, this tragedy might not have happened.

I was tormented by the fact that just a few weeks earlier, Buz had come down with his little daughter Amie, to spend a few days with me in Hove, having separated from his wife. We had all gone kite-flying on the Downs, Buz skimming his kite just a couple of feet above the ground on the long ridge of a brow, before letting it soar. We spent long days on the beach in perfect summer weather; Buz so handsome and tall, lean and tanned, seemingly so full of life, loving the sea. He turned to me at one point and said, 'I could stay in the water forever.' How I wish he had.

The funeral was held in a woodland site in Leicestershire; Buz's coffin a replica of a narrow boat. Pip was asked to be one of the six coffin bearers; he told me how heavy it was, and that as they

*In one scene in *The Ballad of Shirley Collins* filmed in Harvey's Brewery, a great pile of hops are being shovelled; the white sacks bear the name 'Salehurst.' I asked Rob and Tim, the film's directors, if this was intentional, but no, it was a complete coincidence, but such a remarkable one.

reached the grave, he remembered how he used to carry Buz as a six-year-old on his shoulders when we went out to visit Dolly in Bodiam in our early days together.

When we left to drive home, there was a double rainbow in the sky above the burial ground, which was some sort of consolation. My lasting and still heartbroken memory of that sad and dreadful day was of his little daughter's utter bewilderment. Photographs show me standing there wringing my hands… I wasn't even aware that I was doing that – I'd only heard of it in songs:

> *She wrung her hands and tore her hair*
> *Just like a lady in despair…*

Following his suicide, Buz's name was added to the plaque at Butcher's Wood – mother and son together.

THIRTEEN: *Given Time It Will Rise Again*

> *The moon shines bright and the stars give a light*
> *In a little while it will be day*

From the Goby gypsy family, Sussex, collected by
Lucy Broadwood in 1900.

One day in 2003, my mother said she was clearing out a few
things and asked me if I'd like my letters… 'Which letters are they,
Mum?' 'Your letters from America,' she replied. She had kept
every letter I'd written home in 1959, the year I lived in America
with Alan Lomax, the late summer and autumn of which we had
spent in the South and Deep South on the field recording trip
that later became known, through a 13-volume series of Lomax's
recordings, as *The Southern Journey*. I wrote home as frequently
as I could about all the experiences and adventures I was having,
the letters often written at speed in my rare spare time, and they
were full of detail and energy. I showed them to Pip, and he urged
me to write a book about that incredible, unique time, using the
letters as the basis. The letters were all dated, so it was easy to
write it in chronological order. I showed the first draft to David
Tibet who felt that it was mostly about Alan, and not enough
about me.

So I rewrote it, telling the unlikely story of how a girl from
Hastings fetched up in America in 1959 with America's leading
folklorist, a man twice her age, making it much more of an
autobiography. I showed this draft to Pip who pointed out that,
although the book was called *America Over The Water*, by half way
through I hadn't left England! He suggested that I alternate the
English and American chapters – and it worked. I gave it that title
in memory of a conversation I'd had with an old mountain woman

in Kentucky who, on hearing my strange (to her) accent, asked me where I had come from, and when I told her that I had come from England she exclaimed: 'What! England over the water?'

As I was writing it I remembered that ten years earlier, in 1993, Alan had sent me a copy of his new book *The Land Where the Blues Began*, in part of which our 1959 field trip figured. Alan had written on the inside cover 'With much love and great admiration to one of the sweetest singers and ladies who ever walked and graced the green ways of this earth.' Unfortunately, this flattery was somewhat undermined by the fact that he mentioned me just once in the text of the book – on page 330 when he was writing about Lonnie and Ed Young, who we had visited in Como, Northern Mississippi on 21 September, 1959. There was a transcription of a conversation I'd had with Lonnie and Ed, but preceded by the words 'Shirley Collins, the lovely English folk-singer who was along for the trip'. I'd been smarting at this dismissive phrase, anger bubbling under for some while. So I felt it was time to set the record straight, and in the first edition of the hardback of *America Over The Water* I ended with the words: 'We'll see about that. And I started to write this book.'

Then something happened, something changed. In 2004 a Dutch filmmaker, Rogier Kappers, had made a heart-warming, heartbreaking documentary *Lomax The Songhunter* (for which I was interviewed in 2001). Kappers had filmed in Spain and Italy, searching for people that Alan had recorded there back in the 1950s. Not only were Alan's visits still remembered in many places, but memories were rekindled too, of the people who had sung and played for him: instruments were brought out of cupboards or lifted down from shelves, elderly ladies danced as they heard the recordings again, tears and smiles surfacing in equal measure. And then the film moved to Florida where Alan had lived since suffering a stroke; he was in a swimming pool as those recordings were played to him, and the blank gaze that had been so distressing to see was replaced by a beautiful light that came into his eyes as he, in turn, remembered the music, the places, and the people.

As I watched this, I knew that there was something far more important, far greater than my grievance at my being 'along for the trip' and I wrote a new ending for the paperback edition of my book: 'Passionate about traditional music and the lives of working people, Alan Lomax was their champion. His legacy is the books that he wrote and the thousands of field recordings that he made.'

And that made me feel better. In any case, how fortunate, how privileged I had been to have shared that unique and unrepeatable field trip, the Southern Journey. Alan died in 2001.

And when you're on some distant shore think on your absent friend
And when the wind blows high and clear, a line or two pray send
And when the wind blows high and clear, pray do send it, love, to me
That I shall know by your hand-write, how times have gone with thee
'My Dearest Dear': Appalachian song

America Over The Water led me to develop a show of the same name. It started as a simple thing – in folk clubs – just me, with notes, telling the story, and Ian Kearey playing the original tape recordings from cassettes. It wasn't sufficient, nor did it do the story justice, and yet at our second folk club outing, the audience broke into spontaneous applause at the end of Fred McDowell's '61 Highway'. Even so, it had to grow. So I wrote a script for a two-hour long, two-part show, Pip and me reading, Pip enacting various characters from both England and the American South. He has a talent for accents, and was often taken for a fellow countryman by the occasional American in the audience. He spoke the various and varied conversations transcribed verbatim from the original 1959 recordings, along with the songs and music, too, and we added contemporary photographs taken by Alan in 1959, other archive pictures, and some from my own family collection. We worked with Vic and Tina Smith, who operated the sound and visuals. We had an occasional outing with the show, until Alan James, who then worked for the Arts Council, saw us perform it in a London bookshop, The Bloomsbury, and suggested we put in for an Arts Council grant to take it on tour.

It was a successful application, and we were soon on the road taking it to venues all over the country, ranging from arts centres to

Polly Marshall, Shirley and Robert Marshall collecting Shirley's MBE (Pip Barnes).

universities, Cecil Sharp House and the Purcell Room on London's South Bank, the Sidmouth Folk Festival and the Lewes Festival as well as the more modest folk clubs. We still do it occasionally, most recently at the Frome Festival in 2015. But the most memorable was the performance at the Festival Litteratura in Mantova, Italy, in 2008 where, not only were we treated royally by the organizer, Carlo Dusi, we also played in the beautiful, romantic, baroque theatre, Teatro Bibiena, where Mozart had once played. The performance started late as there was such a long queue of people waiting to get in that new levels had to be opened up. And to think I had turned down the booking at first, feeling that an Italian audience wouldn't understand the talk, it being in English. To set my mind at rest, Carlo had asked me to send the script in advance, and he put up a running translation on two large screens on either side of the stage. It turned out to be one of our best performances, and we drew a lengthy and noisy standing ovation. And as much pistachio ice-cream as we could eat…

The success of *America Over The Water* and the pleasure of

performing it, combined with my desire to tell audiences more about folk music, led me to put together a couple of other shows in the same format – *A Most Sunshiny Day*, a brief history of English folk song, and *A Man of No Consequence*, the life and work of Bob Copper; and Pip and I joined forces with Martyn Wyndham-Read on his Australian show *Down the Lawson Track*. I enjoyed doing this work – being on stage talking held no fears for me. But I still didn't dare sing.

Things were on the move! In early 2007 a letter arrived in the post saying I'd been put forward for an MBE. You had to accept by signing and returning the letter, then waiting to see if it was approved. I was thrilled that English folk music had got some recognition, but fretful, too. What if my acceptance letter went astray?

However, all went smoothly. The date to go to Buckingham Palace was 8 May, 2007 – at 10.30am. I'd booked a car to drive us – Polly, Rob and Pip, firstly to pick Rob up from his home in Brighton at 7.30am, then Polly, Pip and me from Lewes at 8am. But an hour passed. A call came from the driver saying he hadn't been able to get an answer from Rob. Rob finally answered his phone and told us his alarm had failed to go off! Eventually he was in the car and heading to Lewes; we all piled in and set off. Thank goodness, I thought, we'd left ourselves plenty of time. The journey went well until we got stuck at Coulsdon behind a car-transporter that had broken down, and we were there for forty minutes – not a police car in sight to sort things out. Eventually we moved, then, as we were driving through Brixton, the driver told us that he desperately needed to relieve himself, as he'd been on the road then for quite a long time. It was urgent, but there was no sign of a public convenience or garage. Polly spotted a Starbucks; we pulled up and as our driver raced in, a police car drew up beside us! The officers got out and told us to move on. I explained our predicament, showed them the Buckingham Palace invitation, and added that we were already late due to the transporter hold up. They replied that the driver had committed an offence, and it would mean points on his driving licence. We pleaded special circumstances, and after they spoke sternly to him, they relented. But more time had been wasted – we should have been at our destination by then. And I was thinking – if this was a movie they'd escort us through the traffic to the Palace, sirens full on! Polly phoned the Palace, explained the position and said we were still at least half an hour's drive away. They were very relaxed at that end, and re-assured us that time was built in to allow for such eventualities, and instructed us that when we got there, we should go to the West Gate entrance; and it so happened that we arrived just in time to walk up the steps behind a uniformed brass band!

Inside, there was plenty of time for me to line up with the other recipients, have a little hook attached to my coat for the medal to be hung onto – so that Prince Charles didn't have to fumble at our bosoms I suppose – and to take in the instructions as to how it all worked. Walk across the ballroom, face the Prince of Wales, take three steps backwards and curtsey, and do it again when you get the signal to leave – a handshake from Charles. I practiced several times, and then it was my turn to walk alone into the huge room with an audience composed of family and friends of all the recipients, and with a band playing tunes from the shows up on the balcony. I executed my curtsey perfectly, and looked up into the kind eyes of Prince Charles. He asked me about my interest in folk song, and when I told him that I'd learned some songs from my grandfather who had been a head gardener on a Sussex estate, he seemed to be on more familiar ground, and we had a warm, albeit brief conversation. I've rather liked him ever since.

When I walked out through the opposite side of the ballroom, my MBE taken from me to be put in its case, my knees buckled, and I shed some tears. What would my republican Mum have made of that!

That same year I was awarded an Honorary Degree from The Open University; in 2008 I was elected President of The English Folk Dance & Song Society, and given the Good Tradition Award at the BBC Folk on Two Awards. It was presented, surprisingly, but delightfully, by Graham Coxon of Blur, who also sang one of my family's songs, 'Just As The Tide Was Flowing'.

In 2011 Tony Engle of Topic Records invited me to compile two collections for *The Voice of the People* series. *You Never Heard So Sweet* was my choice of the 1950s and '60s field recordings made by Bob Copper and Peter Kennedy in Southern England. Three of the singers were Hastings fishermen: Ned Adams, coxswain of the Hastings Lifeboat, who sang 'The Bold Princess Royal', Noah Gillette with his noble historic ballad 'The Bonny Bunch of Roses', and Joe Spicer with his fishing song 'Heave on the Trawl'. The second, *I'm a Romany Rai*, was a two-CD selection compiled from Peter Kennedy's 1964 field recordings of southern English gypsies and the great Dorset gypsy Queen Caroline Hughes. It was a fascinating task, and took well over a year to make my selection, write the notes and transcribe the words. My reward came in 2012 with *I'm a Romany Rai* being voted the *fROOTS* Critics Poll Award for Compilations and Reissues, and I was presented with a heavy plaque, showing the CD cover of a group of gypsies – embedded in a splendid ceramic of the South Downs. It was made by Marion Brandis, a remarkable sculptor who lives just outside Lewes. It's a beautiful thing. And now I've got another one from *fROOTS* – 2016 Album of the Year for *Lodestar*. Unlooked for, but very welcome.

That inspired me to put together two new talks based on both titles, and it was after a performance of the gypsy show at London's Islington Assembly Rooms in September 2013 that I was approached by two tall dark-haired men. They introduced themselves as Rob Curry and Paul Williams, said they were a film-maker and producer and would like to discuss making a film about me, in particular the *America Over The Water* story. I was taken aback, not sure how to respond. They mentioned a film that they'd made with Tim Plester, that they thought I might have seen, *The Way of the Morris*. Then I became really interested: I had seen it three times and loved it, and had been very moved by its telling of the virtual loss of the Adderbury Morris in the Great War, and its revival after. Tim is an actor that I knew of and who was from Adderbury, in Oxfordshire. It wasn't until three years later, around the time the film was finished, that I learned that the idea had been suggested to them by John

Tim Plester and Rob Curry recreating The Southern Journey for
The Ballad of Shirley Collins (Diane Logel).

McMahon of the music promoters Miles of Smiles who had put on
the talk that night. So thanks, John.

I felt that these were people I could trust, so I agreed; but funds
needed to be raised to finance what was going to be a very costly
undertaking. A Kickstarter campaign promoted by Paul Williams
began with a lively fundraising evening with Stewart Lee at Café
Oto in east London in June 2014. Then Earth recordings released a
triple LP set, *Shirley Inspired*, featuring an eclectic number of singers
doing covers of songs I had recorded on past albums; Paul put on
a series of small gigs by some of the artists featured on the album –
and there was enough money to begin filming.

Since it would have cost an inordinate and impossible amount
of money to film in the Deep South of the United States (and in
any case, those 'wide places in the road', those small communities,
would have changed out of all recognition over fifty or more years),
parts of Sussex stood in for Virginia, Arkansas and Mississippi; under

Rob Curry's creative genius, the local landscapes became the Delta! The recreation of the American scenes was cleverly and, I think, wittily done. Rob's research throughout was impeccably thorough, and even led me to things about the Southern Journey that I had forgotten, and for which I'll always be grateful, such as the 1959 recording in Virginia of Horton Barker's 'The Rich Irish Lady', which I learned and recorded for *Lodestar*.

And because there was no actual contemporary footage of the 1959 Shirley in America, the part was played by a young actress, Lotti Maddox, who captured me so well there were a couple of times as I watched the footage that I thought it actually was me. Alan was played by Tassos Stevens – a pretty good likeness, too.

I had told Rob how I'd been inspired, as a fifteen-year old, by *Night Club Girl*, a 1948 film about a Tennessee girl who is discovered singing folk songs in her mountain home and becomes a great success singing in New York night clubs. I'd thought as a teenager that's what I want to be, that's what I want to do!

Rob went hunting for the film, but couldn't find it anywhere. He kept asking me if I'd got the title right – well, I was sure I had, but worried that he might think I'd made the whole thing up! Eventually he ran it to ground from a source in the States, where it had been called *Glamour Girl*. He showed it in the little Electric Palace Theatre in the High Street in Hastings, filling the auditorium with smoke, so that it would be the same atmosphere as I'd seen it in all those years ago. We were all surprised at how good it was, how lovely Susan Reed's singing, and how over-the-top Gene Krupa's drumming. The hero was a bit of a let-down though, he looked as if he'd got coat-hangers on his shoulders – the stiffest, least convincing mover any of us had ever seen. Rob filmed me watching and commenting on it, but sadly it didn't make it into the finished film – there was just so much going on that Rob and Tim wanted to incorporate into it, so it grew to be about much more than *America Over The Water*. When filming began, I wasn't singing and by the end I had made a new album, *Lodestar* for Domino, and was singing in public with the Lodestar Band after a thirty-eight year silence. Recently Paul reminded me that at that first meeting

he had asked me if there was anything I wanted to do; 'I'd like to sing again,' I replied.

To say filming was an adventure would be an understatement. Take the day Rob and Tim wanted to film out at Firle Beacon on the East Sussex end of the South Downs, one of the region's highest points at 712 feet – that's 182 feet higher than Beachy Head! Rob had hired a vintage Buick (as Alan and I had travelled in one in 1959); it had doors only at the front, and I was sitting alone in the back (*see photo above*). We drove very slowly up the winding road to the Beacon, the chaps filming from another car. The driver was muttering something about his brakes, realising that we'd also have to come back down the very steep hill with its many bends. We filmed at the top, made a turn in the car park there, and started back, very, very slowly. We made it down to the village where the crew were waiting and, as the car drew to a halt, the engine caught fire – with me still in the back seat with no door! 'Let me out! Let me out!' I yelled. But no one did! I had to climb over the big cream leather seat, open the door and jump out – but at least by this point Rob and the driver were extinguishing the fire!

Fire figured strongly in the production. The team came down to Lewes Bonfire on 5 November and filmed throughout the evening; and remarkable as this custom is, their filming enhanced the power

Above: Celebrating *The Ballad of Shirley Collins* at The London Film Festival, 2017. *L-R:* Tim Plester, Paul Williams, Shirley, Rob Curry (John McMahon).

and the nobility of it, some of their footage appearing eerily, thrillingly medieval. Throughout all this, Rob Curry requested – insisted – that I wear my 'bonfire coat' for filming. This is a twenty-five-year-old, once-smart navy duffle coat with deep green revers and a leather trim that I had worn at Bonfire for the last fifteen years. It never loses its slightly smoky scent.

It was such a good and talented team; people who knew what they wanted, but were so easy to get along with: directors Rob Curry and Tim Plester, sound recordist Ludovic Lasserre and Richard Mitchell, the cameraman with a remarkable eye for the right shot. Rich and I shared another rather alarming adventure. We were filming locally – more travels in the vintage Buick – but this time it was mounted on a low-loader, a splendidly shiny new one – and very long. They hadn't been able to get it down the narrow street I live on, but had drawn in to Westgate at the top of the road. The driver then tried to turn it to get back onto the High Street, but there wasn't room, so he had to reverse out. By this time I was sitting in my back seat in splendid isolation as usual, and Rich with his camera was strapped securely on to the bar of the low-loader facing me. It was such a narrow corner that it took a good half-hour to get out; cars were backed up in both directions, hooting, people came out of their shops, passers-by stopped to watch, and gave us a round of applause when we finally made it. I felt rather like the Queen, and gave what I hoped they understood was an ironically gracious wave. We proceeded regally down through Lewes until we came to the large roundabout on the Causeway. As the great vehicle turned on a wide circle, the front door of the Buick flew open with a crash; it was a danger to other road users and had to be shut. Rich couldn't reach it, strapped on as he was, so I had to climb over into the front seat, lean far out and try to grab the handle and wrestle the door shut. The driver of the low-loader was unaware of what had happened so we were still moving and the resistance was strong. With Rich yelling encouragement, I finally made it; the door luckily hadn't hit any other vehicles, although there were some very shocked-looking drivers!

We filmed at the remarkable Jack in the Green Mayday celebrations in Hastings, and the footage captures the fun and excitement, the splendour and spirit of the day. We went up to Athelstan Road where I grew up. The houses in the long sloping terrace had become much smarter over the years, the front gardens too. Gone were the simple beds of Michaelmas daisies and California poppies that I remembered at number 117. They still flourished however, hung with spiders' webs, in the dusty, neglected grounds of the big red-brick Anglo-Catholic church where Dolly and I used to practice our tennis strokes against the end wall.

I'd recently seen an exhibition of John Piper's work at the Towner Gallery in Eastbourne, and had been transfixed by his paintings of the Romney Marsh churches. They were so atmospheric you could almost smell the damp and mould of the interiors. I'd been to the Romney Marshes as a child, but not since then, so with friends drove out to explore. I was so entranced by the place that I knew the film-makers must see it. The next visit was to the church of St Thomas à Becket at Fairfield with the producer Paul Williams and the genius author/painter/sculptor Brian Catling, who treated us to a delicious local-caught fish lunch in Rye en route. It's set out on the marsh, a walk away from the road, surrounded by flat grassy land grazed by sheep and interspersed by shallow dykes. We collected the heavy old iron key from a nearby farmhouse, unlocked the solid wooden door of the church, and stepped inside. I was expecting to see the faded white and gold of Piper's picture, but now the high box pews and pulpit were painted a spanking white with shiny black borders, the faded oak beams garlanded with hop vines, since Thomas à Becket is the patron saint of brewers. Reluctant to leave, we sat outside in the warmth of the late summer sun, the silence only disturbed by the occasional bleating of the sheep, and the cawing of rooks making their way home as evening drew on. We gazed across the marsh, letting our eyes light upon the reflecting water in the wide dykes, blue, paling into silver.

On the second visit to Fairfield, with Rob Curry, we filmed an interview with a psychiatrist, Dr John Tully, about my inability to sing, which had been diagnosed as a form of dysphonia, and I was impressed by how revealing it was. And then it was time to leave, and we dashed away, Rob hoping to film yet another sunset on the Downs, which was how the days often ended.

Surprises continued to come out of the blue; one in particular was the last thing I expected. In 2011 I had a phone call from a film-maker, Nick Abrahams. He told me that the Icelandic group Sigur Rós was inviting various directors to enter a competition, funding them to make a short video inspired by any track from their album *Valtari*, and that he, Nicky, was one of them. The track he had chosen was 'Ekki mukk' and his film starred Irish actor Aidan Gillen – would I like to do a voice-over? I was flattered! I asked him what the part was. 'A lonely snail,' he replied! Once I was at the studio, though, it turned out that I was a *friendly* snail, concerned for the lost man played by Aidan. It's a beautiful, moving film and I'm glad I was part of it.

From this first meeting with Nicky a friendship grew, and it was he who made the video for 'Death and the Lady' commissioned by Domino Records to promote the *Lodestar* album. That was a memorable day of filming. Ian Kearey and I drove across to Hythe in Kent, where Nicky filmed us in the ossuary – otherwise known as the bone crypt at St Leonard's Church. This imposing church, still Saxon in part, but mostly Norman, stands in a sloping grassy churchyard high above the town. We were there on a very breezy and bright summer's day; but in the ossuary, the temperature dropped. There are over a thousand skulls there lining one wall, with a high stack of human bones filling the middle of the crypt, said to have been there since the thirteenth century. It isn't the scary place you might think it would be; it feels quiet and tranquil. Nicky had brought with him three 'hooden horses', real horse skulls carried head high, each by a single person, their bodies covered by draped sacking.* They towered over me threateningly in the churchyard, and later chased me, snapping their jaws, across the dunes at Camber Sands.

In July 2016 I was at The Dome in Brighton receiving an Honorary Doctorate from The University of Sussex, where sixteen

---

*These hooden horses were traditionally paraded around South East England at Christmas time.

Shirley collects her Honorary Doctorate from The University of Sussex. *L-R:* Robert Marshall, Shirley, Joe Miller-Marshall, Pip Barnes, Polly Marshall, Laurence Bell.

years earlier Bob Copper had been made an honorary Master of Arts. I was provided with a flowing yellow gown and a rather tall black velvet hat; I worried about it toppling! And how could I have foreseen that a few months later I'd be on the same stage with the *Lodestar* show?

But that's leaping ahead of the making of the *Lodestar* album. Because of the interest being shown in the film (finally called *The Ballad of Shirley Collins*) suggestions were being made about recording a new album. My son Rob (Bobby to everyone else, but always Rob to me) Marshall, who manages the band Asian Dub Foundation, proposed it to Laurence Bell of Domino Records; an agreement was quickly reached, an advance paid, and recording could begin. I knew that I didn't want to go into a recording studio – I still felt far too insecure and vulnerable. I couldn't face singing in front of a young sound engineer with the possibility that he or she might wonder what this old girl was doing singing these strange old songs. So I decided we'd have to record at home in my cottage.

After a couple of false starts, we were ready to begin. Ossian Brown, who later played hurdy-gurdy with the Lodestar Band, suggested that he and Stephen Thrower, who together are Cyclobe, might be the perfect people to do the recording, and that's what they proved to be; endlessly patient, with an intelligent and sympathetic understanding of both my singing and the songs. Ossian's calm, focussed presence felt like a benison; the beauty of his fingers on the keyboard, so delicate, yet drawing out such powerful sounds.

As the recording progressed slowly, it was clear that not only was Ian Kearey holding it all together (like herding eels he said), he was also coming up with brilliant ideas for arrangements. Ian had been a friend for well over forty years; we'd first met when he was a student at the University of Kent, running the folk club, and he'd booked Dolly and me to play there a few times. Up to the age of fourteen he'd described himself as 'a teenage rock kiddy' until he discovered The Band in 1968! Folk music took a hold. He was a founder member of The Oyster Band, and played bass on the Fiddler's Dram's unlikely 1979 hit single 'The Day We Went to Bangor'; he recorded with Gerard Langley and the Blue Aeroplanes, and also with Herbie Flowers. He now plays with the groups Duck Soup, Pigeon Swing, The Sussex Pistols and of course, the Lodestar Band. Our friendship was sealed back in the 1980s, the day I introduced him to Uncle Fred, when they got on like a house on fire.

While I was working at the British Museum he'd occasionally turn up at the end of the day dressed in his rock-bassist outfit of black leather jacket and red trousers, impressing my work colleagues no end as we sauntered along to the Coptic Street Pizza Express.

I had several songs lined up that I had longed to sing for years, and we began with one that particularly enthralled me, 'Awake Awake Sweet England', the fascinating survival of the penitential song written in 1580 by a ballad-writer Thomas Deloney, when the Great Earthquake in London toppled part of old St Paul's Cathedral (see Chapter 9). I had come across it in Ella Mary Leather's *The Folklore of Herefordshire* (the book that Ashley had given me as an anniversary present the day before he

Shirley with Stewart Lee at the fundraising event for *The Ballad of Shirley Collins*, June 2015 (Stephen Hopper).

left me.) No other collector had found the song still being sung; it had simply vanished for three hundred and forty years. What a remarkable find it was and what an extraordinary journey it must have had down through those many years; and over that time, the final verse had morphed into a much jollier May Carol. Ian wrote a guitar arrangement that had an appropriate gravity about it. As we listened to various play-backs of it, I suggested that Ossian might compose a hurdy-gurdy piece to end it, and he came back a few days later with his foreboding 'The Split-Ash Tree'. As he played, we realised that it would fit better after the sombre third verse, so it comes in before the final verse of 'Awake Awake' which ends with the words: 'We wish you all good morrow, God send us a joyful May'. In that case I thought, I'd better add a complete May Carol to sing at the end of the song. I wrote a livelier tune, set it to existing words, and as we listened to the sequence of the three pieces, I fancied having a Morris tune to bring it to a bright and uplifting finale. And if we were going to have a Morris tune, then we should have a Morris dancer. Naturally, I thought of Brighton Morris, my favourite Morris side, who had that year invited me to be their patron (now that's what I call an honour), and asked Glen Redman if he'd allow us to have 'Southover', a beautiful dance and tune which he'd composed, and for John Watcham, Brighton Morris's splendid concertina player to play it. Glen drummed and danced in the cottage; he leaps very high, and we had to keep him clear of the overhead beam! We ran the sequence of the four pieces together; it became the long opening track of the album and a powerful statement of intent.

There were advantages and disadvantages to recording at home. I live on a narrow street, a no-through road, so it's reasonably traffic-free. But there's a nursery at one end of it, so in the morning and mid-afternoon, there are plenty of parents and young children chattering at the tops of their voices, many kids whizzing down the gentle slope on their scooters, and it's enough of an incline for skateboarding teenagers to frequent it. It's surprising how much noise that makes. Also, there's a railway line further down the hill, and trains rumble like distant thunder when they go into the tunnel that takes them to Lewes Station. That's quite alarming for visitors at first!

The advantages of recording at home? You don't have to worry about the cost; you can have as many cups of tea as you want; and best of all, as it turned out one summer's day, the birdsong on the tree-filled high bank at the back. We were recording 'Cruel Lincoln', the centuries-old song about a mason who has built a house for the lord of the manor. He hasn't been paid and he's out for revenge. The kitchen windows were wide open and the bird-song was flooding in. I could hear it as I was singing, and it was on the recording when we listened to the play-back. The sweet, normal everyday sound of the birds was such a contrast to the darkness of the story, so we kept it in; Stephen then put a microphone outside so we could get a clearer recording of the birds. Things grew organically. Ossian had a collection of old wooden organ pipes, and he suggested that he blow across the top of one on the first line of each verse of 'Cruel Lincoln'; remarkably, it added a softly sinister, haunting sound. This version, noted down by Bob Copper from Ben Butcher, a gamekeeper from Popham in West Sussex, had long enthralled me with its almost ordinary tune that holds no indication of the horror that unfolds.

I had always loved (and regretted that I'd never recorded) 'The Banks of Green Willow', collected from Mrs Cranstone of Billingshurst, West Sussex in 1907 by George Butterworth, who based his orchestral idyll of the same title after it, so that had to go on the album with Pip playing a lyrical guitar accompaniment. 'Washed Ashore' (see Chapter 12) had been the last arrangement that Dolly had written for me some twenty years ago; she had set it too high for me to sing, and I hadn't been able to do it. But the regret of not singing it stayed with me all those years. Ian Kearey adapted Dolly's keyboard arrangement to This Instrument, and I re-worked the tune just a little. I also revisited 'Death and the Lady' on the album, as I'd sung it at David Tibet's gig. Ian's slide guitar gave it such a different feel from the original, Dolly's sonorous arrangement on the 1970 album *Love, Death and the Lady*.

Thinking we needed something a bit lighter, I chose 'Old Johnny Buckle' sung by Mrs Hewett from my Topic compilation *You Never Heard So Sweet*. Bob Copper had recorded it in 1955 in her home in Mapledurwell, Hampshire. It's a delightful upside-down nonsense song. The second brighter song I chose was one that I had collected from Ollie Gilbert back in the autumn of 1959 in Timbo, Arkansas, when I had been sent to join 'the womenfolk' while Alan and Ollie's husband Oscar sat in another room drinking his moonshine. This was 'Pretty Polly', one of the many songs that had made it over from the old country to the New World. In England it's known as 'Pretty Polly Oliver', where our heroine dresses as a soldier to follow her sweetheart, and it survived, slightly changed, as happens over the years and the miles. Ollie's version was set in the time of the American War of Independence; she called America the Nunited States (the New-nited), which after all was perfectly logical, and she had one line that had more words in it than the tune allowed: 'I'm a Nunited States soldier from George Washington I came'. At concerts, I'd tell the audience that I expected a round of applause when I'd safely accomplished it… and it always raised a lot of laughter. Ian arranged an accompaniment for This Instrument, making it sound

like a mountain dulcimer. And it was Ian who had sent me the 1922 recording of 'Sur le Borde de L'Eau' made by Blind Uncle Gaspard of Louisiana, and I simply could *not* resist singing it myself, so that had to be included.

'The Rich Irish Lady' was another that came from the 1959 Southern Journey recordings. It had been brought to my attention by Rob Curry, following a piece of his diligent research, when he asked me one day if I remembered blind Horton Barker singing a ballad 'The Rich Irish Lady'. I had to confess that I didn't remember it. I knew I had met him in Chilhowie, Virginia at the time he was visiting his friend, a small tobacco farmer, Spencer Moore, but I couldn't recall Horton singing. This surprised me, as my memory was usually pretty good. Rob sent me the recording of Horton singing through half the ballad, then faltering and saying to Alan in his very gentle voice: 'I'm awfully sorry, sir, I just can't remember the words.' Equally gently, Alan asked Horton if he could *speak* them… And Horton could – and did. So the whole ballad was there, and it was so compelling that I resolved to learn it. And I have Rob Curry to thank for it.

It's a story of revenge, and as its penultimate verse ends with the words 'I'll dance on your grave when you're laid in the earth', I knew we'd need a fierce and vengeful Appalachian mountain tune to round it off. Pete Cooper and Dave Arthur of Rattle on the Stovepipe, my favourite Old Timey band, came up trumps with 'Jeff Sturgeon', a wild Kentucky tune. On the day we were in a studio listening through the tracks Jamie Johnson, the engineer who did the final album mix, turned to me as those final bitter lines came up and asked, 'He doesn't mean it, does he?' As the tune tore in he gasped: 'Oh yes, he does, doesn't he!' And once Pete and Dave were on board, they were used throughout the album.

Previous pages: Recording *Lodestar* in 2016.
Top left: Stephen Thrower, Ossian Brown, Alex Neilson, Shirley Collins.
Bottom left: Dave Arthur, Pete Cooper.
Top right: Shirley Collins, Stephen Thrower, Ian Kearey.
Bottom right: Shirley Collins, Glen Redman, Ossian Brown.

Even in that safe environment of home, though, I was occasionally too nervous to open my mouth to sing. At other times it was frustrating when I felt I wasn't singing well enough, and I was swearing quite a bit. I decided I'd have to do something about that, so I found an old money box to use as a swear box. The rule was that every time I swore, the others would have to put a pound in!! Over the weeks, we found that the best cure was for us all to go through the songs in the morning then, at lunch-time, pop up to Ask on the High Street for pizza and ice-cream. Somehow it miraculously improved my singing in the afternoon!

There was plenty of laughter. At first, Ian got quite used to holding out his hand to collect a half-sucked cough drop from me before I started a song – but not of course if he was playing. When Alex Neilson came down from Glasgow to record the percussion, we had to fit his entire drum-kit in my front room. It filled it. But I wouldn't have missed having him there; he's such a great drummer, and plays with skill and wit, especially on 'Pretty Polly', where he skittered in such an enticing and delicious way that it made me laugh out loud.

Then there was the day we recorded 'The Silver Swan'. Ian had written an arrangement for harmonium. He set up his rather dilapidated portable one and started to play – but not only did the foot bellows creak and wheeze, but when he pedalled, it was out of rhythm with the song. At one point Ossian lay on the floor and tried to pump the bellows by hand, but we were all laughing so much at the ridiculousness of the situation that we had to think of some other solution – it is after all, a serious song. So we wrapped several duvets and blankets round the instrument until it looked as though Ian was in an igloo. But it worked. And when it was safely recorded, we invited Ian's wife Rivka Zoob Kearey to play the exquisite viola part she had written.

Everyone was coming up trumps; Elle Osborne's atmospheric sounds on her cello, and Pip singing so assuredly on 'Awake Awake' and playing a beautiful flowing guitar accompaniment for 'The Banks of Green Willow' exactly as I'd hoped for.

The first person to hear the complete basic recordings was my son Bobby since it was thanks to him the whole thing had happened. We went over to Bexhill to listen to them with Stephen Thrower and Ossian Brown in the studio of their sea-side home. I'd kept Bobby away from the recording sessions, so he had no inkling of what we'd done. He listened attentively then said, 'Mum, I didn't know what to expect. This is amazing!'

He played it at full volume in his car as we drove back to Lewes in the dark across the deserted reed-bordered lanes of the magical and mysterious Pevensey Levels. It must have been something of a relief to him that he had an album he could present to Domino, one that he believed in.

I then had to come up with a title. My daughter Polly was visiting one day, and we sat for hours throwing ideas about; but nothing felt quite right. About an hour after she left, my pink mobile rang. It was a message from Polly – just one word – 'Lodestar'. My heart missed a beat. I looked it up in the dictionary: 'A star that a ship is steered by especially the Pole Star 2) a guiding principle 3) an object of pursuit 4) "lode" (in obsolete sense) "way" "journey"'. I sent a message back: 'YES! PERFECT! THANK YOU!' After all, this music, these songs had been my lodestar for many years, constantly guiding me.

Following the success of *Lodestar* the album, a concert tour was proposed. I wanted it to be a really special evening, with two or three guests playing the first half, chosen on different nights from these willing artists (my wish list): Lisa Knapp, Olivia Chaney, Emily Portman, Naomi Russell, Graham Coxon, Alasdair Roberts, Sam Lee and John Kirkpatrick.

We had Boss Morris, the Stroud women's side formed by Alison Merry, in their vivid costumes, and my beloved Brighton Morris in traditional kits, with their star dancer, Glen Redman, who stole the show every night with his solo spots, becoming a bit of a Morris heart-throb across the country. I wanted the shows to be visually exciting as well, and asked Nick Abrahams to put together a video for each song as back-projection; he came up trumps. They were varied and remarkable, especially the one for 'Death & the Lady' with the extraordinary corn-dollies made by Cathy Ward, sinister, twirling, rather phallic; the sight of Glen leaping in front of them is thrilling, although somewhat unsettling!

Understandably, I had some anxieties about doing the *Lodestar* concerts even though I knew the music was good, played by top-class musicians under the direction of Ian Kearey, all of us good friends who enjoyed working together, along with Pip who also acted as narrator. We were at prestigious venues, too, thanks to Guy Morley (No-Nation) who arranged the bookings in Glasgow, Gateshead, Liverpool, Warwick, Bristol, the Barbican in London and the Dome in Brighton, the Cambridge Folk Festival and the Green Man; as well as obtaining the Arts Council grant that enabled us to do them. How would I fare, knowing that my voice was much lower now? My daughter, Polly, knowing of my anxiety, and with her connections in the music world through her and her husband Chris Taplin's company Shooting Star Productions, (who had already generously given financial support from the start) arranged for the renowned sound engineer Simon Honywill to come on board; and how wonderful that was. I trusted him and I felt secure.

Audiences seemed to get what we were doing, too; a *Guardian* reviewer writing that it was 'a performance of unwavering and revelatory intimacy', while David Suff wrote 'I'm still marvelling at the power and quiet majesty of the evening.'

These recent years have taken me into the company of caring, interesting, talented, creative people – people that I have come to love. There are the songs, too, some that I have known for a long time, but never recorded, and some newly-learned ones that I long to sing. It was the songs, with their unfailing beauty, that brought us together; and it is the Sussex traditions, landscape and spirit that holds us together… until I reach the point where:

Above: Engraving from the tomb of John Cawley, Chichester Cathedral, seventeenth century.

All you that come here the small birds to hear
I'll have you pay attention so pray all draw near
And when you're growing old you will have this to say
That you never heard so sweet, you never heard so sweet
You never heard so sweet as the birds on the spray
From the Copper Family

Epilogue

Last night I had such a lovely dream. I was with a new man whose eyes were grey and silver. We were walking through a field of impossible beauty, with golden flowers so tall they grew above our heads. I had to stand on tip-toe to see the gold – their stems were all white and silver. The path we were on had a double ridge, wide tracks, with other golden flowers growing low to the ground between them. I was troubled because I couldn't remember their name. I stood on tip-toe again to look at the spread of gold in front of us, and whispered to the man, 'It's like the field of the cloth of gold', but I don't think he heard me, and I didn't think he'd understand anyway. But as I slipped my gloved hand into his, I felt in a state of grace. I woke in tears at the sense of loss.
Diary note, 8 November 2014

And they must be the footsteps of our own ancestors who made the whole landscape by hand and left their handprints on everything and trod every foot of it, and the present shapes are their footprints, those ancestors whose names were on the stones in the churchyard and many whose names weren't. And the tales of them and of people living I would take with me, and the songs in my mind, as if everything I thought and felt had to be set in words and music – everything that was true in me.
To Live Like a Man, FC Ball (unpublished novel)

PHOTO CREDITS

All images from Shirley Collins' personal archive, except: cover by SF Said; Toni Arthur: *xiv*; Herb Greer: 74, 84; Brian Shuel: dust jacket rear, 123, 126, 127, 136, 142; David Montgomery: 122; John Harrison: 132, 133; Shirley Collins: 185; Keith Morris: 222; Pip Barnes: 236; Diane Logel: 240; Tim Plester: 242; John McMahon: 243; Toby Amies: 244; Ian Kearey: 246, 247; Ossian Brown: 232, 253; Stephen Hopper: *xii*, 254; Richard Lovett: 253

PUBLISHERS' ACKNOWLEDGEMENTS

Strange Attractor Press would like to thank the following for their roles in bringing *All In The Downs* to fruition: Phil Baker, Richard Bancroft, Ossian Brown, Matthew Browne, Shirley Collins, Rob Curry, Justin Hopper, Bobby Marshall, Polly Marshall Taplin, John McMahon, Alice Measom, Frances Morgan, Guy Morley, Tim Plester, Lorna Ritchie, SF Said, Matt Shaw, Brian Shuel, Katie Stileman, David Tibet, Paul Williams.

Index

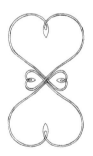

STRANGE ATTRACTOR PRESS 2018